REES HOWELLS'
GOD CHALLENGES
THE DICTATORS
Doom of Axis Powers Predicted

GW00569135

Victory for Christian England and Release of Europe Through
Intercession and Spiritual Warfare, Bible College of Wales

MATHEW BACKHOLER

Rees Howells' God Challenges the Dictators, Doom of Axis Powers Predicted: Victory for Christian England and Release of Europe Through Intercession and Spiritual Warfare, Bible College of Wales

ISBN 978-1-907066-85-6 (hardback)
ISBN 978-1-907066-78-8 (paperback)

British Library Cataloguing In Publication Data
A Record of this Publication is available from the British Library
Hardback first Published in October 2020
Paperback first Published in May 2022

JESUS CHRIST is LORD

On the Day of Pentecost, Peter said, "Repent, and let every one of you be baptised in the name of Jesus Christ for the remission of sins; and you shall receive the gift of the Holy Spirit. For the promise is to you and to your children, and to all who are afar off, as many as the Lord our God will call"
(Acts 2:38-39)

In Memory

Of All the Faithful Servants

Of the Bible College of Wales (1924-2009)

Who Served in Various Capacities

To Train and Thrust Forth More Labourers

Into HIS Harvest Field

In Pursuit of the Gospel to Every Creature

JESUS CHRIST IS LORD

"Go into all the world and preach the Gospel to Every Creature"
(Mark 16:15)

Contents

Foreword: Lessons from God Challenges the Dictators   5.
1. Prophecy and God's Revelations   10.
2. Winston Churchill and the Prophetic Voice   16.
3. Bible College of Wales   25.
4. The History of God Challenges the Dictators   38.
5. Working with the Tabloids   55.
6. The Vantage Point of Historical Victory   59.

    GOD CHALLENGES THE DICTATORS COVER   68.
    INTRODUCTION   69.
    CONTENTS   74.
  I. GOD VERSUS THE DICTATORS   75.
  II. THREE REMARKABLE PREDICTIONS   83.
  III. THE MUNICH PREDICTION   88.
  IV. THE DANZIG PREDICTION   95.
  V. THE GREAT PREDICTION   100.
  VI. THE £100,000 PREDICTION   107.
  VII. PREDICTION OF THE LARGEST BIBLE COLLEGE   115.
  VIII. PREDICTION OF BUYING DERWEN FAWR   120.
  IX. MONEY LIKE MANNA   124.
  X. PREDICTION OF A THIRD ESTATE   129.
  XI. GOD'S HUNDREDFOLD   134.
  XII. PREDICTION OF HOME AND HOSPITAL FOR
     MISSIONARIES   140.
  XIII. THE SUM OF IT ALL   146.

7. Hitler's New Year's Gift   152.
8. Swansea During the War   156.
9. Bible College of Wales – May 1945   166.
10. Judgment on the Nazi Régime   170.
11. Saved for a Purpose   177.
    Epilogue – Every Creature Commission   180.

    Books by Mathew Backholer   187.
    Appendix A – Two Editions and Errors   189.
    Sources and Notes   191.
    ByFaith Media Books   203.
    ByFaith Media DVDs   208.
    ByFaith Media Downloads and Streaming   209.
    Notes   211.

Foreword

Lessons from God Challenges the Dictators

'For the Kingdom is the Lord's, and He rules over the nations. A posterity shall serve Him. It will be recounted of the Lord to the next generation, they will come and declare His righteousness to a people who will be born, that He has done this' (Psalm 22:28, 30-31).

'And Jesus came and spoke to the disciples, saying, "All authority has been given to Me in Heaven and on earth. Go therefore and make disciples of all the nations, baptizing them in the name of the Father and of the Son and of the Holy Spirit, teaching them to observe all things that I have commanded you; and lo, I am with you always, even to the end of the age." Amen' (Matthew 28:18-20).

In the late 1990s, my brother and I joined the community of faith at the Bible College of Wales (BCW) which Rees Howells founded in Swansea, Wales in 1924. During our time as students and then staff, we became close to the elderly staff who knew and prayed with Rees Howells, many of whom had been part of the 120 who had forsaken all nearly three years before the outbreak of World War II (1939-1945). They had laid down their lives and callings to be intercessors for the nations to help train students for the Christian ministry. These experiences were a formidable foundation for our future working with Richard and Kristine Maton, who together spent more than one hundred and twenty years at the Bible College, to publish their accounts of the life and intercessions of Rees Howells' only child, in the two books, *Samuel, Son and Successor of Rees Howells* (2012) and *Samuel Rees Howells: A Life of Intercession* (2012).

During our years at the Bible College, we recall Thursday evenings fondly, when the frail octogenarian Samuel Rees Howells emerged from his private intercessory life, to lead the services, as he reminded us of the spiritual struggles of past and present. Like Rees Howells, Samuel enjoyed reading from the Scriptures and took courage from all of the terrible battles ancient

Israel struggled through. He encouraged us to imagine ourselves inside Jerusalem when it was surrounded by foreign enemies and asked us if we too could believe for deliverance like the Prophet Isaiah. The many examples of mighty miracles of deliverance from foreign enemies on a national level recorded in Scripture were more than historic accounts to Rees and Samuel Rees Howells. They lived through a time when Britain was surrounded by foreign enemies who were both stronger and more effective in warfare. The enemy was at our gates and was about to enter in.

It may be hard to imagine in the present-day, but Britain was literally on the verge of being invaded and occupied within the lifetime of Rees Howells, Samuel and the other prayer warriors at the Bible College of Wales. Together through intercession, they lived through and prevailed in the kind of prayer battles that Isaiah and other Old Testament heroes experienced. Britain like ancient Jerusalem was going to fall to a foreign enemy, but then God said, "No," and the intercessors with Rees and Samuel had to pray God's will into being, with periods of fasting on many occasions.

On special anniversaries at the Bible College of Wales, Samuel Rees Howells would often refer to his father Rees and the special intercessions he fought. He reminded us that, "The Lord's Servant," or, "The Director," as Rees was called by Samuel's generation, had walked costly pathways in the life of intercession that few in the Church understand or have experienced. His victories were great and the burdens, spiritual deaths and delays were challenging.

It is within the context of a war brewing from the mid-1930s onwards and the possibility of *invasion in 1938 and 1939, (*as well as 1940 and in the spring of 1942) that Rees Howells publicly declared in the newspapers that God was going to intervene, and as the situation grew worse into war, he published his conviction in *God Challenges the Dictators* (1939).

Rees Howells lived for the fulfilment of Jesus' Great Commission (the Gospel to Every Creature) and he believed that Hitler (Nazism) and Mussolini (Fascism), the dictators of Germany and Italy, would have to be defeated in order for the peaceful work of world evangelisation to continue. He also saw Stalin of Russia (Communism), as a threat that God could use to defeat the other dictators whilst all three dictators were allies! Hitler and Mussolini were part of the Axis powers of Berlin-Rome.

At the moment when victory seemed to be on the side of the dictators, Rees Howells made several public declarations that shocked some and inspired faith to encourage others. Those mighty nations and dictators which seemed invincible, Rees believed would be smashed because God Himself was against them. The work of reaching Every Creature with the Gospel was being hindered because of the dictators and their end was nigh.

To present his case, in 1939, Rees Howells published *God Challenges the Dictators: Doom of the Nazis Predicted*[1] despite the darkening of the situation. Within the pages, which he began writing *after* war was declared between Britain and Nazi Germany, he pronounces the total defeat of Hitler and Mussolini, and testifies to the way the Holy Spirit led him and the notable answers to prayer he received, which served as a confirmation to God's greater objective.

Rees Howells was born into a poor coal mining community in 1879 with no family money, nor wealthy connections to meet his needs. Having left his poorly paid job in the mine at God's call, he learnt the principles of faith through sacrifice and trial, until his faith was raised enough to support his wife and himself to be trained as missionaries for the South African General Mission, where they arrived in 1915. When they returned to Britain having experienced revival on the mission field across Southern Africa, the Great Depression was in full swing and financial pressures had never been so great. It was at this time that God urged him to believe and receive amounts of money, small as well as large sums, which were needed to purchase four great estates over fourteen years to found a Bible College. This College was founded by faith in June 1924 and without appeals became a house of prayer for all nations, and a bedrock of intercession. Those who lived there can testify that it is no exaggeration to suggest that there was no place like it in the rest of the Bible-believing world.

As Rees Howells explains in his own words, how God led him in *God Challenges the Dictators* you will begin to feel the authentic voice of Rees Howells ringing through his testimonies. The remarkable story of his life of faith is both inspiring and daring, and yet his comments on how God was going to defeat the dictators and in what timeframe became challenging for him. As with all prophecy, we must be careful not to add to, nor take away from what God has said, and adding a date may limit you to something different from what God has planned. Rees Howells knew in his spirit that the mighty dictators would fall, what he was not sure of, after the beginnings of the war and its extension to a global conflict, was the when and how. Consequently, his hope that God would defeat them without the need for a general European war became polemical.

After war was declared on 3rd September 1939, Rees Howells pressed ahead to write and publish *God Challenges the Dictators* and even though the war lasted longer than many had thought (just like WWI – "It will be over by Christmas"), this was a delay, not a defeat, a spiritual battle between the Devil and God. He stayed steadfast that God would defeat the dictators and any questioning of his faith was for him, just another step in the process of the Refiner's fire. If Rees Howells had to die more to the world and its opinions, he was prepared for it.

With hindsight, we can now see that the Lord used Rees Howells' declarations to help sift and shake the staff and visitors of the Bible College of Wales. The evening prayer meetings were packed with locals when Rees seemed unstoppable in his faith. But when war broke out, the chaff blew away, as the sifting and shaking continued. A similar situation can be found in Jesus' teaching in John chapter six, as His followers fell away when they felt confused by the way He was leading them. For Rees Howells, what was left after this challenging time was an army of intercessors ready to stand in the gap, to intercede day and night for the defeat of the dictators and the spread of the Gospel worldwide. They had come through the Refiner's fire and were purged of all need of man's approval and praise. This indifference to the opinions of the evangelical world was still notable to the very last days of the Bible College under the leadership of Samuel Rees Howells. "We are not seeking popularity are we?" asked Samuel at the College. "It was a cross that was given to our Lord. The popularity of the religious, of the evangelical world – what does that mean? To a true man of God, a man that has been to the cross and is broken at the cross – what does it mean?"

The apostle Paul declared: "I have been crucified with Christ; it is no longer I who live, but Christ lives in me; and the life which I now live in the flesh I live by faith in the Son of God, who loved me and gave Himself for me" (Galatians 2:20).

What then can we learn from Rees Howells' experience with the predictions, declarations and statements in this book? Our experience of anointed declarations of faith is that there is a danger of reading more into a prediction or prophecy than first meets the eye. It is often only when a something is fully fulfilled or an event comes to pass that we discover precisely what the Lord was relaying to His people, a nation or an individual. "For My thoughts are not your thoughts, nor are your ways My ways," says the Lord (Isaiah 55:8). Due to this fact, we believe it is important for believers following the Holy Spirit to be careful not to add their own spin or biased interpretation to any prophecy, nor to read more into any Spirit-led utterance; not to take something out which was inspired, and to be very careful not to add a timeline or date, unless directed by the Lord. God will not be restricted by our additions, timelines or interpretations, when we mistakenly add to, or take away from, what He has spoken.

This book serves as an important historical document on the lessons of faith and prophecy that Rees Howells and his team of intercessors learnt during the twentieth century. It helps place us in the midst of those exciting years of faith and provides guidance for anyone who moves in the prophetic.

There is far more to receive from this book than the thought provoking questions of the war, as we feel Rees Howells' excitement burst forth from the pages, and as we ponder what we can learn from a difficult time in the life of the Bible College of Wales.

The monetary figures for the year 2020 have been included within the text in parenthesis [ ] to give a contemporary value of costs and are calculated using the Bank of England's inflation calculator. They are based on the year an amount is mentioned; therefore £100 in 1924 with inflation calculated for 2020 would be different than £100 in 1932 or for 1939.

My brother and I will never forget reading for the first time a 1939 red hardback edition of *God Challenges the Dictators* more than twenty years ago at Rees Howells' Bible College of Wales, and pondering the examples and questions it poses. We pray that you too will be blessed by the positive examples of faith it contains.

Paul and Mathew Backholer,
ByFaith Media
www.ByFaith.org

www.facebook.com/ByFaithMedia
www.instagram.com/ByFaithMedia
www.pinterest.com/ByFaithMedia
www.youtube.com/ByFaithMedia
www.twitter.com/ByFaithMedia

Chapter 1

Prophecy and God's Revelations

After the Spirit had rested on the elders of Israel and they prophesied, Moses replying to Joshua, said, "Are you zealous for my sake? Oh, that all the Lord's people were prophets and that the Lord would put His Spirit on them" (Numbers 11:29).

Thus says the Lord, "And it shall come to pass afterward that I will pour out My Spirit on all flesh; your sons and your daughters shall prophesy, your old men shall dream dreams, your young men shall see visions; and also on My menservants and My maidservants I will pour out My Spirit in those days" (Joel 2:28-29).

Rees Howells (1879-1950) was a great man of God and he often had a column or more in the local newspapers of South Wales from the mid-1920s onwards, recording his and the Bible College of Wales' achievements. From the mid-1930s, Rees Howells' news from his College or his 'predictions' or 'prophecies,' as the newspapers called them expanded from local periodicals of South Wales to national ones across England, into America and even as far away in Australia and Papua (Papua New Guinea).

A 1938 Newspaper Cutting

Some of the local newspapers had Rees Howells as the front page headline. Rees was known as the 'Welsh Prophet' a 'divine' who often made 'predictions' as the secular press wrote.

One headline from June 1935 was: 'Swansea New Vision, College To Fulfil Biblical Order; another, from July 1938: 'Bible College £10,000 Prophecy Comes True' [£674,400 in 2020], one from September 1938: 'Prophecy Brings £500' [£33,720], and for December 1939: 'Amazing War Prophecies of Welsh Pastor.'

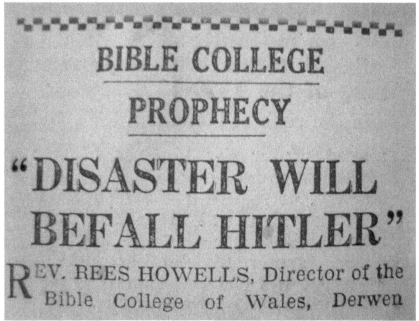

BIBLE COLLEGE

PROPHECY

"DISASTER WILL BEFALL HITLER"

REV. REES HOWELLS, Director of the Bible College of Wales, Derwen

A 1939 Newspaper Cutting

Rees Howells' son, Samuel Rees Howells (1912-2004) would often preach on the prophets of the Bible and the challenges they embraced. He would never allow the College to forget that these people were ordinary men and women, just like us, who had to believe God in the worst of circumstances. The apostle James wrote: 'Elijah was a man with a nature like ours, and he prayed earnestly that it would not rain; and it did not rain on the land for three years and six months. And he prayed again and the heaven gave rain, and the earth produced its fruit' (James 5:17-18). Elijah had to believe that an entire nation could be turned back to God, when Jezebel and Ahab had all the power and used it to turn the nation to false gods. There were many other examples that Samuel cited of identification, agony and the gained position of intercession that leads to authority. "Daniel believed Him," said Samuel. "There wasn't a shade of doubt and there was no need then for Daniel to proceed with that prayer. He caused the people to go back to their land, wasn't that impossible? (Daniel 9). The Holy Spirit is with us and He is giving us an opportunity of believing Him."

Samuel Rees Howells told the College that there is much prayer in parts of the Church, but little believing. Samuel was looking for people to believe with him that God would intervene in international events, just like He did in the Old Testament in response to the faith of the prophets.

Doubt is the currency of the flesh, but believing is the currency of the Spirit and the Bible warns that without faith, it is impossible to please God. 'But without faith it is impossible to please Him, for he who comes to God must believe that He is, and that He is a rewarder of those who diligently seek Him' (Hebrews 11:6). "There's hardly any believing in the Church today," said Samuel. "What does He want from us today? It is to believe Him in the impossible! We need to go back to these things. It's a different world all together." The angel Gabriel said to the Virgin Mary, "For with God nothing will be impossible" (Luke 1:37). Jesus said to the rich young ruler, "The things which are impossible with men are possible with God" (Luke 18:27).

These were the challenges Samuel presented to all. Think of Esther and Mordecai. Those two people were entirely responsible to believe for every Jew in the world's largest empire to be saved. Could we do the same?[1]

Understanding Prophecy

For a prophet, a man of God such as Rees Howells, leading up to war against the dictators, sometimes the prophecies or revelations were given in quick succession, at other times, weeks or months could pass before he received a word from the Holy Spirit that had to be spoken publicly, written down or made public to Christendom at large. As Michael Backholer in *Prophecy Now, Prophetic Words and Divine Revelations* wrote:

Some prophecies are plain and easy to understand, others are not. Some have a play on words, or rhyme has been incorporated, whilst others can have two meanings or are written as a riddle, and are designed to be thought over and pondered (Mark 4:11-13 and 1 Corinthians 2:14). Yet others are given in figurative language (John 16:25), whilst some are analogies or allegories – living parables.

All are edifying, to build up, however some are pointed and are an indictment to the Body of Christ – the Church, and many professing Christians, and even Christian workers. 'Do not despise the chastening of the Lord...nor be discouraged when you are rebuked by Him, for whom the Lord loves, He chastens...' (Hebrews 12:5-6).

'We also have the prophetic word made sure, which you do well to heed as a light that shines in a dark place, until the day dawns and the morning star rises in your hearts, knowing this first, that no prophecy of Scripture is of private interpretation, for prophecy never came by the will of man, but holy men of God spoke as they were moved by the Holy Spirit' (2 Peter 1:19-21).

Prophecy is an important gift for the Body of Christ and must not be despised, disregarded or neglected, but heeded.
- 'Pursue love, and desire spiritual gifts, but especially that you may prophesy' (1 Corinthians 14:1).
- 'He who prophesies speaks edification and exhortation and comfort to men...he who prophesies edifies the Church' (1 Corinthians 14:3-4). To edify means to 'build up,' and a word of rebuke spoken in love is still edifying as godly sorrow can lead to repentance (2 Corinthians 7:10).[2]
- 'Do not quench the Spirit. Do not despise prophecies' (1 Thessalonians 5:19-20).

Prophecy needs to be weighed, judged, often prayed through and tested, because many false prophets, as well as deceiving, lying spirits are in the world, trying to deceive and beguile.
- 'Test all things; hold fast what is good' (1 Thessalonians 5:21).
- 'Beloved, do not believe every spirit, but test the spirits, whether they are of God; because many false prophets have gone out into the world' (1 John 4:1).

A prophecy, revelation or prediction can be from God, of the flesh, from the evil one, or a combination, as some people can start in the Spirit, but wander into the flesh as they prophesy beyond their faith.
- 'To whom have you uttered words? And whose spirit came from you?' (Job 26:4).[3]

- 'Having the gifts differing according to the grace that is given us, let us use them; if prophecy, let us prophesy in proportion to our faith' (Romans 12:6).

The Bible reveals that by the mouth of two or three witnesses every word shall be confirmed and established.
- 'This is the third time I am coming to you. 'By the mouth of two or three witnesses every word shall be established' ' (2 Corinthians 13:1).

Prophecy is often conditional and we have to fulfil our obligations to our covenant keeping God. If we have not completed our part (e.g. abiding in the Vine, John 15), then we cannot expect God to do His. God will not be mocked by our lifestyles – sins of commission (what we know is wrong and still do) or sins of omission (what we neglect to do which we should do). In addition, God cannot be cajoled into fulfilling His Word when we have neglected His revealed will as found in the Holy Bible. James stated we should be doers of the Word and not hearers only, otherwise we deceive ourselves (James 1:22).
- Many prophecies, visions or revelations of revival (or other) can be prayed over to see the fulfilment of the will of the Lord, to 'pour out His Spirit' (Joel 2:28) and to 'pour water on him who is thirsty and floods upon the dry ground' (Isaiah 44:3). In 2 Chronicles 7:14, in regards to revival, God states, "If My people who are called by My name will humble themselves and pray and seek My face, and turn from their wicked ways, then I will hear from Heaven, and will forgive their sin and heal their land." In the same way that Daniel understood that Jerusalem, and its surrounding land, would be desolate for seventy years according to the Word of the Lord under Jeremiah the prophet (Jeremiah 25:11-12). Knowing that the time had been fulfilled, Daniel prayed for Jerusalem to be repaired and re-inhabited (Daniel 4:2-4). He 'stood in the gap' (Ezekiel 22:30) on behalf of the people, prayed, fasted and made confession to God for his sins, the sins of his forefathers, and pleaded for God to fulfil His Word (Daniel 4:3-19).
- The revelation from Jesus Christ given to John for His followers needs to be read, heard and kept, and blessed are the Christians who obey (Revelation 1:3).

'But to each one of us grace was given according to the measure of Christ's gift.... He [Jesus] Himself gave some to be apostles, some prophets, some evangelists, and some pastors and teachers, for the equipping of the saints, for the work of ministry, for the edifying of the Body of Christ, till we all come to the unity of the faith and the knowledge of the Son of God, to a perfect man, to the measure and stature of the fullness of Christ. That we should no longer be children tossed to and fro and carried about with every wind of doctrine, by the trickery of men, in the cunning craftiness by which they lie in wait to deceive, but speaking the truth in love, may grow up in all things into Him who is the Head – Christ – from whom the whole Body, joined and knit together by what every joint supplies according to the effective working by which every part does its share, cause growth of the Body for the edifying of itself in love' (Ephesians 4:7, 11-16).

Understanding God's Revelations

- 'Surely the Lord God does nothing, unless He reveals His secret to His servants the prophets' (Amos 3:7).
- Hanani the seer said, "For the eyes of the Lord run to and fro throughout the whole earth, to show Himself strong on behalf of those whose heart is loyal to Him..." (2 Chronicles 16:9).
- '...Those who seek the Lord shall not lack any good thing' (Psalm 34:10).
- 'Delight yourself in the Lord and He shall give you the desires of your heart' (Psalm 37:4).
- 'As the eyes of servants look to the hand of their masters, as the eyes of a maid to the hand of her mistress, so our eyes look to the Lord our God until He has mercy on us' (Psalm 123:2).
- '...Those who seek the Lord understand all' (Proverbs 28:5).
- "For I will pour water on him who is thirsty, and floods on the dry ground; I will pour My Spirit on your descendants, and My blessing on your offspring" (Isaiah 44:3).
- 'Thus says the Lord, the Holy One of Israel, and His Maker, "Ask Me of things to come concerning My sons; and concerning the works of My hands..." ' (Isaiah 45:11).
- Jesus said, "Seek first the Kingdom of God and His righteousness..." (Matthew 6:33).[4]

Chapter 2

Winston Churchill and the Prophetic Voice

'Therefore I exhort first of all that supplications, prayers, intercessions, and giving of thanks be made for all men, for kings and all who are in authority, that we may lead a quiet and peaceable life in all godliness and reverence' (Titus 2:1-2).

Moses and the children of Israel sang this song to the Lord, saying, "I will sing to the Lord, for He has triumphed gloriously! The horse and its rider He has thrown into the sea! The Lord is my strength and song, and He has become my salvation; He is my God, and I will praise Him; my father's God, and I will exalt Him. The Lord is a man of war; the Lord is His name" (Exodus 15:1-3).

When it was evident to Rees Howells that a delay in the fulfilment of the prophecy and declaration of the 'doom of the dictators' was necessary, he stood firm despite those who claimed his failure. His reputation was of little consequence to a man who had been crucified with Christ (Galatians 2:20) and the will of God was his utmost priority. Rees found sympathy for Moses who had boldly prophesised, proclaimed and predicted the liberation of the Hebrew slaves in Egypt (Exodus 5) only for it to become much harder for the brick-making slaves. During the Ten Plagues of Egypt, a number of times Pharaoh told Moses that the Hebrew slaves could "Go" and then hardened his heart and changed his mind. At other times, God hardened Pharaoh's heart so that God's power and signs could be displayed across Egypt, told as a memorial for all generations, and that He would be glorified (Exodus 5-11).

The intercessors at the Bible College of Wales were in a similar situation, delay meant death to self, and apparent failure not only within Christendom, but from the glaring eyes of the newspaper reading world. But just as Moses would lead Israel out of Egypt at a later date than hoped or expected, and with the Hebrew slaves experiencing greater suffering under their taskmasters, so the dictators would fall! But at a time when God's good, pleasing and perfect will would be accomplished. In addition, the spirit of Nazism had to be expunged from the Third Reich, which had indoctrinated a generation of Germans and influenced others. If a 'general European war' or a 'world war' was necessary after 1939 for the dictators' defeat and the Jews to return to the Promised Land, Israel – so be it! However, for Rees Howells it was always "a battle between the Devil and the Holy Ghost," as he often said. With this confidence, Rees Howells wrote and published his book within three months of the outbreak of war with Germany, without amending any prophecy, prediction or declaration. As the years passed he stood firm and as unmovable as a large rock and encouraged Winston Churchill who served from May 1940 to July 1945, with his letters and his book, *God Challenges the Dictators*.

The preceding Prime Minister, Neville Chamberlain served from May 1937 to May 1940 was also sent a copy of Rees Howells' book, alongside members of the Government. Whilst a Specimen Chapter of 32-pages was sent to every Christian Minister across Britain, 20,000 copies, to encourage prayer and stimulate faith.

British Government and Fishing at Penllergaer

In a letter dated 4th December 1939, to A. J. Russell, Rees Howells' literary agent, he wrote: '…We do feel that there is going to be a very great blessing with this book. The prediction is the great thing. As it is so well put out I think Members of the Government will read it. Of course I shall send a copy of the book to Mr [Stanley] Baldwin [Prime Minister of Britain on three occasions] and to the Prime Minister [Neville Chamberlain], so when you come to visit Penllergaer [Rees Howells' fourth estate of 270 acres], maybe some of these will be there at that time. I am sure the Prime Minister would like to do some fishing in our lake. It is a great place for trout fishing, and the river through the estate is nearly two miles long, so it is a splendid place for anyone who likes anything like that. I may write the history of the College very soon, and I could send it to you in about five chapters at a time, and that will keep me in touch with you, which I shall want to do in the future.'

To Prime Minister Winston Churchill

On 26th March 1942, Rees Howells wrote to Prime Minister Winston Churchill who replaced Neville Chamberlain in May 1940. The following is a copy of that letter. Rees Howells had three secretaries during the war years and copies of letters sent to, and received from, were often kept at the Bible College of Wales.

The Rt. Hon. Winston S. Churchill, C.H., M.P.
H.M. Prime Minister and Minister of Defence
10 Downing Street
London, S.W.1.

My dear Prime Minister,

I have been asked to write an article on the war, to be published in about 180 daily papers in America. As next Sunday is a National Day of Prayer, I am sending the article to some of the English papers, that the people may read it for Sunday, and I wanted to send it to you personally.

Since you became Prime Minister, we have followed you daily with our prayers. We have a College, Secondary Schools, a Hospital and a Missionary Home, and we have always had prayer meetings each evening with about 150 present. During the war, we have had two prayer meetings each evening, and for over a year now, without a single break, we have had prayer meetings from 7pm till midnight. As you are the Leader of the State, you have had a very special place in our prayers, and what a hero you have been to these young students! They all say that you are the only man who could have kept up the courage of the country, to lead it to victory after the colossal disaster of Dunkirk.

Over two years ago, I was led to send out a Book of Predictions: "God Challenges the Dictators: Doom of the Nazis Predicted." I sent out 20,000 copies of a Specimen Chapter, one to every minister in the country. At that time, people did not realise, that this was more than a European War; it was a war with the Powers of Darkness. That was the reason why I called the attention of all the clergy to call on God to come to England's aid, because it came as a revelation that God will have to intervene to bring the Nazis to their doom and deliver Christian England. [God's will be done, on earth as it is in Heaven].

In the Book, we predicted three impossibilities:
The Emperor of Abyssinia [Ethiopia] to be restored to his throne.
God to give the College £100,000. [£674,400 in 2020.]
The Doom of the Nazis.

The Lord has fulfilled the first two, and I am sure He is about to do the third.

We all want you to be the Prime Minister when the Victory comes, and as we feel sure that it will come soon, and that is why I wanted you to get this Article. We had a promise of a visit from

Mr & Mrs Chamberlain, when he was Prime Minister. They knew that we were upholding them in prayer, and we wanted him to spend a holiday fishing on our Penllergaer Estate. After the war we should like to have a visit from Mrs Churchill and yourself.

If the country will send a real cry up to God on the National Day of Prayer, we feel sure that the prayers will be answered. I have been led to offer £50,000 [£2,360,450 in 2020] as War Bonds [money loaned to the government to help the war effort], free of interest at Whitsun [Pentecost], if the Lord has not by then brought the Nazis to failure. This will make the war cost more to us, until the Lord will deliver Christian England from the menace of the Nazis....

I am enclosing you a Specimen Chapter of the Book. I hope some of the leading Papers will take up this article, because we need prayer, along with our war effort, and the two together [faith and works, intercession and military strategy] are sure to win.

May the Lord bless you abundantly.

Yours sincerely [Rees Howells]

Second Letter to Prime Minister Winston Churchill

On 26th March 1942, Rees Howells wrote a second letter to Prime Minister Winston Churchill with an Article for the London newspapers. On a separate typed sheet of paper attached with a paperclip to the letter, Rees Howells wrote: 'As I am late for the London papers, if this Article is favourable to you, I wonder if you would pass it on to one of the London papers. I don't mean in any official way. I only want the London district to have it for Sunday, the National Day of Prayer. The South Wales papers will have it from here.'

The Rt. Hon. Winston S. Churchill,
10 Downing Street
London

I am impressed to write to you before the NATIONAL DAY OF PRAYER next Sunday, the following Article.

Our country has come to know by this time that this is not a EUROPEAN WAR, but a Holy War, a war between God and the Powers of Darkness, as General Smuts said last November:

"I look upon this war as one of the great religious wars of the world." This was not an ordinary war, he said. It involved all the things mankind had struggled for through centuries – freedom, conscience and religion; freedom to shapes one's own life and destiny; freedom to be the custodian of one's own soul. It was a question whether those ideals should survive, or whether the world should listen to a dictator, to a man who might be the Devil himself." He continued: "Before I did not believe there was such a thing as anti-Christ, but I believe it today. I see what incarnate evil means in this world."

Two years ago (December 1939), the Bible College of Wales published a Book:

GOD CHALLENGES THE DICTATORS
DOOM OF NAZIS PREDICTED

It was stated plainly in the book, that this is not a European War, nor is it a war against flesh and blood, but against "principalities, against powers, against the rulers of the darkness of this world, against spiritual wickedness in high places," and that God would have to intervene in a miraculous way, as He did in Biblical times, to deliver Christian England; because these powers of darkness could never be fought by "carnal weapons."[1]

In the Book, were three Impossible Predictions:

1. That Emperor Haile Selassie was to be restored to his throne in Ethiopia. [He was forced into exile in May 1936].

2. That the Bible College of Wales would give £100,000 to build Homes, Colleges and Schools in the Holy Land, for those Jewish children who had been thrown out of Greater Germany; this £100,000 to be a thank-offering to God for delivering the world from the menace of the Berlin [German] and Rome [Italian] axis.

3. The Doom of the Nazis, and the deliverance of Christian England.

1. The Emperor Haile Selassie has been restored to his throne.

While in residence in England, the Emperor had word through some missionaries, that Rev. Rees Howells, the Director of the Bible College of Wales, had taken in Abyssinian [Ethiopian], Spanish and Jewish refugees, and that he had bought Penllergaer, the estate of the late Sir John Llewelyn to take in 2,000 Jewish refugees; so a request came from the Emperor that he would like to visit the College and the estate.

When the Emperor drove through a mile and a quarter of rhododendrons and azaleas, and saw the fishing lake of 20 acres on the way to the [Penllergaer] Mansion and knowing that the

Director had thus taken on himself a liability of over £20,000,[2] [£1,348,000 in 2020] and knowing that it would cost more than that each year to keep 2,000 children;[3] with tears in his eyes, he said, "We can easily believe that God has prepared Heaven for man, if He has prepared all this for refugee children; this is the nearest place to my idea of Heaven." Then he told of a proverb used in Ethiopia: "The man who has only God to look to, can do all things and never fail." And turning to the Director [Rees Howells] and his wife [Lizzie Howells] he said: "God will never fail you." He had heard how God had sent nearly a quarter of a million pounds (£250,000) to the College [£16,530,000 in 2020], by prayer and faith alone; and many of the gifts came in large sums – twenty of £500, [£33,720 per £500 in 2020] ten of £1,000 each, [£67,440 per £1,000 in 2020] and one gift of £10,000 [£674,400 in 2020].

On the Emperor's second visit to the College, which lasted nearly a fortnight [two weeks], the Director told him, how God had revealed to him, that he would rob the Fascist dictator [Mussolini], and give him back the throne of Ethiopia to the Emperor. [Mussolini had invaded Ethiopia in October 1935]. As proof of the Director's conviction, he offered to the Emperor Penllergaer Mansion as a private residence until God would restore him to his throne.

The following week the Emperor was called to London (direct from Penllergaer), and from there straight to Egypt; and what a joy there was in the College where a personal cable from the Emperor to his friend, the Rev. Rees Howells: 'You will I know share in my joy at entering my capital. I send you this telegram in remembrance of past sympathy and help. Emperor Haile Selassie.'

2. A gift of £100,000 to be spent after the war in the Holy Land, for educating Jewish children. [This was Ramallah School, north of Jerusalem then under Jordan's jurisdiction].[4]

The war breaking out has hindered Mr Howells from having more than a few Jewish children in the College. But the Lord has provided this large gift; more than two-thirds of it already in hand [more than £67,000], and negotiations are being made to release the remainder of the gift [through sale of land]....

3. Doom of the Nazis Predicted.

If Christian England will do what God said to King Solomon: "If My people, which are called by My name, shall humble themselves, and pray, and seek My face, then will I hear from Heaven, and will forgive their sin and heal their land" (2 Chronicles 7:14), the Director feels that God will answer our country and bring the Nazis to their doom....

God will intervene as He did in Bible times, and raise Christian England again to be His chosen power for evangelising the world, and bless our King and Queen, and the Prime Minister."
End of Letter.

The National Day of Prayer – 29th March 1942

The National Day of Prayer was held on Palm Sunday, 29th March 1942. Rees Howells wrote an Article which was very similar to that which was sent to Winston Churchill above and it is not therefore necessary to repeat. However, the final paragraph on the last page, (page 3), reads: 'For over a year now, without a break, the College has had two prayer meetings each evening from 7pm till midnight [in 1944 there was a short break in between and reconvening between 9:30-10pm], and God, who has answered for Ethiopia and the *£100,000 will answer for Christian England, and will raise her again to be His chosen power for evangelising the world.'

*Rees Howells notes on page 2 of the Article: 'Before Whitsun (Pentecost) the greater part of the £100,000 will be paid over to the College.

Rees Howells the Squire

When I first read the letters that Rees Howells wrote to Winston Churchill and other members of the British government, I was quite stunned because he wrote as if they were good friends. How did a miner of working class origins have the boldness to write to these upper class government officials with such ease? Firstly, Rees Howells was a son of the King of Kings and Lord of Lords, blood-bought and Spirit taught. Secondly, he was a man of God who was not only filled, but consumed with the Holy Spirit and had been dealt with to the core over many decades. There was no fear of man in him, but fear of God and being obedient to the Holy Spirit at all times, at whatever cost.

Rees Howells was brought up as a working class man in the valleys of South Wales and during his period of intercessions before he went to the mission field in 1915, he had been introduced to people such as Lord Radstock and John Gossett of London, upper class people. In addition, Rees Howells met and associated with a number of high profile Christian leaders across

Britain and from overseas, before and after his time on the mission field of Southern Africa. He was a conference speaker and was much in demand to preach in pulpits and to speak at other meetings. Rees Howells, a former miner gradually got accustomed to meeting with people from a higher social class than himself who themselves were fascinated with this minister of religion who was filled with the Holy Spirit.

In Southern Africa during a period of revival Rees Howells had been asked to meet the Queen of Swaziland who inquired why her people were going after his God. Rees proceeded to tell her and the chief men who were present, how her subjects had met the living God and then told her the Good News of Salvation.

Before the first estate which became the Bible College of Wales was bought, Rees Howells had been invited to tea with Sir William and Lady Maxwell at Cardoness House in Gatehouse of Fleet, Scotland. In 1923, Rees Howells and his wife Lizzie, bought Glyn Derwen, which was later contracted to one word, Glynderwen, this was the first of four large estates in Wales each with a Mansion and outbuildings; plus a very large mission hall with accommodation in Paris, France. Sir Percy Molyneux had also befriended Rees Howells and the Bible College of Wales.

Two years after the Bible College of Wales was founded Herbert M. Vaughan wrote *The South Wales Squires* (1926). It is a fascinating window into an era long past of wealthy squires, or the not so wealthy ones, with their Big Houses and family estates and how the social class system was in operation amongst three principle counties of South Wales of: Carmarthen, Cardigan and Pembroke. The last few chapters are focussed around the Welsh Land Commission (1893-1895), Land Acts for Wales, the Welsh Church disestablished (1920), and the Squires and disestablishment. The author writes of a struggle of a landowner with an income of *just* £2,000-3,000 [£122,480-£183,720 in 2020] per year and annual rent of £500-£1,000 [£30,620-£61,240 in 2020] and how heavy taxation, losses in income and WWI brought an end to many land-owning squires across Wales. Yet here was Rees Howells, a skilled miner and former missionary buying up these Big Houses or Mansions and their estates: Glynderwen (1923), Derwen Fawr (1929), Sketty Isaf (1932), and Penllergaer (1938-9) with its 270 acres! During the course of Rees Howells' Directorship of the Bible College of Wales (1924-1950) until he was promoted to glory, he would often buy plots of land, fields which were adjoining to one of his three main central Swansea estates of Glynderwen, Derwen Fawr and Sketty Isaf and sell other plots of land as a need arose or when led to. Many of the houses and bungalows that were built in the immediate vicinity of the Bible College of Wales in the 1940s and 1950s were built on land formerly owned by Rees Howells. In addition, the Bible College of Wales also owned or operated property abroad including a ministry in Paris, France; at Ramallah, north of Jerusalem within Jordan's jurisdiction, now Israel, and a work in Lebanon, Beirut.

Rees Howells was friends with Haile Selassie the Emperor of Ethiopia who sent a number of his family and relatives to the Bible College School (later known as Emmanuel Grammar School) and even one member of the royal household was a student at the Bible College of Wales for a brief period. Rees even offered the Penllergaer Mansion (sometimes referred to as Penllergaer Hall) to the Emperor and his royal entourage for his own private use.

Rees Howells could write to Winston Churchill and other members of the British government because even though he was just a man writing to other men, he had more Big Houses, Mansions, acreage of land and money than most of them! However, Rees Howells only ever claimed to be the *steward* of God's properties, though his name was the principal signature on all the title deeds of every estate bought, alongside the names of three to five trustees.

True to the Letter

Six months after the War in Europe had ended, Rees Howells wrote to Rev. S. H. Dixon in London, England, enclosing a copy of *God Challenges the Dictators*.

I give you this word of explanation on the book. It was revealed to us that the Devil had entered into Hitler and those followers of his who are awaiting their trial today [Nuremberg Trials of November 1945 to October 1946], and that this war was not a European War, but that God challenged the Dictators. Keep this in your mind when you are reading it. The book is in two parts, and the predictions have become true to the letter. (7 November 1945).

'Blessed be the Lord, Because He has heard the voice of my supplications! The Lord is my strength and my shield; My heart trusted in Him, and I am helped; Therefore my heart greatly rejoices, and with my song I will praise Him' (Psalm 28:6-7).

Chapter 3

Bible College of Wales

'This is the Word of the Lord to Zerubbabel, "Not by might nor by power, but by My Spirit," says the Lord of hosts' (Zechariah 4:6).

'Now faith is the substance of things hoped for, the evidence of things not seen. For by it the elders obtained a good testimony. By faith we understand that the worlds were framed by the word of God, so that the things which are seen were not made of things which are visible' (Hebrews 11:1-3).

I am very familiar with the history of the Bible College of Wales (BCW), Rees Howells' life and the surrounding area. I lived on the Glynderwen estate for four years, firstly as a BCW student, then as a staff member and have been entrusted with much of its oral and written history for future generations, a posterity who will serve the Lord (Psalm 22:30). These have included the publication of *Samuel, Son and Successor of Rees Howells: Director of the Bible College of Wales – A Biography* by Richard Maton and *Samuel Rees Howells: A Life of Intercession* by Richard Maton, Paul Backholer and myself, Mathew Backholer.

As a student and staff member of the Bible College of Wales I was able to speak to many of the elderly staff who were with Rees Howells as BCW students from 1935-1939 (all of whom are now with the Lord) until he went to receive his Heavenly reward in February 1950. After that the Rev. Samuel Rees Howells (Rees and Lizzie's only child) became the Honorary Director until he was promoted to glory in March 2004, aged ninety-one and these 'elderly' staff as I knew them, all served faithfully under Samuel Rees Howells and were of a similar age.

In June 1924, the Bible College of Wales was officially opened by Rees Howells' in Blackpill (bordering Sketty), Swansea, Wales. Rees and his wife, Lizzie Hannah (also known as Elizabeth), were former missionaries at Rusitu Valley, Gazaland, (near Portuguese East Africa, and now in present-day Zimbabwe), where they saw revival from 1915-1917, which was still continuing in 1920 after two years of their absence. In early

1917, Rees and Lizzie Howells attended the annual South African General Mission (SAGM) conference at Durban, South Africa, for three weeks and the Holy Spirit visited them. Under the SAGM, Rees Howells was commissioned to travel to all the SAGM mission stations in Southern Africa for six months, which was extended to two years. He travelled to the countries of Swaziland, Pondoland, Bomvanaland, Tembuland and Zululand, over 11,000 miles and saw revival in every mission station![1]

In the summer of 1922, Rees Howells attended the Llandrindod Convention in Wales, and the following year, the Howells' felt led to resign from the SAGM as they were called by God to start a training college for missionaries.

In 1923, they were staying in Mumbles, on the edge of Swansea Bay. The Mumbles Road, skirts Swansea Bay and as they were walking along the promenade they saw a large estate called Glyn Derwen, which was later contracted to a single word Glynderwen. This estate with a stream running through it was purchased by faith in October 1923 and thus the Bible College of Wales was inaugurated on Whit-Monday, Pentecost in June 1924. The local paper called it 'God's College.' This estate had three entrances, two on Derwen Fawr Road of Sketty, Swansea, and one on the Mumbles Road, Blackpill, Swansea.

In the subsequent years, Rees Howells purchased two other estates along Derwen Fawr Road, called Derwen Fawr and Sketty Isaf, purchased in 1929 and 1932 respectively, and both were opened one year after purchase. A fourth estate, Penllergaer, consisting of 270 acres in Penllergare, Swansea, was purchased in September 1938 and opened the following year. (Please note that Penllergaer Mansion is spelt differently than the Penllergare area). In 1939, Rees Howells wrote: 'Thus was founded the largest college of its kind in the country, with at one time, more than one hundred and forty students in residence.'[2]

Every Creature Vision 1934

On 26th December 1934, known as Boxing Day in Britain, Rees Howells received the Every Creature Vision. It was interpreted as laying the responsibility of his team of intercessors to believe for Every Creature to be reached with the Gospel within three decades. The Good News of salvation is that Jesus died for all, but people need to repent, to turn from their sin and put their faith in the finished work of Jesus Christ. He took their punishment at Calvary, was crucified, died, buried and rose from the dead, so

- 26 -

that we can have eternal life in Him. For all who believe and accept God's gift of grace, having faith in the atoning and finished work of Jesus Christ.[3]

The theology of the vision was based on Jesus words, "Go into all the world and preach the Gospel to Every Creature" (Mark 16:15) and, "This Gospel of the Kingdom will be preached in all the world as a witness to all nations, and then the end will come" (Matthew 24:14). On New Year's Day 1935, Rees Howells shared this vision with the College body, and the Every Creature Vision was central to their mission for the rest of their lives.

The *Twelfth Anniversary Booklet,* 1st June 1936, stated that 120 students and staff members were 'called out,' surrendering their mission calls to God, and the 'fire of God fell on 29th March 1936.' It also stated that 170 staff and students were praying and interceding three hours a day for the fulfilment of the Every Creature Commission.

During times of prayer, intercession and worship, when there were breakthroughs in the Spirit; the College body knew that prayers had been answered; Rees Howells would often say that he had "shot out into space" and the glory of God would be evident on him. He was a man who read the Bible on his knees and due to his incessant reading of the Word, turning the pages back and forth, he needed to replace his Bible annually.

Rees Howells in the *Twelfth Session Annual Report* of 1936 stated that during the first twelve years of the Bible College of Wales' existence, God delivered them day by day and had sent gifts amounting to over £25,000 without a single appeal to man, and without a committee, council or denomination behind them. In July 1938, a gift of £10,000 [£674,400 in 2020] was given to the Bible College of Wales and was seen as a seal, a sign for the Every Creature Vision.

Paul Backholer in *Samuel Rees Howells, A Life of Intercession* wrote:

In 1924, Rees Howells was led to found a Bible College by faith alone, and ten years later he received the Every Creature Vision from God, accepting personal responsibility to intercede that every person would hear the Gospel. Rees invited everyone at the Bible College of Wales to receive the Holy Spirit, and the responsibility for the Every Creature Vision on the same terms that he had accepted them. The entrance fee to this life of faith, he explained, is a full and complete surrender to the Lord. There can be no compromise with God.

This Vision from God placed upon the College staff a personal duty to intercede for the Gospel to go to the world, and to bind any strong man (spiritual power) in the heavenly realms that hindered the progress of the Gospel (Mark 3:27). Rees had learnt that all conflicts on earth are rooted in spiritual battles in the heavenly realms and that intercession has to prevail in this realm for events on earth to be transformed. This was also the experience of the prophets and apostles in the Bible. Paul wrote about it in Ephesians 6:12, 'For we do not wrestle against flesh and blood (against human beings, dictators or failed / evil governments etc.), but against principalities, against powers, against the rulers of the darkness of this age, against the spiritual hosts of wickedness in the heavenly places.' Their call therefore, was to spiritual warfare in the heavenly places as led and guided by the Holy Spirit.

This Vision and the College's personal commitment to it were put to the test during World War II (1939-1945), when in accordance with Ephesians 6:12, Satan raised up Hitler to challenge God's plan.

This was for: Gospel liberty, freedom of conscience, worldwide missionary endeavour and to annihilate the Jewish race. Satan had to be bound and the Holy Spirit led the College staff and students in a prolonged intercession for the demise of this threat to dominate the world. Before World War I (1914-1918), Germany and Britain were the biggest missionary sending nations in the world and this, followed by World War II (1939-1945) greatly curtailed men, women, financial resources and safe passage to the mission fields of the world.

Paul Backholer continued:
The believing and faith that the Holy Spirit gave at that time enabled Rees to declare publicly the complete defeat of Hitler. He was confident that Divine power and authority were available to overthrow any spiritual powers restricting the proclamation of the Gospel in every country of the world, for the fulfilment of the Every Creature Vision.[4]

Every Creature Conference 1936
Rees Howells began the annual Every Creature Conference in 1936 which was very popular during the summer, a Christian spiritual retreat. Up to one thousand people would attend with

three hundred being accommodated in the first three estates of Glynderwen, Sketty and Derwen Fawr. However, the first conference took place in 1925 on the Glynderwen Estate and forty ministers attended. This was before the cleavage.

In 1932, a Missionary Conference of the Evangelical Union of South America was held at Derwen Fawr from 24th-28th June. One week later, Rees Howells held a Summer School for Ministers at Derwen Fawr from the 2nd-8th July. They were a precursor to the Every Creature Conferences that were first called the Every Creature Missionary and Intercessory Conference. They were held over two weeks from July into August and staff and students would vacate their rooms for guests and live under canvass. A big marquee (tent), additional toilets, seating and catering facilities were all rented. Most guests shared a room, but some rooms were available for single occupation but not at a reduced rate. Some guests who had prior permission would bring their caravans and pitch on site.

The first Conference of 1936 could accommodate three hundred guests and the cost for attendees was subsidised by the Bible College of Wales. Rees Howells was aware of the possibility of overcrowding, and people taking advantage of their generosity, and urged those who desired to join them to exercise their faith for the financial provision they needed to attend. In one letter he described God's financial provision as a 'seal,' the evidence that the Lord wanted the person to attend.

In 1938, the name of the Conference was shortened to Every Creature Conference, then later, Missionary Conference. The Worldwide Evangelization Crusade (WEC) held a Conference at the Bible College of Wales (BCW) in 1937 and for some years afterwards in early July. There was also an Intercessory Conference held in 1941 at Derwen Fawr.

Rees Howells' BCW and Norman Grubb's WEC were very close, both being faith ministries, and many of the BCW graduating students joined the WEC organisation over the decades. In 1935, more than thirty graduating BCW students were accepted as WEC missionaries! Norman Grubb was delighted because BCW students had lived 'by faith,' trusting God for their needs and had been biblically trained with relevant subjects and teaching for the mission field, including tropical medicine. They had been trained for the mission field, spiritually, academically and practically. In addition, Rees Howells was thrilled that BCW students had callings to different fields of labour in need, to reach Every Creature and all nations for Jesus Christ.

The Every Creature Conferences were initially held for two weeks spanning July and August but were later reduced to one week in duration. The 1938 Every Creature Conference (ECC) had seventy booklets printed in German, noting the international demand. The 1939 ECC booklet had a print run of 1,250. The last Conference was held in 1964.[5]

Visitations of the Holy Spirit from 1936

The blessing of God came in Easter 1936 followed by the Christmas holidays of 1936 and the following Easter of 1937. These times of blessing were amongst the Bible College of Wales (BCW) community (and the Preparatory School) on all three of the BCW sites. The main visitation of the Holy Spirit took place in the Prayer Room at Derwen Fawr on 29th March 1937, during the Easter Holidays and lasted for three weeks, though God's presence abided for much longer and transformed the very atmosphere of BCW, as staff and students knew that He was present, as they walked on holy ground.

The Prayer Room was where the meetings took place during the holidays, as the majority of the students had returned home and so it was not necessary to use the Chapel or the Conference Hall. When I was a student at BCW, the Prayer Room was where all thirteen weekly meetings took place. Hung on the wall, behind the pulpit was an old world map to remind all of the Every Creature Commission.

In the College's *Twelfth Session Annual Report* of 1936, Rees Howells wrote:

While there is a dearth of students in most Colleges, the Bible College of Wales cannot accommodate all the applicants. Last year [1935] there were 90 students in residence and over 30 of them joined the same Mission, the Worldwide Evangelization Crusade (WEC), and others went to Japan, China etc. More than a hundred applicants for this new term have been accepted, and others are asked to wait until the New Year.

The College is prepared to accept all those who have been "called" by the Holy Ghost, provided that they can prove their "call" by asking the Lord to send them £10 [£610 in 2020] to clear the first term's fees [or £30 per year]. After that they can enter the School of Faith, and during three years training they will learn the way to take all their needs from God's Treasury, proving the promise: "But my God shall supply all

your need according to His riches in glory by Christ Jesus"
(Philippians 4:19).

The Threat of Adolf Hitler to Europe

Adolf Hitler, like many German soldiers from the Great War
(1914-1918), believed that Germany could have won, but their
leaders had capitulated and signed an Armistice which came into
effect on 11th November 1918. It took six months of negotiating
by the Allied forces at the Paris Peace Conference before the
Treaty of Versailles (Traité de Versailles) was signed in June
1919. In what became known as the War Guilt clause (Article
231), Germany had to 'accept the responsibility of Germany and
her allies for causing all the loss and damage,' disarm and pay
reparations, which were crippling to the German economy.

In March 1936, Adolf Hitler, sent his soldiers into the Rhineland,
a demilitarised zone in Germany and broke the Locarno Treaty
which had been signed after the First World War (1914-1918) in
1925. This threw Europe into a crisis; Germany had broken her
agreement; should she be punished, but no European country
wanted or was prepared for war to enforce the treaty.

Miss Doris M. Ruscoe, the headmistress of the Preparatory
School (which was previously known as the Bible College School)
recollected that after Lent 1936, with the rise of Hitler and the
threat to Europe, the school staff participated in the College
midday meetings and in the evenings. Though they were wearied
and burdened, 'over and over again in the meetings we were
lifted into another realm and were renewed and refreshed day by
day,' she wrote.

Britain Prepares for Attack

As has been previously stated, it may be hard to imagine in the
twenty-first century, but from 1936-1942, Britain was on the verge
of being attacked and invaded by the Third Reich. In July 1935,
His Majesty's Stationery Office (HMSO) published *Air Raid
Precautions*, four years and two months before war was declared
on Germany by Britain. This was followed by *Anti-Gas Training*
(February 1936), *Medical Instructions* (December 1936), *The
Part of the Police* (February 1937), *New Arrangements for Local
Anti-Gas Training* (July 1937) and in 1938, *The Protection Of
Your Home Against Air Raids* was issued by the Home Office
and printed under the authority of HMSO.

Other HMSO handbooks which were issued and projected from
1937 were: 1. *Personal Protection Against Gas*, 2. *First Aid For*

Gas Casualties, 3. *Medical Treatment of Gas Casualties*, 4. *Decontamination of Materials*, 5. *Structural Precautions Against Bombs*, 6. *Air Raid Precautions in Factories and Business Premises*, and 7. *Anti-Gas Precautions for Merchants and Shipping.*

An 8-page pullout booklet *War Emergency Information and Instruction* was also printed in 1939 and was issued to every household in Britain. On the front cover it stated: 'Read this leaflet through carefully and make sure that you and all other responsible persons in your house understand its contents.

'Pay no attention to rumours. Official news will be given in the papers and over the wireless. Listen carefully to all broadcast instructions and be ready to note them down.'

On the back page, the last sentence in capitals read: 'KEEP A GOOD HEART: WE ARE GOING TO WIN THROUGH.'

In 1940 in Nazi Germany an 88-page book issued by Military High Command, Berlin, was published detailing the German invasion plans for Britain. It was called: *Militärgeographische Angaben Über England, 1940* (Military Geographical Indications About England, 1940), though the English edition is known as *German Invasion Plans for the British Isles, 1940*.

On 16th July 1940, Adolf Hitler said, "As England, in spite of her hopeless military situation, still shows no willingness to come to terms, I have decided to prepare, and if necessary to carry out, a landing operation against her. The aim of the operation is to eliminate the English mother country as a base [of the British Empire] from which the war against Germany can be continued and, if it should be necessary, to occupy it completely."

Adolf Hitler initially wanted to appease Britain with a treaty of peace, but he had consistently broken his word and treated people, leaders and countries with contempt. As an antichrist who set himself up as a god, he persecuted the Jews and imprisoned Evangelical Christian ministers and others – he had to be stopped, militarily and spiritually. There needed to be a team of intercessors, a united group who would stand in the gap on behalf of the land, who could pray through the war as the Allies fought in the air, sea and land to liberate Christian Europe from the dictators. God had raised up a group in Swansea under the leadership of Rees Howells at the Bible College of Wales.

Full Surrender, Intercession and Revival

On 29th March 1936, many of the staff and students of the Bible College of Wales dedicated their lives fully and unequivocally to

God as they laid down their lives to become intercessors. Living martyrs, those led by the Spirit to stand in the gap on behalf of others, thus changing world events in the pattern of the prophets of old such as Moses, Elijah, Isaiah and Jeremiah. From that moment on 'the Spirit was at work in the college,' wrote Norman Grubb. At that time virtually all of the school teachers would have been present, most of whom lived on site. The Bible College of Wales was a tight-knit community of believers, but the consecration only strengthened their bond as intercessors for the Every Creature Vision, believing that the Great Commission could be accomplished in their generation, which Rees Howells had put before the staff and students on 1st January 1935.

The College diary recorded for 29th March 1936: 'The most wonderful day in the College so far. Big day of surrender and many take up the challenge of martyrdom.' 30th March 1936: 'Fire fell on sacrifice. Holy Ghost descended on the evening meeting. Went on knees and someone started the chorus, 'Welcome, welcome, welcome! Holy Ghost we welcome Thee.' Liberty and power so great we continued singing this one chorus for a full hour.'[6]

Miss Doris M. Ruscoe wrote: 'As proof that the Holy Spirit had accepted the intercession of March 29, the days that followed were literally days of heaven on earth. The Holy Spirit was poured out upon us and we prayed, sang and worshipped through the Easter Vacation.' For the next five years, during the war years of 1939-1945, due to conscription most lectures had to be suspended (there was none in the first year of war), but the college would have up to seven meetings a day (though three and then four were standard) as they stood in the gap on behalf of Great Britain and Europe against the Nazi régime and its allies – the dictators. During that period of intense battles against the principalities and powers of darkness the meetings were varied. 'For we do not wrestle against flesh and blood, but against principalities, against powers, against the rulers of the darkness of this age, against spiritual hosts of wickedness in the heavenly places' (Ephesians 6:12).

Miss Doris M. Ruscoe wrote: 'There were quiet meetings when the Lord dealt deeply with us, revealing self, self-motive, things we had not realised in us until the light of God showed them. Sometimes the Holy Spirit revealed Himself in all His majesty and godhead; sometimes we were broken at the foot of the cross.' At other times 'the Holy Spirit would break through' giving assurance that the prayers of the intercessor had been answered, or the will of God was revealed for a certain situation. 'Then the [Conference] Hall was full of God's presence and prayer turned to praise and worship. At times like these there was such a release in the Spirit.'[7]

During the Christmas holiday of 1936, the Bible College of Wales gave much time over to prayer and 'there was an increasing consciousness of God's presence.' One staff member broke down and confessed her need for more of the Holy Spirit; then He met with a group of girl students and as He revealed their sin, they wept for hours before Him, but the climax of the visitation was in the 1937 Easter Holidays.

Dr. Kingsley Priddy, a staff member wrote: 'As those days of visitation went on, we were just prostrate before His feet....' The Holy Spirit revealed to them that whilst many of them had surrendered all at the altar the previous year, [meaning Easter 1936, to do anything for God as part of the Every Creature Commission], He had come to show them self, the crucifixion, the Saviour, to warn them of the trials that lay ahead [all the disciples had failed Jesus] and that He had to do through them what they were not able to do themselves. The Holy Spirit showed them, 'There is all the difference in the world between *your* surrendered life in My hands and I living *My* life in your body.'[8] One by one the Holy Spirit met with those present, 'one by one we broke in tears and contrition before Him...' so wrote Dr. Priddy, 'one by one our wills were broken; we yielded on His own unconditional terms.'

The Holy Spirit in His glory permeated the College grounds and the students found themselves talking in whispers, being 'awed by the holy majesty of His Person,' so much so that they hardly dared raise their voices in the meetings. From Christmas 1936, up until 29th March 1937, they had been carried away with singing and shouting their praises, but this was different – and for many of them, they would spent the next twenty, forty or even seventy years of their surrendered lives in faithful service at the College until they passed into glory.[9]

In January 1937, the Person of the Holy Spirit was revealed to staff and students alike – 'never-to-be-forgotten days...which produced an indescribable awe in the presence of the ineffable holiness and majesty. Day after day we were on our faces before Him,' so wrote Miss Doris M. Ruscoe, 'and often night was as day as His hand was upon us.'

Easter 1939 was especially memorable as Rees Howells, "The Director," as he was known, based his messages on Romans 6 and 'for days the Holy Spirit rested on the College as one and another realised their identification with the Lord Jesus in His death and resurrection.'

In August 1939, Miss Doris M. Ruscoe declared: 'Never was the Holy Spirit more manifest in the College...Over and over again we were taken 'beyond the veil' in the meetings and over and over again we were lost in a spirit of praise and worship.... Over and over again the Holy Spirit broke through in the meetings with new revelations of Divine grace and renewed assurance of final victory. At such times we sang and sang, hymns of praise and worship, sometimes even national songs, especially in the late meeting in the Blue Room.'[10] The Blue Room was where Rees Howells received the Every Creature Vision, a front room on the first floor of Derwen Fawr House.

When I was a staff member at the Bible College of Wales (BCW) I spoke to Miss Ruth Williams, then in her eighties and very active, the personal assistant of the Rev. Samuel Rees Howells. She was then the matriarchal figure of the Derwen Fawr Estate and had previously worked as a teacher at Emmanuel Grammar School on the Glynderwen Estate. I asked her what it was like when the Holy Spirit came. She told me that during the Christmas Holidays of 1936, as a BCW student staying with her parents who lived at Treherbert, at the head of the Rhondda Fawr Valley, she was asked by Rees Howells to return to BCW as something special was happening (she lived 53 miles away, around ninety minutes by train). When she entered the Prayer Room, she found the students and staff, standing on their chairs, waving their handkerchiefs in the air, a sign of jubilation and victory during that era. I asked her, "What did you think of that?" To which she replied in her usual witty self, "I thought they had all gone mad!" Ruth Williams passed into glory in February 2008, aged eighty-nine.

Nurse Catherine Orsman, another labourer at the College passed away four months later, aged ninety-nine. She was born in India, as was her younger sister Margaret, both of whom joined the BCW community in the mid-1930s. Their dad had been an officer in the British Army and was stationed in India for some years. The Orsmans and Miss Williams (as she was known) were undoubtedly welcomed through the gates of Heaven with the acclaim, "Well done, good and faithful servants," as had many other Bible College of Wales staff members who were held in such high regard in their day. The memories of these dear saints linger on in the minds and hearts of those who had the privilege to know them, to sit at their feet and to have fellowship with them.

Nation of Israel

The 3rd September 1938, saw the Bible College of Wales begin its intercessions for the re-establishment of the nation of Israel when Mussolini gave the Jews in Italy a six month eviction notice. Israel as a nation saw the fulfilment of Bible prophecy in May 1948 when a nation was born in a day! (Isaiah 66:8). The British Mandate to govern the Holy Land was about to expire and Israel declared its independence, with the USA, followed by other countries, acknowledging the State of Israel.

In June 1967, Jerusalem was back in the hands of Israel after the Six-Day War, and in May 2018, America opened its embassy in Israel's capital, Jerusalem, recognising Israel's sovereignty over Jerusalem, as its undivided capital, whilst other countries pledged to follow suit.

At the end of November 1938, the Penllergaer Estate of 270 acres, the Bible College of Wales' fourth estate was purchased as a home for Jewish refugees – the 'City of Refuge' as it was referred to in the newspapers, and the estate was opened the following year. Thus the home for Jewish refugees and the re-establishment of the nation of Israel were one intercession with two dividing branches.

On 16th September 1938, the Chief Rabbi in England, Dr. J. H. Hertz proclaimed a Public Fast Day for Sunday: when prayers were offered for world appeasement in general and for the "amelioration [changing for the better] of the terrible position today of Jews all over the world." On the same day the Archbishop of Canterbury put out a request that next Sunday 'shall be observed as a National Day of Prayer in this time of crisis,' as recorded the local *Evening Post*. 'To emphasise its national significance, the King [of England, George VI] has given his wholehearted approval to this call to prayer.'

In January 1939, the Lord told Rees Howells that a gift of £100,000 was to be given to the Jews – this was published in the *Western Mail* on 29th May 1939: '£100,000 expected by Bible College – New Schools for 1,000 Jewish Refugee Children.' Rees Howells in *God Challenges the Dictators* wrote that 'the sale of the properties would be dedicated to the "Cities of Refuge" for the Jewish children. In other words we were prepared to make an offering to God of £100,000 – the value of our College property – for helping the children of His Chosen people. Because we were prepared to do this, we were observing a rule of faith whereby we might confidently look to God for an equal sum for our genuine needs.'

Rees Howells believed he had to sell all three estates (Glynderwen, Sketty Isaf and Derwen Fawr) and use that money as a first-fruit offering unto the Lord for the Jews. The Lord tested Rees and like Abraham of old he was found willing to sacrifice whatever the Lord wanted, but like Abraham with Isaac on Mount Moriah, he was not called to perform the literal sacrifice.[11]

In July 1944 it became known to Rees Howells and the Bible College community that four million Jews of Europe had been murdered by the Nazi régime. This made Rees Howells and his team of students and staff even more determined to see the nation of Israel, re-established in the Holy Land, according to Bible prophecy. In addition Rees Howells speaking in July 1944 noted, (and I paraphrase), "Why would any Jews of Europe want to go back to Germany or be resettled in Europe? They want to be settled and safe in their own Land of Promise."

When the war was over, entire days were given over to intercession for the re-establishment of the nation of Israel, a Jewish State, especially from October to November 1947 when the United Nations (UN) were in discussions, and a vote was cast on 27th November in the UN headquarters in New York, USA.[12]

A BCW Hymn about Beloved Israel

John Rocha was a boarder at Emmanuel Bible School. He had Jewish ancestry whose father was a missionary and associated with the Mildmay Mission to the Jews. John became a teacher at the school in 1948 and emigrated to Israel in 1977. He wrote:

During the time that the Jewish people were being persecuted by Hitler and the Nazis...[the following] song was composed by Ardis [Butterfield] a member of the Bible College of Wales fellowship. We frequently sang this song in the meetings at that time. I am still encouraged as I sing it!

Oh, Israel, beloved and chosen
Thine hour is drawing near,
When out of thy great tribulation
Thy name God will lift up on high!

Oh, cry out and shout!
Thou dweller of Zion
And praise ye the Lord!
For great is the One in the midst of thee,
Declare ye His doings abroad![13]

Chapter 4

The History of God Challenges the Dictators

'The Preacher sought to find acceptable words; and what was written was upright – words of truth. The words of the wise are like goads, and the words of scholars are like well-driven nails, given by one Shepherd. And further, my son, be admonished by these. Of making many books there is no end, and much study is wearisome to the flesh. Let us hear the conclusion of the whole matter. Fear God and keep His commandments, for this is man's all' (Ecclesiastes 12:10-13).

'For we do not wrestle against flesh and blood (against human beings, dictators or failed / evil governments etc.), but against principalities, against powers, against the rulers of the darkness of this age, against the spiritual hosts of wickedness in the heavenly places' (Ephesians 6:12).

In September 1939, just days after Britain declared war on Germany when they ignored Britain's ultimatum to retreat from Poland, Rees Howells began writing what would become *God Challenges the Dictators*. The first reference was on 6th September 1939 at the 6.45pm meeting when Rees Howells said, "It is God who went against this system [Nazism] is what I want to write in my book.... It is a fight of the Holy Ghost against the Devil...." Rees had hoped to get the book published by 10th October 1939, (his sixtieth birthday) as noted in the meetings of 28th and 29th September, though this was not possible.

God Challenges the Dictators was first published as a paperback edition with card covers by the Western Mail & Echo Ltd., Cardiff and London; followed by a hardback edition, red board covers with a black dust cover by Simpkins Marshall Ltd of London.

It was split into two sections and drew largely from the *Twelfth Session Annual Report* (1936) and the *Fourth Every Creature Conference* (1939) booklet.

Part I – War Predictions (Chapters I-VI).

Part II – Predictions Fulfilled (Chapters VII-XIII).

The paperback and hardback editions page numbering stops at 160, but the following un-numbered page is a statement of accounts for the year ended 31st March 1939.

God Challenges the Dictators: Doom of Nazis Predicted was written from early September to the end of November 1939, with minor corrections over the first few days of December. The last chapter was penned by the 25th November 1939 and the first edition, paper card cover was published in early December 1939. The hardback edition was published in the first week of December 1939 and reprinted in January 1940, out of an initial print run order of 20,000 copies. Rees Howells gave signed copies to members of staff, from "the Director." Like himself they had all made great personal sacrifices, left all to follow Jesus Christ, to make disciples, and sank their lives into the Bible College of Wales.

On 16th October 1939, Western Mail & Echo Ltd, a printer who published local newspapers sent Rees Howells a quote:

10,000 8vo books [a printing term describing the format of a book] DIVINE PREDICTIONS FULFILLED, 120 printed pages including five pages of halftone illustrations, coarse grain blocks and paper cover printed on front in two colours and on the 4th page and spine in one colour, for £195.

20,000 ditto £341.

50,000 ditto £780.[1]

Author A. J. Russell of London

A. J. Russell of Woodlands, London and then of Finchley, London, an author, helped edit and proofread *God Challenges the Dictators* and had contacts within the newspaper and magazine industry. He was a member of the Authors' Club at 2 Whitehall Court, London, S.W.1. Over several months, Rees Howells sent A. J. Russell cheques of £5 [£337 in 2020] and £10 [£675 in 2020] for proofreading, revising of the text, advice, additions and for A. J. Russell's promotion of the book within his sphere of influence because 'a labourer is worthy of his hire' (1 Timothy 5:18). This also included favourable reviews being hand-delivered to national newspapers in Fleet Street, London, alongside a copy of the book for the newspapers' perusal of which A. J. Russell and a Mr Barwell were a part of. A. J. Russell was not only a friend and supporter of the work of Rees Howells with their near daily correspondence, but appears that he was also acting as his advocate and literary agent to promote and boost sales of *God Challenges the Dictators*.[2]

In a letter dated 2nd November 1939, to A. J. Russell, Rees Howells wrote: 'Now I have the manuscript nearly ready. As you would notice on the prospectus I sent out, we have nearly a hundred on the staff [some would have been called up for the war effort or left, as the College ceased all lecturers for the first year of the war; lecturers thereafter were sporadic, but no student paid any fees for the duration of the war!]. There are over twenty degree people here, and one of them has been through the manuscripts. She had a very great distinction in English and is a gold medallist. The thought that came to me about yourself was that you might read through them, and you could put some headings [in] that would make the book attractive.

'In my prediction I said there was going to be no European War, and the prediction was fulfilled when Italy, [and] Spain dropped out of it, and isolated Germany. This fulfilled my prediction to the letter.'

In a letter dated 14th November 1939, to Rees Howells, A. J. Russell wrote: 'Dear Mr Rees Howells, Your MMS [manuscript] contains a number of really good things.' The following part of the letter is written in bullet point style:

- Not having had a vision as to its future I cannot predict [the number of books that will sell]. But I have had a shot at the MSS to make it read a little more popularly.
- There was rather more to do with it than I had gathered.
- You will notice that I have re-written the first chapter and have made quite a lot of minor changes in the other.
- I have also put in cross-heads where they will be useful.
- The chapter headings I have shortened so that they will come up more sharply in the book.
- You will see something like this [very frequently and will gather that it means a new paragraph.
- This kind of argumentative narrative needs smaller paragraphs to retain attention than a novel. It is important.
- If your typist is unable to follow the interlineations your printer will do so quite easily. If not refer anything back to me.
- A number of these sentences were inverted and these I took the liberty of returning to their feet. [Whilst Rees Howells was fluent in English his first language was Welsh].
- Your introduction has not yet come to hand. What is URGENTLY NEEDED is a VERY CLEAR description of

exactly how and when and where the predictions were received.

- Also a general description of the Founders [Rees and Lizzie Howells] and the after-life of the students [what they have done after graduation, which mission fields do they labour in]. Something should also be said to show that those who cannot raise half-fees still get admission [because the students learnt a life of faith].

In a letter dated 16th November 1939, to A. J. Russell, Rees Howells wrote: 'This is just a word to acknowledge the MSS [manuscript], which we received yesterday. We have only had time to re-type about five chapters, and to put it mildly, we are more than pleased with the way you have made it a living book. I am positive that God is behind it, and that thousands and thousands will be blessed through it, because nearly all the Daily Papers took up the predictions, from the *Daily Herald* to the *Daily Mail,* and especially the weekly periodicals.'

Changing Book Titles and Subtitles

In an undated letter, which was probably written on 17th November 1939, Rees Howells to A. J. Russell wrote: 'We sent you a letter with the last post. Now we are sending you the MSS complete with the "Contents" showing the chapters. Also the title "GOD CHALLENGES THE DICTATORS" and in the middle of the cover I want to put our school motto "EMMANUEL." I enclose a pattern of it. At the bottom of the title page will be "THE DOWNFALL OF THE NAZI REGIME PREDICTED."

'When you return them, we shall send them to the printers. Any suggestions you would like to make concerning the cover and the title, will you please do so. This will be your last correction before it goes to the printer, and then you will get the proof when we get it from them.'

The book title and subtitle went through five specific revisions:

- DIVINE PREDICTIONS FULFILLED (16th October 1939).
- GOD CHALLENGES THE DICTATORS: THE DOWNFALL OF THE NAZI REGIME PREDICTED (16th November 1939).
- Similar to above was GOD CHALLENGES THE DICTATORS: THE DOWNFALL OF THE NAZI REGIME. This was found on an early typed manuscript (no date) on the Introduction page.

- Inside another manuscript (there were three in total) and similar to above with no date was: GOD CHALLENGES THE DICTATORS: DOOM OF THE NAZIS PREDICTED. But the first definite article 'THE' has been crossed out in blue ink, reading: GOD CHALLENGES DICTATORS. The definite article was soon restored being central to the title.
- GOD CHALLENGES THE DICTATORS: DOOM OF NAZIS PREDICTED (unspecified date between 17th November and 4th December 1939). The school motto of 'EMMANUEL' never made it onto the cover (letter, 17th November 1939), but the Emmanuel School ensign, a world globe without any text was placed in the centre of the front cover on the dust-jacket.
- The book grew in length from 120 pages from the first quote of 16th October 1939 to 164 pages with the last page numbered at 160, the statement of accounts and the remaining three pages of the hardback being blank; 164 pages in total.

When Rees Howells spoke of his book from 1939-1949, or when there were advertisements promoting *God Challenges the Dictators* in the newspapers from 1939-1940, sometimes the subtitle would be: *Doom of Nazis Predicted* and at other times *Doom of the Nazis Predicted* with the definite article 'the' added. Rees Howells wrote to A. J. Russell on 4th September 1944, then residing at Harvington, near Evesham, who had been his editor and literary agent for *God Challenges the Dictators* from 1939-1940. He wrote the title plus the subtitle: *The Doom of the Nazis Predicted and the Death of Hitler*. A section of the phantom subtitle *"and the Death of Hitler"* was never part of the book's title. Five years and three months later, Rees Howells speaking at the 7pm meeting on 15th December 1949, said, "I had to be very sure when I put that title on my book: *The Doom of the Nazis Predicted and the Death of Hitler*. This was just sixty days before Rees Howells was promoted to glory on 13th February 1950.

It may have been a potential title that Rees Howells had considered in 1939, or one he had *initially* intended to put on the cover, but was advised against it. Whatever the correct answer, history does not reveal, but it does show that the BCW secretaries and scribes who recorded Rees Howells' sermons and typed his letters and teaching notes did not alter them, but put them down as they were dictated.

First Public Reading

On Saturday, 25th November 1939, Dr. Kingsley Priddy read *God Challenges the Dictators: Doom of Nazis Predicted* by Rees Howells to those who were present in the Conference Hall on the Derwen Fawr Estate. The meeting began at 5.45pm and ended at 9pm. More than two hundred students and staff would have been present, though it is possible that the number was nearer 250 with some of the older boarders attending from Emmanuel School plus friends and visitors to the College, which was common. The meeting would have begun and ended with a hymn and there may have been a Scripture reading and possible prayer. However this meeting was unique and different than any other meeting that was held at the College during the war years.[3] The original 1939 *God Challenges the Dictators* can be read in under two hours, though for some it will take longer, however when reading aloud in a public forum accomplished speakers will slow their reading to give the audience time to digest what is being said. A meeting of 3 hours and 15 minutes in duration is the longest service that occurred during the war years.

Dr. Kingsley Priddy was on the medical team and in 1950 became the Headmaster of Emmanuel School, later to become known as Emmanuel Grammar School.

Rees Howells in his only published work wrote: 'This Introduction was written during the very weekend [25-26th November 1939] when the German magnetic mines were beginning to blow up British and neutral ships.'

At the 9.30am meeting of 26th November 1939, Rees Howells said, "This is one of the darkest days since the war began. Germany has crippled our navy by laying thousands of magnetic mines all around our coasts, so that London and other ports are closed. This comes after Mr Churchill's speech of a week or two ago, saying that our Navy was still 'the mistress of the seas.' But not so now. Unless our experts find something to counteract it, we will be starved out before Germany. What of the sending out of the book and the predictions in this dark hour?"[4]

Rees Howells was eager to get his book out to help the country to pray, to inspire faith and trust in the living God over a righteous and just cause. The Nazis with their antichrist spirit had trampled over countries and their borders, annexing them, imprisoning and killing opponents. They had put Evangelical ministers who opposed the Nazi régime into prisons and concentration camps, and had been persecuting the Jews in Germany since the early

1930s, and in Nazi-occupied European countries from the late 1930s until the destruction of the Third Reich in 1945.

Get it Printed before Christmas 1939
In a letter dated 29th November 1939, to A. J. Russell, Rees Howells wrote: 'I want to get it out by Christmas.' In a letter dated, 4th December 1939, to A. J. Russell, Rees Howells wrote: 'The book that was revised and revised and revised [sic] came back, and I think it was worth all the revisions. We are more than pleased with it.' On the same day *God Challenges the Dictators* went to the printers in Cardiff, Western Mail & Echo Ltd, which was just over forty miles by road from Swansea.

In a letter dated 4th December 1939, Rees Howells reveals that he had ordered 20,000 copies of *God Challenges the Dictators* with the option of ordering 50,000 copies within the month from the printers, Western Mail, in Cardiff, Wales.

Printers in London and Cardiff
On Friday, 15th December 1939, Rees Howells took the morning train from Swansea, Wales, to London, England, and returned by 8.30pm. It was a 320 mile round trip by train. In London he saw the Censorship Bureau and the printers Simpkin Marshall Ltd. *God Challenges the Dictators* passed for publication on the same day and was signed by G. M. M. of Press and Censorship Bureau. Due to the war, books had to be cleared before publication.

On the following day, Rees Howells travelled in the morning to Cardiff to see the printers. In the evening, Rees Howells took the 7pm meeting and spoke on 2 Samuel 2. He said, "I can sing this Psalm of David tonight, perhaps in a deeper way even than David did. What perfect guidance God has given me these last days concerning the book. What perfect guidance over the censoring of the book. I wired to make an appointment with the censor and how quickly it was all done. Then again how the Lord has worked to get the best publisher in London to take the book without it being reviewed. What a book! What a title!.... I do not want any credit for it."

On the morning of Monday, 18th December, Rees Howells returned to the printers in Cardiff to discuss money and quantities. It was not good news, but Rees knew – God is sovereign. He is in control of all things and all things are under His control.

On 18th December 1939, Rees Howells revealed in a letter that the printers, Western Mail could only print about 5,000 copies per week and needed to be paid monthly. Rees Howells asked A. J. Russell to speak to larger printers in London to see if orders of 100,000 to 200,000 copies could be printed weekly and paid for in half-yearly instalments on 30th June and 31st December, which were the same fiscal terms as Simpkin Marshall Ltd.

On the morning of Wednesday, 20th December 1939, Rees Howells travelled to London to see the printers. A typed copy of the 7pm meeting revealed: 'Director [Rees Howells] came back from London triumphant again in securing his object, i.e. of getting in touch with a large printing firm. He had said he fixed up everything with the largest printing firm in the country (Penguin), and said that if it came to him needing 1,000,000 copies a week of his book from them, he would get them! How wonderful! Director was more than pleased with the business terms arranged between these printers, the publisher and himself. He said he could hardly believe that what had happened in London was true. The Lord, nothing less than removed mountains for him in a few minutes. He came back convinced in a greater way than ever that the Holy Ghost is the Creator in business and finances as He is in Creation. Director overjoyed.'

The Cost of a Book
The 1939 card cover copy was originally sold for 1/- per copy, plus postage 4d., 12 copies sent for 13/- (which includes postage); 50 copies, £2 12s. 6d. (including postage); 100 copies £5 5s. 0d. (including postage).

The hardback edition of 1940 was twice as expensive at 2/- (two shillings) and every once in a while a copy appears on eBay, Amazon or Abebooks (sometimes a seller lists the same book on multiple sites). From 2004-2020 when I have been following the prices of God challenges the Dictators, I have known of only twenty-one copies bought and or sold from across the United Kingdom and America. The prices have ranged from a low of £15 plus the cost of postage to just over £200 plus the cost of postage.

Books Sold 1939-1940
On 8th December 1939, Rees Howells in a letter to A. J. Russell wrote: 'There is great excitement concerning the book. One person has just ordered 100 this afternoon, and another 50, one 40 and so on.

On 20th December 1939, one London bookseller ordered 75 copies.

GOD CHALLENGES
THE DICTATORS

DOOM OF NAZIS
PREDICTED

REES HOWELLS

Printed in Great Britain
by
Western Mail & Echo Ltd., Cardiff and London,
and Published by
The Bible College of Wales, Swansea.

—

1939

Passed for Publication 15 December 1939

By the end of the year, 29th December 1939, 20,000 copies had already been printed by the Western Mail. They would have used their printing press in London as well as the one in Cardiff as they could only print around 5,000 copies per week. Rees Howells believed that they wanted to print the next 30,000 copies as part of a total package of 50,000. In the same letter to A. J. Russell, Rees Howells reveals: 'Now in the Spirit we do feel that God is going to use the book in a very great way, because the printer has made 2,500 of the incorrected [sic] ones and nearly all those have been sold, and of the corrected ones, 500 have been sent to Simpkin Marshall [a publisher with distribution access] and he wired last night to send another 1,000 immediately.' One bookshop ordered 700 copies to date (29th Dec. 1939). Another bookshop in London ordered 50 copies, then another 50 and then another 50 copies until Rees Howells informed them that they could order via Simpkin Marshall (of London), whilst 'one shop in Swansea sold nearly 50 copies every night.' This reveals how popular Rees Howells was on his home turf.

A. J. Russell sent a Post Office Telegram to Rees Howells of Darwen [sic] Fawr Swansea, dated 29th December 1939. 'Have induced Purnells [Purnell and Co, publisher] accept fourpence [4p per copy] provided half total [invoice be] paid with immediate order they guaranteeing supply hundred thousand about one months time, some earlier = Russell.'

These numbers are quite astonishing as most publishers would have an initial print-run of between 1,000-1,500 books for a first-time author. The danger with many first-time authors is the self-belief that their book will sell in large quantities, when in reality most are disappointed with the low volume of their sales. This is why many books only have a single print run, which are removed from bookshelves within six weeks if not selling in sufficient quantities, as they are taking up valuable retail space.

Rees Howells was a popular man of God with well-known spiritual credentials and had a proven track record within Christendom, though not without his critics and those who opposed him and his ministry. Rees Howells was actually self-publishing the book *God Challenges the Dictators* (paying to get a book printed) because if he had submitted the manuscript to a publisher it would often take 18 months until publication, and only if the publisher was willing to take on a new author, whilst some are left waiting for six months or more, only to be turned down. Going direct to a printer, Rees Howells was able to avoid publishing bureaucracy and get the book into print within one month to utilise the spiritual climate, to instil and stimulate faith in the face of overwhelming odds when fear of invasion was sweeping the land. As Adolf Hitler and his Nazis stormed across Europe removing Christian freedoms, and later tried to annihilate the Jewish race like Haman of the old Persian Empire, as recorded in the book of Esther from the Bible.

In less than two weeks after *God Challenges the Dictators* was printed 'nearly 1,000 people from all parts of the British Isles sent for a copy each, and that only through reading a small article in one of the daily papers...besides 100s of others who ordered through their agents,' so wrote Rees Howells.

In a letter dated 9th February 1940 to A. J. Russell, Rees Howells wrote: '...We are receiving orders for the book all the time, and only the day before yesterday we heard from Simpkin Marshall Ltd that Wyman [bookshop] had sent for a hundred.... Although we thought that many more of the books would have gone by this time.... As you do say, there is a very great deal of jealousy about the book, and there has been re: the College. The standard the College has raised up in a life of faith [a standard of believing faith against all odds] has caused from the beginning, and that is how the College has had thousands of real followers, because of the life of faith and the standard.... We are having letters every day from people who have been blessed through reading the book. Many of the Welsh papers have reviewed it, which were most favourable.' Rees Howells had a proven record.

Two weeks later on 23rd February 1940, Rees Howells wrote to A. J. Russell: '....The meetings are very, very great. We had another call from Simpkin Marshall Ltd for a further 1,000....'

Book Production War Economy Standard

God Challenges the Dictators was published at the end of 1939, three months before paper rationing was introduced in Britain in March 1940. From this time onwards, publishers and printers had their paper supplies cut by 60% from the previous two years as the raw materials were needed for the war effort.

The Ministry of Supply and the Publishers Association agreed on a Book Production War Economy Standard (BPWES) to help preserve paper supplies which came into effect on 1st January 1942. On the copyright page books were stamped with an open book logo with a lion on top facing west. The text on the book's open pages covering four lines was: Book Production War Economy Standard. Below the logo was: This book is produced in complete conformity with the authorised economy standard.

The Book Production War Economy Standard was only a voluntary agreement but for any publisher or printer who did not sign up to it, they had their allotted rationed paper cut further! For those who did sign up there was to be less white space on every page (smaller margins), smaller font (type) and paper quality and binding were not as good as they were pre-war. In Britain, paper rationing was discontinued in 1949.

GOD CHALLENGES
THE DICTATORS

DOOM OF NAZIS
PREDICTED

By

REES HOWELLS

Printed in Great Britain
by
Western Mail & Echo Ltd., Cardiff and London,
and Published by
The Bible College of Wales, Swansea.

—

1939

A 1939 first edition Specimen Chapter of 32 pages bound with two staples. The Specimen Chapter used the Title Page as the Cover with the Copyright Page on the reverse side. It was stamped at the top in red ink Specimen Chapter.

Specimen Chapter Edition

A paperback Specimen Chapter edition in booklet form was also published. In some letters or meetings it was referred to as a "booklet" whilst at other times as a "pamphlet." This was a 32-page booklet, which included the Introduction, Chapter 1 and two pages of chapter 2, plus the Contents, and had the same title *God Challenges the Dictators*. It appears that the Specimen Chapter was born out of a printing error (or inspired it) and was used as a form of advertisement. So good was the providential "big mistake" that others were printed to order. Rees Howells said "...It was wonderful how the Spirit had got over so many difficulties concerning the book, and what seemed *a big mistake turned out to be a big victory and blessing*. I sent the first 32 pages in a cover as a Specimen copy of the book to the world. What an advertisement this would be!"[5]

The Specimen Chapter of 32-pages was one fifth of the full book of 160-pages. Originally, 14,000 copies were ordered on 23rd December 1939, 4,000 less than was initially intended. However, a further 6,000 copies were printed at a later date taking the total to 20,000 copies, or 640,000 printed pages! These Specimen Chapter editions were dated 1939 and 1940, the same as the hardback editions.

For Every Minister in the Country

At the 7pm meeting on Boxing Day, 26th December 1939, the fifth anniversary of the Vision, Rees Howells commented, "Picture an army of ministers reading the book!" On the following day at the 9am meeting he said, "I was only thinking this morning, I don't believe in all my life I have ever picked up a book full of predictions." At the 7pm meeting on 29th December 1939, Rees Howells noted that about 10,000 pamphlets (Specimen Chapters) had been sent out and he hoped the ministers would see the Vision (Every Creature) as revealed by the Holy Spirit.

An unnamed typist in a set of shorthand notes for Friday, 29 December 1939, noted: 'Director is all day in prayer for ministers – the Holy Spirit is after them!'

Dr. Kingsley Priddy preached at the 9am meeting and Rees Howells took the 7pm meeting.

By the 3rd January 1940, 'every minister in the country had one of those little booklets,' wrote Rees Howells.

ORDER FORM

To: The Secretary,
        The Bible College of Wales,
            Derwen Fawr, SWANSEA, Glam:

Please send .... copy of the
                            copies

*SHILLING EDITION   of "God Challenges the
TWO SHILLING EDITION
Dictators" to the following address:

M...

    ....

        ....

(in block letters)
            * cash
    I enclose postal order for ....
                cheque

to cover cost and postage.

Postage rates: 4d one copy of the shilling ed:
                6d "   "   "   " two "   "

Date.................................

*Please cross out the one not required.

A 1939 Order Form for *God Challenges the Dictators*. One Shilling Edition (card covers) or the Two Shilling Edition (hardback). This typed Order Form which is on light salmon pink paper would have been enclosed with the 20,000 Specimen Chapter editions sent to every minister in the country. It is highly probable that an Order Form was also enclosed with every purchase of the book which was processed at the Bible College of Wales to help with future orders.

23 DEC. 1939

GOD CHALLENGES THE DICTATORS

DOOM OF NAZIS PREDICTED

Rev. REES HOWELLS

Bible College of Wales, Swansea

LONDON
SIMPKIN MARSHALL, LTD
STATIONERS' HALL COURT, E.C, 4
1940

CAN BE OBTAINED FROM ALL BOOKSELLERS 1/- NET

A 1940 first edition Specimen Chapter of 32 pages printed by Simpkin Marshall, LTD (of London, England), as opposed to the 1939 first edition, published in Cardiff, Wales. Notice how the 1940 edition has the title prefix of Rev. added, whilst under Rev. Rees Howells' is: Bible College of Wales, Swansea.

20,000 Envelopes

The cost of posting 20,000 Specimen Chapters would have been quite significant. 20,000 'booklets' had to be packed in 20,000 envelopes, sealed by licking the sticky gum and then taken to the Post Office. 20,000 stamps had to be bought, assuming that there was a single value stamp to cover the weight of the envelope and each stamp had to be stuck to the envelope!

At the 7pm meeting on Wednesday, 27th December 1939, Rees Howells gave part of his testimony and traced his experience of the new birth (conversion), fellowship with the Saviour, how the Holy Spirit came in to possess him, and the cleansing through the blood of the Lord Jesus Christ. An unnamed typist in a set of shorthand notes revealed: 'He [Rees Howells] mentioned the book and the envelopes in connection with sending out the pamphlets to the ministers – Hitch over the Western Mail – but [the] Director [Rees Howells] got in touch with the Managing Director of the manufacturers, who is going to send 10,000 envelopes first thing tomorrow at 7/6d. per 1,000, whereas from the Western Mail he was paying £1 per 1,000. Real guidance in this today.' (£1 in 1939 is approximately £67 in 2020. 7/6d is just over one third of £1, or approximately £22.50 in 2020. Thus Rees Howells in today's money would have saved around £445 for 10,000 envelopes direct from the manufacturer).

Total Print Run

It appears that whilst Rees Howells had the option of a total of 50,000 copies of God Challenges the Dictators (4th December 1939), all the evidence suggest that no more than 20,000 copies were printed, plus 20,000 Specimen Chapters. What is known is that Rees Howells was interested in an additional 30,000 copies, but there is no evidence to suggest that they were printed. 20,000 copies were ordered and 2,500 copies were error copies. It is possible that due to these error copies the total print run could have been 22,500, or the 2,500 error copies were accepted (because they were sold) as part of a total of 20,000 copies.

In the late 1980s, before the rise of the internet and online ecommerce, boxes of God Challenges the Dictators were taken out of the loft of the Men's Hostel and destroyed or thrown away, though one copy resided in the library and all the elderly staff members had their own books. The war was long past and the College was in a new era, though some of those commissioned with literary destruction kept copies for themselves. It was the duty of the male students to maintain the boilers at Derwen Fawr and Sketty Isaf, to keep the fires stoked with firewood, and some of the books were burnt. Ashes had to be regularly raked out and scrunched up paper was needed to get the fire going (even if it was the words dictated by Rees Howells) alongside kindle (small pieces of wood, or parts of a hardback), before split logs were placed inside. The Derwen Fawr boiler was in an underground chamber next to the library, opposite the Bake House, in the same quadrangle as the Men's Hostel. The Sketty Isaf boiler was also underground near the potato shed at the end of Sketty Isaf.

Rees Howells' Letters 1943

In a letter dated, 22nd May 1943, replying to David Prytherch of Chepstow, England, Rees Howells' Assistant Secretary wrote: '...As regards literature, owing to the restrictions on paper by the Government nothing has been printed recently concerning the work here, although the Lord is continuing to bless the work in a wonderful way, and during the war we have been a family of 200 [around 70 were children] and the Lord has abundantly supplied. "God Challenges the Dictators" was printed during the *first week of the war and is all coming true to the letter – we wonder if you have read this?' *Rees Howells actually began to write it then, though as the Bible College had a small printing press in their printing room on the Derwen Fawr Estate, did they have some samples printed?

On the same day, 22nd May 1943, Rees Howells wrote to Corporal C. Workman of Shrewsbury, England: 'After we left you yesterday we couldn't get away from that meeting in Bath. Dr. Symonds [a medical member of staff] and myself felt sure that it must all be of the Lord, and I hope there will be a wonderful outcome of it.' Rees Howells then goes on to talk of an 86-year-old missionary to Japan, Miss Evans, 'is enjoying the provision that the Lord has made for her' in the Missionary Home (on Sketty Isaf Estate, opposite the Derwen Fawr Estate).

'I am enclosing one of my books to you [*God Challenges the Dictators*] and while you read it if you only bear in mind that we said Hitler failed to make a European War at Munich [in 1938], and we said it's God [who] made war on the three great systems of Nazism, Bolshevism and Fascism and it seems He will smash them with that "stone" that came out of the mountain – the Holy Spirit and they will never remain again [Daniel 2:44]. In reading the book, if you begin reading at the buying of the College and School etc. you will have a better insight into predictions of the war.'

Chapter 5

Working with the Tabloids

Haman said to King Ahasuerus, "Then let this robe and horse be delivered to the hand of one of the king's most noble princes, that he may array the man whom the king delights to honour. Then parade him on horseback through the city square, and proclaim before him: 'Thus shall it be done to the man whom the king delights to honour!' " (Esther 6:9).

'The chariots of God are twenty thousand, even thousands of thousands; the Lord is among them as in Sinai, in the Holy Place. You have ascended on high, You have led captivity captive; You have received gifts among men, even from the rebellious, that the Lord God might dwell there' (Psalm 68:17-18).

Rees Howells was media savvy and knew how to connect to his audience through the medium of public speaking, annual booklets and newspaper articles to reach a much larger audience. Editors and journalists always want a story and Rees Howells was a man with many messages, predictions and words which the people of Wales, Britain and beyond needed to hear. Some articles were published in newspapers as far away as Australia.

It was Benjamin Franklin who popularised the phrase, "God helps those who help themselves," and so with Rees Howells, he applied faith and works to what he was called to do. He prayed and he made known the forthcoming publication of *God Challenges the Dictators* through précis (summary of the text), review copies sent to newspapers, the Specimen Chapter Edition of 32-pages, excerpts, many press releases and adverts.

In a general press release dated 12th December 1939 from Rev. Rees Howells:

Your review of my latest book "God Challenges the Dictators," which as suggested by the title, has a topical appeal, will be appreciated. The book deals with the founding of the Bible College of Wales, now worth £150,000, [£10,116,000 in 2020] on two shillings [approximately £6.74 in 2020], and goes on to refer to my predictions on world affairs, given considerable publicity at the time, and since proved to be correct. It also forecasts the fate which will befall Hitler and his supporters. I am taking the liberty of enclosing a précis, and would appreciate a copy of the paper containing your comments – should you be kind enough to review the book. Thank you in anticipation, faithfully yours, Rees Howells, Director.

THE BIBLE COLLEGE OF WALES

OPENING OF THE

SECOND TERM

OF THE

SIXTEENTH SESSION

THURSDAY, JANUARY 11th, 1940.
MEETING AT 2 p.m.

ALL WELCOME.

THE NEW BOOK

"GOD CHALLENGES THE DICTATORS"

"DOOM OF THE NAZIS PREDICTED."

by

REV. REES HOWELLS, Bible College of Wales.

Publishers :—
Simpkin Marshall, Ltd., Stationers' Hall Court, E.C.4.

Can be obtained from all Booksellers.
1s. Net.

Newspaper Advertisement January 1940
17 weeks after war broke out between Germany and Britain

- 56 -

Australian Newspaper Article

The following report contains the correspondent's interpretation of Rees Howells' predictions. Hitler had already annexed Austria, Czechoslovakia and had invaded Poland and was at war with Britain and France. It was published in *The Cairns Post,* in Australia, 11th January 1940: HITLER'S DOOM. PROPHESIED BY WELSH PARSON. WHAT GOD HAS TOLD HIM. (From a Special Correspondent by Air Mail). LONDON, December 23.

The war will never develop into a general European conflict, according to Rev. Rees Howells, Director of the Bible College in Wales [sic]. The prediction is one of a number of extraordinary prophecies about Hitler and the Nazi régime published this week under the title of "God's [sic] Challenge [sic] to the Dictators: Doom of the Nazis Predicted." The author, a former missionary, has already won distinction by his strange gift of prediction. He founded his famous college in Swansea with a capital of 2/- [shillings], "because God told him to do so." He now holds property worth £150,000 [£10,116,000 in 2020]. Here are some of the other things which Mr Howells tells us: Though the Allies may perhaps find themselves hard pressed, the struggle will end with the overthrow of Hitler and the final doom of the Nazis.

It has been foreshown to Mr Howells that God will intervene in the war and that He will Himself deal with Hitler. Mussolini's decision to remain neutral at the outbreak of war was prompted not by any ordinary diplomatic strategy, but by Divine guidance. "The unseen hand of God Himself was at work." There can be no future alliance between the European-dictators to the prejudice of the Allied cause. God will prevent it. "Not only shall we see the downfall of Hitler, but the same fate will overtake all those blood-thirsty leaders of the Nazi régime." Those of them Mr Howells declares, who do not take refuge in suicide will be thrust, into their own concentration camps, there to endure the horrors they have themselves inflicted on the Christians and Jews."[1]

Newsreel footage later revealed that at some of the concentration camps which were liberated by the Allies, German soldiers who had been guards at the camps were forced to bury the dead of those whom they had held captive. Thousands of survivors who were emancipated and unable to digest food or ate too much solid food, having been starved for months or years also died after liberation. Hitler took his own life in an act of suicide, as did some senior Nazi figures before and during the Nuremberg Trials. The verdict and results at the end of the trial on 2nd October 1946 was: twelve Nazis were sentenced to hang to death, three were given life imprisonment, two were given twenty years, one was given fifteen years and another was sentenced to ten years in prison.

A Number of other Australian newspapers ran articles about Rev. Rees Howells and his war predictions; some citing his Bible College and his book *God Challenges the Dictators.* These articles range from 70 words to no more than 500 words and are all very similar to the article above, but edited to fit the column space. The following are the headlines from each article, the newspaper in which it was printed, date and page number:

1. PRAYER AND FAITH. *Western Star and Roma Advertiser* (Toowoomba, Qld), Friday, 8 January 1940, page 3.
2. HITLER'S DOOM Prophesied by Welsh Parson Former Missionary Predicts Course of War. *The Armidale Express and New England General Advertiser* (NSW), Friday, 12 January 1940, page 3.
3. WAR PROPHECIES. *The Gloucester Advocate* (NSW), Friday, 26 January 1940, page 4.
4. WAR PROPHECIES Fate Of "Bloodthirsty" Nazis. *The Mercury* (Hobart, Tas), Friday, 26 January 1940, page 5.
5. WAR PROPHECIES. *Dungog Chronicle: Durham and Gloucester Advertiser* (NSW), Tuesday, 30 January 1940, page 3.
6. WAR PROPHECIES. *The Port Macquarie News and Hastings River Advocate* (NSW), Saturday, 10 February 1940, page 6.
7. MISSIONARY PROPHESIES NAZIS DOOM. *The Evening News* (Rockhampton, Qld), Wednesday, 21 February 1940, page 2.
8. CLERIC PROPHESIES GIFTS. *Cairns Post*, Wednesday, 19 March 1940, page 2.

Relating to one prediction, Rees Howells wrote: '...Was not only displayed on the news-bills of the *Evening Post* and the *Western Mail,* but also on those of the *Daily Mail* and other London [in England] newspapers, which, following the great publicity given to it by the local press.... People read it in Germany, Italy, and even in the Holy Land.'

Chapter 6

The Vantage Point of Historical Victory

'For whatever things were written before were written for our learning, that we through the patience and comfort of the Scriptures might have hope' (Romans 15:4).

'To the intent that now the manifold wisdom of God might be made known by the Church to the principalities and powers in the heavenly places, according to the eternal purpose which He accomplished in Christ Jesus our Lord, in whom we have boldness and access with confidence through faith in Him' (Ephesians 3:10-12).

Before you read the very words and thoughts of Rees Howells in the midst of the greatest conflict of intercession in his age, we invite you to read the thoughts of those who spent their lives at the Bible College of Wales, and how this book and the events told within can be interpreted from the vantage point of historical victory. Richard Maton, the author of two books on the life of Rees Howells' son Samuel Rees Howells, Miss Doris M. Ruscoe an intercessor with Rees Howells from 1932 onwards, and Norman Grubb, a close friend of Rees Howells (and his biographer) explain what we can learn from these events.

A Declaration of Faith
The following comments concerning *God Challenges the Dictators* are by Richard Maton the author of *Samuel, Son and Successor of Rees Howells* and Principal of the Bible College of Wales from 1979-2002.

Rees Howells had known the threats posed by Adolf Hitler and the Nazi Movement but, being fully convinced that the Holy Spirit had complete mastery over all powers of darkness in the world, he was totally confident in making a prediction that there would be no General War in Europe. This he made publicly, even writing to the Prime Minister, Mr Winston Churchill, and publishing a book, *God Challenges the Dictators* in December 1939, which was split into two parts. It was not a prophecy as such, but a declaration based upon the total believing the Holy Spirit was giving him for the demise of this evil system in Europe, a quality of faith that very few have exercised. Nothing would prevent the fulfilment of the Vision the Lord had given Rees Howells in December 1934 [the Every Creature Vision / Commission]; every knee would bow to the eternal Son of God. Of course, from this assurance he used, on several occasions, the Lord's Name which brought complete confusion and mistrust into the minds of people who had, up till then, become ardent followers of this 'Welsh prophet.'

Samuel [Howells, the only child of Rees and Lizzie Howells] remembered very vividly how that prediction, and all his father's plans to assist the Jewish refugees and eventually enable them to settle in land purchased in the Holy Land (modern day Israel), all publicised widely in local and national newspapers, had come crashing down. He had lived every minute of those dark days, when even his own personal faith was tested to the limit.

He had endeavoured, as best he could, to stand alongside his father and was inclined to agree that, had the whole nation turned to God for His help, the story might have been different. However, Rees Howells had not wavered in his total conviction that the doom of the Nazis would one day be realised throughout the world.[1]

Testing and Sifting

In *Samuel Rees Howells: A Life of Intercession*, a chronicle of Samuel's intercessory life, Richard Maton explains that Rees Howells was led to give no explanation by way of justification for the outbreak and spread of World War II (1939-1945). Instead, the intercessors had to allow the full implementation of the death to their reputations to do its work, to prepare them for the costly intercessions ahead, where man's opinions must have no influence upon them.

When war broke out, at that crucial point, the Lord had shown Rees that it was necessary that he should experience this failure in the world's eyes so that full focus and attention could be given to the spiritual conflicts which were to ensue. No explanation should be given by way of justification. Death to reputation is an essential ingredient for all intercessors to follow. In spiritual warfare, Christians take delight in the concept of fast and decisive victories, but this was not the case with the prophets, nor is it often the case in the Church. 'What you sow is not made alive unless it dies' (1 Corinthians 15:36).

The whole question of failure is one which every intercessor has to face at some point in his or her ministry and Samuel had faced it alongside his father in 1939. The war did proceed and the bitter struggle lasted for six years. Samuel recalled the ignominy of those days when even the Christian world kept them at arm's length, so he himself would not flinch in later years when he was plunged into further depths to see the development of God's covenant plans for the blessing of the world in his day. ['...Before honour is humility,' Proverbs 15:33].[2]

Life Out of Death

Miss Doris M. Ruscoe, a close friend of Rees Howells, a fellow intercessor and the Headmistress of the School for Missionaries' Children, as it was first called, believed all of Rees Howells' declarations concerning the war would bring resurrection life out of death. The intercessors died to the world and the world to them, and through this, the private life of intercession in the Holy Spirit could flow unhindered. In her book *The Intercession of Rees Howells* she notes:

Never was the Holy Spirit more manifest in the College than in the month of August 1939. Over and over again we were taken 'beyond the veil' in the meetings, and over and over we were lost in a spirit of praise, and worship. Rees Howells was confident that there would be no war and believed this right up to the fatal day of 3rd September when war was declared because of the Nazi attack on Poland. He was always like a lion in a test, but as he went back to the Lord, day after day seeking an explanation, the conviction grew within him that God had a purpose in the war, that without it the three great dictators, Hitler, Mussolini and Stalin [of Nazi Germany, Fascist Italy and Bolshevist Russia] would override the world. During the next months of what came to be known as 'the phoney war' because there was little action of vital importance on either side, he produced a small book, *God Challenges the Dictators* (GCD).

From the beginning he pronounced 'the doom of the dictators,' committing himself to this in an absolute and final way. However dark the situation might be he never swerved from this commitment and held on to it throughout the years of war. Assured that the war could not last long [which was after GCD had been published] he predicted its end by the following Whitsuntide [Pentecost], May 1940, the very time when Hitler's Panzer regiments broke through the Allied lines and began to roll over Europe....

On Whit-Monday (Pentecost Monday) crowds flocked to the College meetings held in the open air, many curious, most disbelieving. Was it failure? To the press, to the crowds, there could be no other conclusion, but as Rees Howells went back to the Lord, he began to understand. The great principle of intercession is *life out of death*; the corn of wheat must die before the new life can spring forth from the ground.

Rees Howells saw the glory that would have come to himself and the College if the prediction had come to pass. He said, "The glory and the credit for victory in this war must come to the Holy Spirit and not to man. God has declared war on the Devil and it is God who will give the victory."

Hitler boasted that he would set up a Nazi régime throughout the world which would last for a thousand years, a direct challenge to the Millennial Reign of Christ. Rees Howells took this public 'death' with perfect acceptance as from God and threw himself into the battle against the dictators, the conflict in the heavenlies, and we followed him with complete confidence in the final victory. There were to be days of darkness, oppression and burden in the spirit, but also days when we were caught up into those heavenly places of which the apostle Paul speaks, days of heaven upon earth.

From the human standpoint it is clear that an early and abrupt end to the war would have left the dictators, their governments and their armies still strong and powerful, *still a threat to the world.* To us it seemed that we were baptised into the conflict in a new way. Rees Howells never defended the prediction of 1940. He was not new to this kind of 'death' and knew that in the end there would be a resurrection. He reiterated 'the doom of the Nazis' [throughout the war years] and of the dictators and carried on the struggle of faith with ever deeper conviction. The crowds were no longer interested in the College and for the next few years we were literally shut in with God. [Though there were occasional public meetings in the chapel on the Derwen Fawr Estate which were advertised in the local press: All were welcome].

Day by day Rees Howells wrestled with the Word of God, especially the positions of faith of the men of the Old Testament, believing that God is the same today and that the Holy Spirit could be equal to these positions today. We saw the setbacks that Moses experienced in Egypt as the enemy through Pharaoh and the magicians defied him. But Moses knew that God had one final weapon that would bring about the deliverance of the people from Egypt – deliverance through the death of the firstborn.

In the days of Hezekiah God allowed the enemy to take all the fenced cities of Judah and to come right up to the walls of Jerusalem itself before He spoke the word of deliverance through the prophet Isaiah, that God Himself would defend the city for His own sake. The strange plot of Judges 20 demonstrated the mystery of God's ways in some situations. Twice the men of Judah asked counsel of God and went up against Benjamin, only to be driven back each time with great slaughter. But after a National Day of Prayer and fasting the word of assurance was given and victory came on the third attempt. So throughout those years, in a real war situation, the Word of God came alive to us in a new way and daily the Holy Spirit sustained us as we fought on, knowing that the real battle was in the heavenlies, and over and over again seeing the outcome of a spiritual victory demonstrated later in the actual fighting.[3]

Standing Firm

Rees Howells always stood firm to his prediction even on the day that Britain declared war on Germany on 3rd September 1939. He said, "If I had a choice again about making this prediction I would make it tonight, although it has gone much farther than we thought it would. Hitler must be put out of the way, because if he isn't, he will come up again in another two years. I want to know that the Holy Spirit is stronger than the Devil in the Nazi system. This is the battle of the ages and victory here means victory for millions of people."

On the day of the declaration of war, he published the following statement: 'The Lord has made known to us that He is going to destroy Hitler and the Nazi régime, that the world may know that it was God and God alone who has scattered the dictators. Three and a half years ago, the College prayed this prayer for weeks and months, and we firmly believe He will now answer it. He has isolated Germany so that He may get at this evil system, which is the Antichrist, and release Germany, the land of the Reformation. He will deal with the Nazis as He dealt with the Egyptian army in the time of Moses. God will cause Hitler to fall on the battlefield or by a mutiny or a great rising in Germany against the Nazis.'

To summarise, Rees Howells discerned three great advantages of the struggle he faced based on his public declarations of the defeat of the dictators. He had already published accounts in the newspapers and was working on his book *God Challenges the Dictators*. First he saw it as an opportunity for the true intercessors to emerge, who were seeking God's will, instead of the glory of being in a company who were always right. Second, he doubled-down on his belief that God would defeat the dictators, with the understanding that all they were experiencing was a delay. Third, their death in the eyes of the world was a victory to work of the Holy Spirit in them.

A Delay

Norman Grubb was a lifelong friend to Rees Howells (they first met in 1928) and the Bible College of Wales, and he found in Rees a friend and mentor, as well as an unmoveable pillar of faith who stood firm during storms and trials that all ministries experience. When Grubb was called to lead the great missionary agency Worldwide Evangelization Crusade, (now known as WEC International, founded by the famous Cambridge Seven missionary, C.T. Studd, Grubb's father-in-law), whilst it was close to collapse in 1931, it was Rees Howells who aided Grubb practically and with spiritual guidance to save the sinking ship. Whilst others fled from Grubb during the troubles, Rees Howells provided the assistance (including finances and trained Bible College students, taught in the life of faith) necessary to keep the ministry alive which now serves in more than seventy nations as a witness to Jesus Christ.

Rees Howells' willingness to stand with Norman Grubb during any trial and stay firm regardless of people's opinions developed a reciprocal loyalty that safeguarded their friendship during the testing period for Rees and the Bible College of Wales.

When Rees Howells went to be with the Lord in February 1950, Norman Grubb was *very* keen to publish an account of his life, in order that others could derive benefit from the lessons the Spirit of God had taught him through experience. Grubb had spoken to

Rees Howells some years before about this. Grubb had received such guidance from Rees that he felt a real burden to chronicle his lessons of faith and intercession. The staff at the Bible College of Wales used Rees Howells' writings and notes to produce the first draft for Norman Grubb, which he edited, pulling together various themes and included teaching on intercession etc.

In the book *Rees Howells Intercessor* by Norman Grubb we find the following account:

So far from the declaration of war shaking him [Rees Howells] and those with him [students and staff of the Bible College of Wales], it only sent them more determined than ever to their knees. They were now called in a new way to pay the vow they had made three years before – to give their lives over "to fight the battles of the Kingdom, as really as if called to fight on the Western Front." This stand of faith against war in order that the Gospel might not be hindered, was proved to be God's way of placing upon that company a responsibility from which they could never come free, until the enemy that God was dealing with should be destroyed.

When, after a month of hostilities, an offer of peace was made by Hitler, the College stood with the Prime Minister in stating that war must be continued, "until Hitlerism is overthrown," even though, like so many more, the College had much to lose by its continuance. The conviction of the College was expressed in the title of a book which Mr Howells wrote in the opening weeks of the war, and which was published in December, 1939, called: *God Challenges the Dictators – Doom of Nazis Predicted....*

Although his confidence was that God would intervene to deal with the enemy, he wrote: 'We may have many a set-back before He does so...it may be that we, like the Israelites (referring to Judges 20), will have to cry out to God in our extremity for the help which will certainly come.' It is truly remarkable to look back now and realise that these things were in print before the end of 1939....

In spite of this apparent set-back, as we read the diaries of the daily College meetings, three meetings on most days, we find ourselves among certainly not a fearful, not even chiefly a praying company, but rather among those who are already on victory ground, when all around men's hearts are failing them for fear; and what gave them such clarity and assurance that theirs was the victory, was the outward 'death' of the prediction! If we say God was not with them, we may well ask ourselves this question: "Was there anywhere else in the whole of Britain or America or elsewhere among God's people another such company, maybe a hundred strong, who were on their knees day by day, holding fast the victory by faith, while our soldiers across the water were retreating mile by mile, whole countries surrendering, and the enemy within sight of their goal?"

From this time on, through all the years of the war, the whole College was in prayer every evening from seven o' clock to midnight, with only a brief interval for supper. They never missed a day. This was in addition to an hour's prayer meeting every morning and very often at midday. There were many special periods when every day was given up wholly to prayer and fasting.[4]

In the College meetings just before Whitsun (Pentecost) 1940, when Rees Howells had believed the war would end, he said, "Through God we made the prediction, through God we stand to it, and through God we are going against the enemy. He tells me tonight, 'Don't you fear because of that prediction you have sent out, don't you fear the Nazis.' I think what a glory it is that we don't need to change our prayers one bit, in spite of the present developments. I am so glad that it has been the Kingdom we have had before us all the time in the last nine months, and I haven't a single regret. The Lord has said, 'I am going to deal with the Nazis.' It has been a battle between the Holy Spirit and the Devil which we have been fighting for four years."

On 10th May 1940, the German 'Blitzkrieg' began, a lightning war, where armoured vehicles and troops sped through neutral Belgium and Holland, circumnavigating the French Maginot Line which had been heavily fortified and defended after WWI (1914-1918), to enter France by attacking neutral countries.

On Whit-Sunday, 12th May 1940, Rees Howells said in the 9.30pm College meeting, "We shall never defend the prediction. The point is, can God put a doubt in us who have really believed? If the Lord tells you that *this delay is for His glory,* then you must take victory in it. There is no glory in delay, unless there was faith to put it through...I can really thank Him for the delay. I wouldn't be without this experience for the world. Very strange that what is death in the eyes of the world, is victory to the Holy Spirit."

At the 7pm meeting on Whit-Monday, 13th May 1940, Rees Howells said, "It doesn't matter how many set-backs we get in the College we are going to pray the land of Germany back to God!"

At the 9am meeting on the following day, Rees Howells said, "We could never have had a greater death than in this prediction being delayed. But we are not going to have resurrection on one point more than has gone to the cross. I preached victory yesterday without a visible victory. There is a death in every grade, but as really as you die, there will be fruit to a hundredfold. We are going up to the battle and I am as sure of victory as of the dawn. If you know you have faith for something, would you not go on until you got it? I would like this to ring out to the world: The Lord, He is the God!"

This central section of the book is the full text of *God Challenges the Dictators: Doom of Nazis Predicted* by Rees Howells, 1939 with annotations. You may have noticed that on the front cover of this book that the word 'Nazis' has be replaced with 'Axis Powers' *(Rees Howells' God Challenges the Dictators, Doom of Axis Powers Predicted)*. This title helps separate it from the hardback collector's edition *God Challenges the Dictators: Doom of the Nazis Predicted* which was released on 13th February 2020, on the seventieth anniversary of Rees Howells promotion to glory, and the eightieth anniversary of its first publication in December 1939. This book was first released on 10th October 2020, 141 years to the day that Rees Howells was born.

AMAZING WAR PROPHECIES OF WELSH PASTOR

TOMORROW WILL BE PUBLISHED A BOOK BY THE REV. REES HOWELLS, DIRECTOR OF THE BIBLE COLLEGE IN WALES, CONTAINING SOME EXTRAORDINARY PROPHECIES ABOUT HITLER AND THE NAZI REGIME.

A Newspaper Article from December 1939

An original dustcover / jacket from Rees Howells' book converted into greyscale. The original colour is black with white lettering, with the continents in white, whilst the oceans and rays are in red. The cost was 1 shilling (1/-). Round 2 shilling stickers (2/-) were placed over the circle denoting the price difference between the card cover edition and the hardback edition. This was the most economical way rather than having two sets of artwork. Some editions of the hardback do not have the 2 shilling stickers on its dustcover. Incidentally, when Rees Howells went to buy Glynderwen Estate in 1923 he *only* had 2 shillings in his pocket.

INTRODUCTION

This is an unusual book. It differs in many respects from any book that has been written in this generation. Because it contains a number of prophecies which concern everybody, some of which have already come true, we believe that it is essentially a book for all to read and ponder deeply. It may bring much good to many people. If it does no more than give vision and a sure foothold to some who are wrapped in mists and walking uncertainly, it will have served a useful purpose at this time of crisis.

We are assured that it will do much more, for it has a vital message for many nations. It has an especial message for you in this country, and if you believe it, you may be comforted "by the comfort wherewith we ourselves are comforted of God" (2 Corinthians 1:4). We have not been afraid nor dismayed since it was revealed to us, "for the battle is the Lord's.... Stand ye still and see the deliverance of the Lord with you" (2 Chronicles 20:15, 17).

In the second part of the book, the predictions described concern the founding and development of a Bible College, Bible College Schools, Hospital, etc. These are given in order to show the reader the many years it has taken the College to come to know the voice of God, and to give those greater and wider predictions that relate to war and peace, the rise and fall of dictators, and epochal events that are yet to be. It does not shy at those immensities which are of absorbing interest to all. Moreover what is written here is not mere guesswork, but the sure word of prophecy, proof that God still speaks through His servants, and shows them things that are to come.

The title, *God Challenges the Dictators,* and its subtitle, *Doom of Nazis Predicted*, convey at once to the reader the reason why the book is sent out at this time. Keep it by you and check future events with what is here recorded.[1]

On that fatal day, September 1st 1939, Hitler hurled this defiance at the world:

"As a National Socialist and a German soldier I enter upon this struggle (war with Poland) with a stout heart.... One word I have never learned: that is, surrender. I have once more put on that coat that was the most sacred and dear to me. I will not take it off again until victory is secured or I will not survive the outcome."[2]

Our Prime Minister in his well-balanced and temperate broadcast to the German People on September 4th, said,
"I regret to have to say it – that nobody in this country any longer places any trust in your leader's word. He gave his word that he would respect the Locarno Treaty; he broke it. [In March 1936, Adolf Hitler sent his soldiers into the Rhineland, a demilitarised zone and broke the Locarno Treaty which had been signed at the end of World War I (1914-1918)]. He gave his word that he neither wished nor intended to annex Austria; he broke it [12 March 1938]. He declared that he would not incorporate the Czechs in the Reich; he did so [29 September 1938 and invaded on 15 March 1939]. He gave his word after Munich [30 September 1938] that he had no further territorial demands in Europe; he broke it. He gave his word that he wanted no Polish provinces; he broke it [he annexed a number of provinces in October 1938, making what became known as the Danzig Corridor or the Polish Corridor]. He has sworn to you for years [views made public since the mid-1920s] that he was the mortal enemy of Bolshevism; he is now its ally [23 August 1939, with the Hitler-Stalin Pact]. Can you wonder his word is, for us, not worth the paper it is written on?
"In this war we are not fighting against you, the German people, for whom we have no bitter feeling, but against a tyrannous and forsworn régime which has betrayed not only its own people but the whole of Western civilisation and all that you and we hold dear. *May God defend the right.*"

Mr Chamberlain had previously said, "There is hardly anything that I would not sacrifice for Peace, but one thing I must except, that is the liberty that we have enjoyed for hundreds of years, and which we will not surrender," and the whole of the British Empire stood behind him by saying, "Hitler's Peace we unitedly reject."
God also predicted beforehand through the College, that He will not surrender Protestant Germany, the land of the Reformation, to Hitlerism (the Antichrist). So, if Hitler says that he will die before he will surrender, the Allies that they will not surrender, and God says that He will not surrender, this war is going to be a fight to a finish – "the survival of the fittest."

This introduction was written during the very weekend [25-26 November 1939] when the German magnetic mines were beginning to blow up British and neutral ships. Only a week before, Mr Churchill had said over the wireless that we had cleared the high-seas, and not a German ship was to be seen, that our blockade [which began in September 1939] was nearly perfect and complete; and then suddenly came the magnetic mines. Shocked at this unexpected blow [London and other ports were closed and there was fear of starvation due to the amount of imported food going to the bottom of the sea unless a solution could be found quickly], we consoled ourselves by saying we had struck a bad patch. Yet Hitler has boasted that Germany has other diabolical inventions to unloose. But don't be alarmed at Nazi threats.

"Man's extremity is God's opportunity." When God told the College on September 9th, 1939 to send a prediction to the *Daily Press* that "God will Intervene in a Miraculous Way to End the War" – had God then foreseen that man could not end it? Is the day coming when our country will have to look to God, and to Him alone, to deliver us from this black spectre of Hitlerism? Will God have to step in as He did in Biblical times to deliver our nation, because we are fighting solely for freedom and religious liberty? Although we show clearly in the early chapters of this book that God has promised to "intervene to end the war," we have many a setback before He does so.

Open your Bibles to the Book of Judges to where God told Israel to go against Benjamin, because they refused to give up those men who had committed a certain folly in their tribe (Judges 19-20). And it is for exactly the same reason that England and France have gone against Germany, asking them to give up those Nazi leaders who have committed crime after crime against their own people, the German Jews, and the smaller nations round them, the Czechs, the Poles, and the Austrians.

The Benjamites in all only numbered twenty-six thousand men that drew sword, while Israel (Judah) numbered four hundred thousand men that drew sword. God was with Israel, and sent them against Benjamin, but Benjamin killed the first day no less than twenty-two thousand men. The second day again the Benjamites killed of the Israelites eighteen thousand men that drew sword; so in two days these sturdy fighters had killed forty thousand – nearly double their own number! But remember this – the Benjamites were fighting for their lives, while Israel (Judah) was only fighting for a principle. This seems to be a true illustration of the war today between Germany and the Allies. Whilst we are fighting for a principle, Hitler and the Nazis are fighting for their lives; the Nazis do desperate things because they are a thousand times more desperate than we are. Hitler knows well that he is making a last bid to save his life of crime, as do his Nazi leaders whose consciences must give them much uneasiness; and they will use every evil device to help them, as they did in Poland, and are now doing with their magnetic mines in the North Sea.

So Christian England will have to do today as the Israelites did in their day: "The children of Israel inquired of the Lord, saying, 'Shall I yet again go out to battle against the children of Benjamin my brother, or shall I cease?' And the Lord said, "Go up; for tomorrow I will deliver them into thine hand" (Judges 20:28). It may be that we, like the Israelites, will have to cry out to God in our extremity for the help, which will certainly come. The Benjamites made their last desperate bid to save the tribe, but God wiped them out on that day. And it may be the same with Germany, who are today intact (for so far it has only been a war of blockade), and they will have to be desperate indeed before they will voice the word "surrender." For have not all the Nazi leaders, like Hitler, pledged themselves to die before they surrender? They know already what is coming to them.

This Book of Predictions is nothing if not opportune. May it be a warning to England to stand to the end under the shadow of the Almighty, and to obey His constant guidance. May we cry to God as did the people of Nineveh when Jonah predicted their doom. The ruler of that mighty city "arose from his throne, and he laid his robe from him, and covered him with sackcloth, and sat in ashes," and he called all his people to "cry mightily unto God: yea, let them turn everyone from his evil way.... And God saw their works, that they turned from their evil way; and God repented of the evil....and He did it not" (Jonah 3:1-10).

If God saved wicked Nineveh when it repented and cried for help, He will save Christian England, and He will even save the Modernists in Germany (the New Theologians), who have made such a mockery of the Book of Jonah. Even though their New Theology, so misled them, today these "Reverend Storm Troopers" would be ready to sit in the seat of the Ninevites, in "sackcloth and ashes," repenting of their folly in handling the Word of the Lord so lightly.

If they had followed their own countryman "Saint George Müller" (1805-1898) they, like him, would have really believed that the

Bible was the Word of God. That modern "St. George" [patron Saint of England] made Orphanages in Christian England, maintaining two thousand orphaned children by prayer and faith alone, to be a great object lesson to all. He drew out of God's Treasury a million and-a-half pounds without a single appeal to man. And the Bible College of Wales which issues this book, and which works on the same principles, will also draw out of God's Treasury Millions of pounds to carry out its own Vision: "The Gospel to Every Creature in the next twenty-five Years."[3]

If every man and woman in Christian England will cry to God as the Ninevites did, and continue to cry until God will answer, God will intervene as He did in Bible times, and raise England again to be His chosen power for evangelising the world.

The sending out of this Book of Predictions, in the darkest hour of the war, has cost more to the Founders of the College [Rees and Lizzie Howells] that any of the former predictions. Predictions are always open to criticism until their fulfilment. Many of the Prophets of old were put in prison, like Jeremiah and Micaiah, until their predictions were fulfilled. Then those who disbelieved and criticised were condemned, and the Prophets were praised. So the College will be fully compensated for any criticism, if the hundreds of thousands of wives, mothers and children who will be separated from their loved ones this Christmas, will take comfort in knowing that God is on their side; that He will bring their loved ones back again, when peace will be upon the earth, and goodwill towards men.[4]

Fierce may be the conflict
  Strong may be the foe,
But the King's own army
  None can overthrow.
Round His standard ranging,
  Victory is secure,
For His truth unchanging
  Makes the triumph sure.[5]

CONTENTS

Part I

The War Predictions

Chapter

I.   God Versus the Dictators
II.   Three Remarkable Predictions
III.   The Munich Prediction
IV.   The Danzig Prediction
V.   The Great Prediction
VI.   The £100,000 Prediction

Part II

Predictions Fulfilled

Chapter

VII.   Prediction of the Largest Bible College
VIII.   Prediction of Buying Derwen Fawr
IX.   Money Like Manna
X.   Prediction of a Third Estate
XI.   God's Hundredfold
XII.   Prediction of a Home and Hospital for Missionaries
XIII.   The Sum of it All

Chapter I

GOD VERSUS THE DICTATORS

Since March 1936, the Western democracies have done everything in their power to avoid a clash with the dictators. Meanwhile, the dictators under a cloak of National Revival in their countries, have been scheming and planning among themselves to dominate the world by force and bloodshed.

Before the 1914 War there was only one autocratic Government in Europe, and that was Russia. For centuries there had been a struggle between Monarchism and Republicanism; whether kings by heredity or the masses were to rule.

People who had emigrated to America from monarchical countries, like Russia and Germany, found liberty, because the people of the U.S.A. were ruling the destiny of that great country through their representatives in Congress and their Presidents whom they elected every four years.

George Washington, who won liberty and independence for America, said: "The nation which is incapable of winning its Parliamentary freedom is unworthy to exist." The common people should, through their deputies, be ruling the national destiny. That was why Lincoln brought in the Act of Emancipation, so that not even the rich should rule over any man, whether he be black-skinned or white. "The wind shall blow and the rain shall fall," said he, "on no man who goes forth to unrequited toil."

Those who emigrated from Russia to the United States found a wonderful freedom, and men like Lenin and others went back to their country and preached revolution and Communism. They were willing to risk their lives to emancipate two hundred million peasants out of the bondage of an autocratic Czar.[1]

In the uprising that followed hundreds of thousands were killed, others were exiled to Siberia, or deported; yet no military force could ever extinguish the urge for liberty now greatly stirring in the Russian people.

WESLEY SAVES ENGLAND

It was through Wesley's Revival [the Evangelical Revival 1739-1791][2] that England in the eighteenth century was saved from a revolution and a civil war. Ferocious laws figured on the Statute

Book; justice itself was cruel and vindictive. Judges swore on the Bench, and even chaplains cursed while they preached. Men who refused to plead on capital charge were pressed to death; and up to the year 1794, when the vicious law was repealed, women were publicly flogged.

At this dark period of our history the Church of England had lost its power. The clergy were discredited and our public life was flagrantly corrupt. In those dark days, only a spiritual revolution could save England. It came through God raising up John Wesley (1703-1791)[3] for his colossal task. Only another Wesley can save Germany, Russia or Italy, the countries of the military dictators, today.

THE UNHOLY ALLIANCE

In twenty years two menacing figures, Hitler and Stalin, have given their countries a greater set-back than England has progressed by the last two centuries of civilisation. Before Wesley's Revival, our Parliament was unreformed; two-thirds of the House of Commons were elected by the privileged rich, like the Duke of Norfolk, who nominated eleven members, Lord Lonsdale, nine members; and so on.

No less than three hundred M.P.s were returned by one hundred and sixty persons, while large cities were unrepresented by even a single member. Whilst politics were at a low ebb, Christianity was a living force, and the conscience of the masses was deeply quickened. Christianity was re-born in the individual heart, and the country, awakened to the truth of the Gospel, found again that it was the "power of God unto Salvation to all who believe" (Romans 1:16). Once again it was more than an outworn creed and a dead ritual; it was the thing most needful in life.

Hardly a branch of the social life of our country was unaffected by that Revival. The new effort to establish the Reign of God on earth reached to the Universities, the Army, the Navy and to every class of people. Even politics responded to the Revival. The Secret Ballot came, and at last the masses controlled the destiny of England. King Edward VII (1841-1910) and his Prime Minister, Sir Henry Campbell-Bannerman (1836-1908) were both democrats, in no way inferior to any President and Premier of the French Republic. King George V (1865-1936) was also a great democrat and so also is our present King. But countries like Russia and Germany, who were ruled by sword and rifle, by Czar and Kaiser (titles which meant the same – Cæsar) were, through their Socialist leaders, reduced to a state of revolution and civil war, to gain the liberty they saw here, in America and other democratic countries. Great changes came to them and to Italy as well. But in these changes, which are only transition stages, they have fallen into the hands of ambitious dictators, who have ruled the masses by a vile discipline, by rod and revolver, and secret police, destroying both Parliament and Democracy, and replacing these by a reign of terror, more or less terrible according to country, under their respective dictators.

STALIN

These three dictators have undergone amazing experiences. They have suffered much themselves, but have exacted from their fellows a hundredfold more. Stalin, the man from Georgia [formerly part of the Russian Empire], escaped from prison six times. Once he was in exile near the Arctic Sea, in Kuleika, which he called the empire of eternal snow. It was while there, he says, that even his stubborn nature was broken. His life among "dangerous criminals," and the silence of the north, transformed that fiery rebel into a very quiet man. But it did not change his evil nature.

When, after Lenin's death, Stalin came to power, he soon deported his rival, Trotsky, the man who, through his writings, had brought Soviet Russia into being. Trotsky too, had suffered much, he had been twice deported, had spent four years in a dungeon, and altogether had passed over twelve years in prison under the late Czar. Under Lenin he built up the Red Army, and sincerely endeavoured to give Russia the widest democracy. Because Trotsky maintained that Stalin's methods were only an imitation of the autocratic rule of the Czars – "ruling from above the masses below," Stalin plotted against Trotsky. When illness came, and Trotsky could not defend himself, Stalin exiled him, and deprived him of Soviet citizenship. Trotsky then had to live in the only country that would offer him refuge, Mexico.

During Stalin's bloody purge, every one of his fellow Revolutionists who took a leading part in Lenin's Government, were executed, and likewise everyone who had dared oppose the ambitions of this peasant dictator from Georgia. When a youth, Stalin had passed four years in an Orthodox Seminary at Tiflis, but the only use he made of the Christianity he was there taught was to put down the Church of God, and to replace God's Sabbath by a weekly pagan holiday.

This then is the man who has planned to impose his savagery on the Christian democracies. But as sure as there will come the downfall of Hitler and the Nazi régime – for God has revealed it – the time will also come when Stalin will pay the full price of his murderous life. God said to Cain: "The voice of thy brother's blood crieth unto Me from the ground and now thou art cursed" (Genesis 4:10).

The Devil has used and may yet use this man to be the greatest foe to the Church that the world has ever known, but the stone that Daniel saw, in his tremendous vision: "The stone that was cut out of the mountain without hands" (Daniel 2:45), will break in pieces this Stalin and the other blood-thirsty dictators as well.

MUSSOLINI

The fate of modern Italy was decided when Mussolini mobilised the Fascist forces, and threatened to march on Rome. The Italian Government resigned, whereupon the King of Italy invited Mussolini to form a Government; so the Duce became dictator of the new Italy. The old proportional representative system was done away with, and a new electoral law was put in force, parading the dictator's slogan: "Let parties die and the country be saved," and so the Fascist Totalitarian State was brought into being.

Mussolini proceeded to make war on Libya [in North Africa] and Abyssinia [now Ethiopia, in Africa]. When Germany decided to aid Italy in Abyssinia and Spain; Italy passed laws against the Jews. And so the Axis was formed. Italy then demanded Corsica [an island close to Italy and France], Nice [in Southern France] and Tunis [in North Africa]; and she took Albania [to the right of Italy, on the Balkan Peninsula in south-eastern Europe]. Italy had also helped Franco to overthrow the Liberal Government in Spain, and the Nazis rejoiced at the great danger thereby created for us in the Mediterranean. So, slowly but surely, the Berlin-Rome and Spanish Axis was forged, and only God, and God alone, could have foreseen that it had no sure foundation and would soon snap before our astonished eyes.

It was a tragedy that German support of Italy should have brought about the downfall of Abyssinia, a country known in Scripture as Ethiopia. Yet Ethiopia had been opened to the Gospel, and her missionaries were welcomed by the Emperor;

and it seemed that the Bible prophecy was coming true: "Princes shall come out of Egypt; *Ethiopia shall soon stretch out her hands unto God"* (Psalm 68:31). But for a time it seems the door there has been shut against the Gospel.

ITALY MAY CHANGE

However, from the day the Berlin-Rome Axis was broken, Italy began to turn to the democracies for refuge and help against Bolshevism and Soviet Russia, which are being used in the plan of God to break the evil Nazi régime, by stopping their further penetration into the Balkan and Baltic States.

ADOLF HITLER

Enough has been said in the Government's "Blue Paper" and "White Paper" concerning the "Treatment of German Nationals in Germany," to reveal the bestial and brutal treatment of human beings by Hitler and his co-assassins the "power-drunk adventurers of the Third Reich." Adolf Hitler, the German dictator in less than six months after coming to power, abolished the provincial governments, suppressed or murdered all political parties except the National Socialists, who are the only party in Germany today. Whoever attempts to organise another political party is punished with imprisonment or death.

Like Stalin, Hitler soon began to lift up his bloodstained hand against the Church of God. He has bitterly persecuted the Evangelical Churches. He regards allegiance to any other ruler than himself – even the God of Heaven – as treason. If the Evangelical Church sets God above the State, and worships Him and not the dictator, as it must do, its members are imprisoned like political offenders. Hitler the Antichrist appointed the Army Chaplain Müller[4] (1883-1945), who has bowed the knee to Baal, to be Reich Bishop [in 1933] to carry out his decrees, as did the Satraps in the time of Darius of old. It was these Satraps, who accused Daniel before the King of Babylon, saying that they actually "found Daniel praying and making supplication before his God," and not to the King, so they forced him to cast Daniel into the den of lions, though even the heathen King was sorry and said: "Thy God whom thou servest continually, He will deliver thee" (Daniel 6:16). And He did.

HITLER'S FATE

The Bible College has predicted that the God of Daniel will deliver Pastor Niemöller[5] (1892-1984) and the hundreds of other German Evangelicals who have followed him to the concentration camps (Hitler's dens of lions). It affirms that their places will one day be occupied by the fanatical Nazi leaders, "the power-drunk adventurers," if any of them escape a speedy death. Just as Darius treated those who accused Daniel, so will the Nazis be treated, for they have afflicted Germany and God's servants most sore.

After the downfall of the Nazi régime there will be a new Government in a new Protestant Germany. It will cause men to "tremble and fear" before the God of Martin Luther and the God of Martin Niemöller: "For He is the living God, and steadfast for ever, and His Kingdom that which shall not be destroyed, and His dominion shall be even unto the end" (Daniel 6:26). So then, the God who delivereth His people, will deliver the oppressed in Germany, the land of the Reformation, and will call out again from that enslaved country thousands of missionaries afire for God to take the Gospel to Every Creature.

THE HEAD OF GOLD

God passed judgment on the proud Kings of Babylon, and through Daniel he said of Nebuchadnezzar (the "Head of Gold" of the famous Image): "Thou, O King, art a king of kings: for the God of Heaven hath given thee a kingdom, power and strength and glory. And wheresoever the children of men dwell...hath He given into thine hand, and hath made thee ruler over them all. *Thou art this head of gold*" (Daniel 2:37-38). But when that ancient Overlord challenged his three Hebrew governors – Shadrach, Meshach and Abednego, saying: "Do not ye serve my gods, nor worship the golden image which I have set up? Who is that God that shall deliver you out of my hands?" The answer they gave to their proud king is now going to ring out through Germany: "Our God whom we serve is able to deliver us from the burning fiery furnace, and He will deliver us out of thine hand, O Hitler."

When he saw "the form of the fourth like the Son of God" walking in the fiery furnace with the brave Hebrew servants of the Living God, who were thus triumphantly delivered, the King of Babylon made a solemn decree "that every people, nation and language, which speak anything amiss against the God of Shadrach, Meshach and Abednego, shall be cut in pieces, and their houses be made a dunghill, because there is no other God that can deliver after this sort" (Daniel 3:29).

THE WRITING ON THE WALL

The God of Heaven predicted through Daniel, that Nebuchadnezzar, King of Babylon (the "Head of Gold") should be driven from men, and "thy dwelling shall be with the beasts of the field, and they shall make thee to eat grass like oxen...till thou know that the most High ruleth in the kingdom of men, and giveth it to whomsoever He will" (Daniel 4:25).

So if the God of Heaven delivered the "three young men" who trusted Him from the burning fiery furnace, and delivered Daniel from the lion's den, and humbled Nebuchadnezzar the mighty King of Babylon, surely He will deliver His faithful servants from the puny dictators of this decadent Twentieth Century.

WEIGHED IN THE BALANCES

If the "Head of Gold," which represented Babylon, and the "breast and arms of silver," which represented the Second world-empire, Media and Persia, failed to compel the Jewish captives to worship the state or the kings of Babylon, then surely those "two toes" out of the "ten toes" of Nebuchadnezzar's vision – the unspeakable Bolshevist and Nazi dictators – as the Bible predicted, can never unite against the Living God. Thus saith the Lord: "They shall not cleave one to another, even as iron is not mixed with clay" (Daniel 2:43). And where the "Head of Gold" failed, there is no chance for the "insignificant little toes" to succeed; and we can say of them, as Daniel said to Belshazzar: "And thou, his son, O Belshazzar, hast not humbled thine heart, though thou knewest all this; but hast lifted up thyself against the Lord of Heaven" (Daniel 5:22-23).

Therefore, the verdict given of Belshazzar was "God hath numbered thy kingdom, and finished it...thou art weighed in "the balances, and art found wanting" (Daniel 5:26-27), and – believe it or not – God has given a similar prediction through the College regarding Hitler, who has put people in prison because they did not worship himself and the State before God. Likewise, the same thing will happen to the other dictators unless they take warning from the downfall of Hitler and the Nazi régime, which is imminent.

The Penllergaer Mansion from the West-side elevation. The main drive was more than 1 ¼ miles long, lined with rhododendrons and azaleas (at the opposite end of the building, out of view). It was the Bible College of Wales' fourth estate in Britain and consisted of 270 acres.

Chapter II

THREE REMARKABLE PREDICTIONS

Among the many predictions made by the Bible College of Wales since it was started with the sum of two shillings only [£6.74 in 2020], are three outstanding ones.

They were: a prediction of a gift of £10,000, [£674,400 in 2020] another that God would give the offer of the Gospel to Every Creature in the ensuing thirty years, and that there would be No (General) European War during that time. Because these predictions were unique and apparently impossible of fulfilment they were eagerly seized upon by many of the newspapers, including the London dailies, and given wide publicity. By the Welsh Press the predictions were also given great prominence. The news-bills mention them in large type. As the man in the street read them he rubbed his eyes in more than mild surprise. Here are some of the news-bills relating to the predictions:

1. Swansea £10,000 Gift Prophecy Comes True. (28th July, 1938).
2. Swansea Bible College Chief and His "No War Prediction." (30th September, 1938).
3. Swansea Bible College Chief's New Prophecy On War. (11th September, 1939).

From an article in the Swansea *Evening Post* of July 22nd, 1938, the following is taken:

There are rejoicings at the Bible College of Wales, Derwen Fawr, Swansea, that the College's first £10,000 gift, the coming of which was predicted at the last Conference [Every Creature Conference] – has been paid into the College Bank Account.

An article in the *Western Mail* of July 23rd, 1938, stated:

£10,000 GIFT PROPHECY COMES TRUE. The Bible College of Wales, whose reliance on Faith to produce money to carry on its manifold activities is widely known, has just received its first gift of £10,000. This donation was predicted at a College Conference some time ago, and the Director, the Rev. Rees Howells, believes that it will be the first of many such gifts to be received.

REVEALER OF SECRETS

Those who earn say four pounds a week know that it would take them fifty years to earn ten thousand pounds. If they could live on two pounds a week it would take them (not allowing for compound interest) a hundred years to save ten thousand pounds. Consequently the man in the street is baffled when he hears that someone, who has only faith in his vision to support him, says that he has received from God his Father a substantial gift of not less than ten thousand pounds. It is natural for anyone, hearing that such a prediction had come true, to say: "Who would not serve so rich a Father?" And when the ordinary man reads on the news-bills, or in his newspaper, that one man has had faith enough in his Heavenly Father to draw from Him ten thousand pounds, a deeper impression is made upon him than if he had listened to ten thousand sermons.

Such a prediction, when fulfilled, rouses great interest and becomes the table talk of thousands. Though our pseudo-astrologers and our Spiritualists often attempt to interpret the future, with laughable results, the man in the street is not really carried away. He knows without being told that only God can foresee events. Occasionally through circumstances or knowledge of the past, men sometimes guess the future with a moderate degree of accuracy; but not very often. The greatest men of every generation have proved how hopelessly wrong they are whenever they have forecast the trend of world events. The man who has managed to make one good guess seldom if ever contrives to guess right twice in a lifetime. Yet it has been done time and again by the Founders of the Bible College of Wales.

Whoever heard of a person foreseeing with absolute certainty that he was going to have a gift of ten thousand pounds from some person or persons unknown? Surely the man who dares foretell such an absurdity will get himself ridiculed; he will certainly get nobody to believe him, no newspaper to publish what he says, or to display it on its news-bills. That is unless his prediction has come to pass – as did ours of the impending gift of ten thousand pounds.

Guessing and hoping and feeling that a thing is going to happen can never produce that state of certainty that comes to one when God draws aside the curtain of fate, and allows His servant to get a vision of the future. Prediction, substantiated by the event, has more than once elevated the prophet to a position of high authority in the land. Two such men were both taken as captives to foreign countries, and these two – Joseph and Daniel – were each raised to the position of Governor or Viceroy in the country of his compulsory adoption.

For what reason? For predicting the future. Yet both testified that predicting the future was the province of God. Said Daniel: "There is a God in Heaven that revealeth secrets, and maketh known what shall be in the latter days" (Daniel 2:28).

After years in prison, suffering under a false charge, what else in this world could have raised Joseph in one day to be the ruler of Egypt save the fact that he was able to foretell the seven plenteous years followed by the seven years of famine? To those who did not understand, here was a mere slave ruling Egypt. Yet when Joseph interpreted his dream Pharaoh saw not a slave but "a man in whom the Spirit of God is" (Genesis 41:38). What a difference!

And so, for eighty years Joseph taught the senators of Egypt wisdom. And he showed both wisdom and the love which comes from God alone when he said to his trembling brothers who had sold him to slavery: "Be not angry with yourselves that ye sold me hither, for God did send me before you to preserve life. Tell my father that God hath made me lord of all Egypt!" (Genesis 45:5-9). What a man! What a brother! What a son! What a message to take to an aged father! And this because there is a God in Heaven who revealeth secrets!

Are those days of the open vision gone forever? Surely not. They are with us again today. For God still opens the future to His chosen servants. To the Bible College of Wales, through whom a number of predictions have been made already, God has more than once opened the future, as this simple narrative attempts to show. If the College remains obedient to His leading the open vision should be seen again and yet again.

THE "EVERY CREATURE" VISION

Five years ago there was given to the Director of the College a remarkable Vision. It foretold:
1. That God would give the offer of the Gospel to Every Creature during the next thirty years.
2. That God would call forth Ten Thousand people who would believe the Vision, and would send them out as His Witnesses unto the uttermost parts of the earth.
3. That God would open His Treasury to finance the Vision – the first gift to be £10,000.

Great Christian leaders of the last generation, men like J. Hudson Taylor, John R. Mott, A. B. Simpson and others, preached the possibility of Evangelising the World in their generation. But not one of them could say like Moses that God had commissioned him to do this great thing, or, had given him a sign as He did Moses, "And thou shalt say to Pharaoh thus saith the Lord, Israel is my son, even my firstborn...and if thou refuse to let him go, behold I will slay thy son, even thy firstborn" (Exodus 4:22-23).

When Pharaoh drove Moses and Aaron out of his presence, and set task-masters over the children of Israel, Moses was already aware, for God had told him so in Midian that the time was coming when He would slay his firstborn. And though by sending the frogs, flies, hailstorms, locusts and darkness, etc., God failed to induce Pharaoh to let Israel go, yet Moses knew that this last and most drastic sign, this killing of the firstborn would make Pharaoh thrust them forth – and so Pharaoh did.

As the slaying of the firstborn was a sign to Moses, so God's promised gift of £10,000 was a sign to the College which announced its coming beforehand, though yet unaware who was the donor-to-be. When the prophecy was fulfilled, it was felt to be a confirmation and, a sign to all that the College Vision was of God and neither man nor Devil would be allowed to hinder God from putting it through.

All interested in the evangelisation of the world know by experience that this can never be accomplished in their generation unless they receive a bigger blessing and greater power than was conferred on Christian leaders who lived before them, men like Martin Luther, William Carey, David Livingstone, D. L. Moody, and William Booth. Nearly two thousand years have passed since the Risen Lord gave the Command: "Go ye into all the world and preach the Gospel to Every Creature" (Mark 16:15), and yet not a third of this world has had the offer of salvation. So no existing organisation, striving its utmost, can do in thirty years what other excellent organisations, controlled by splendid Christians, have failed to do in two thousand years. But, when God gave the Vision to the College He also said: "I am coming down to do it," even as He said to Moses in Midian: "I am come down to deliver them out of the hands of the Egyptians?" (Exodus 3:8).

Even as Moses was given signs that he had been commissioned, so were the Founders [Rees and Lizzie Howells] of the College given signs with their commission, and one of the signs was the fulfilled prophecy of the Gift of £10,000 [£674,400 in 2020].

NO EUROPEAN WAR

Although the College has had numerous other gifts of as much as £500 a time, and ten single gifts of £1,000 a time, yet this special gift of £10,000 was different. And that is the reason why it is so much stressed in this volume. It was to be a *sign,* a *special sign* and a confirmation that the College Vision of the Gospel to Every Creature in thirty years was of God, and that God the Holy Ghost would put it through. In the days of Samuel the Word of God was precious because there was no open vision. "Where there is no vision the people perish" (Proverbs 29:18).

It is doubtful whether there has been really open vision since the days of Martin Luther. Through Luther God brought about the Reformation[1] [1517] when countries were changed and delivered from the yoke of Rome [Roman Catholic Church] into the glorious liberty of the children of God through believing that – 'THE JUST SHALL LIVE BY FAITH' (Romans 1:17).

We believe that the College Vision is a further maturing of the Promise God gave through the Prophet Joel: "In the last days, saith God, I will pour out of my Spirit upon all flesh" (Joel 2:28-29) – Every Creature! So then, this country is being prepared for an epoch-making event.

Through the fulfilment of one prophecy – the prediction of £10,000 – it is being prepared to take from God, another prophecy, one that will startle the world, that there will be "No (General) European War for thirty years."

The £10,000 Gift concerned only the College. It was a sign that God wanted to give to those who had received and believed the College Vision. But this wider prediction of "No European War" is one that concerns the whole world, especially the Continent of Europe. Yet this prophecy was being repeated when it seemed that a *General* European War had already broken out! Nevertheless, the One who gave the Vision, and confirmed it with the gift of £10,000 has also made it known to us, that the bawling boastful dictators of Europe, can never make a General European War. The manner in which God made known this prophecy will be described in the next chapter.

Chapter III

THE MUNICH PREDICTION

After the arrival of the £10,000 [£674,400 in 2020] the next great test of the College Vision was the threat of a General European War. How could Every Creature be reached with the Gospel in thirty years, and how could ten thousand young people be trained and sent out as witnesses to the Lord unto the uttermost parts of the earth if a war like that of 1914 [to 1918] were repeated? For in the event of war, all the young people of military age would be called up, and College properties would be taken over for hospitals, etc. The 1914 war lasted four years, nearly every country in Europe was involved and millions were killed, but as Lord Baldwin told us, the next war would end civilisation!

In March 1936, just fifteen months after the College Vision was given Hitler marched his troops into the Rhineland [a demilitarised buffer zone]. He defied Britain and France, and the Treaty of Versailles [signed at the end of WWI (1914-1918) on 28 June 1919], and many expected France to defend the Treaty by declaring war on Germany. Then Britain, Italy and the other countries of Europe would have been drawn into war; and the Devil would have defeated God's plan of giving the Gospel to Every Creature in this generation.

The policy and propaganda of the Third Reich, the Nazi Government, were first to abolish trade unions and other organisations among the working classes. The German Pacifist Movement was also put down, anti-war publications were banned, and a nation of sixty million people were carried away with the slogan, "Peace with Armaments." The Press was soon muzzled; it became the mouthpiece of the Government, and journalists became political soldiers of Hitler. Education was also reorganised on the basis of "a nation in arms," military instruction was systematically given in schools, and the school teacher became a drill-sergeant. In an address to German teachers, Rust, the Prussian Minister of Education, said: "Gentlemen, you are the Storm Troop leaders of German education."

"REVEREND" STORM-TROOPERS

The only church that received Government support was the church that supported national defence as conceived by the Nazis. The right of the church to exist was only recognised so far as it agreed with Hitler's teaching. The Prussian Press Service even announced that many of the young pastors of their churches had been asked to be allowed to join the Storm Troops. But in the Evangelical churches resisters were harried and arrested; those who entertained unapproved ideas disappeared without being brought to trial; numbers were placed in concentration camps, where they saw and endured many horrors. So the pastor, who would escape persecution, had to be a spiritual storm-trooper, the school teacher an educational drill-sergeant, and the journalist a soldier with a lying pen.

Under the new Prussianised laws of Germany, criticism of the Nazi doctrine, their policy of "guns before butter" was equivalent to treason. For the first time in Germany, the land of the Reformation, freedom of thought, freedom of expression and freedom of worship were forbidden. Those who resisted were persecuted; the spirit of Antichrist was imposed on one of the greatest Protestant countries in Europe. So God led the College to pray against Hitler and the Nazi régime.

PRAYER AGAINST HITLER

During the crisis in March, 1936, lectures and everything else were put on one side, and the College was given up to days of prayer and fasting. The conflict, "was not against flesh and blood but against principalities, against powers, against the rulers of the darkness of this world" (Ephesians 6:12). For three whole weeks over one hundred and twenty young people [largely students of the Bible College], who had been called to the Vision, *prayed until they prevailed with God to avert a European War.* On Sunday, 29th March 1936, they all made a vow to God that they would give their lives on the Altar, for God to use them to extend His Kingdom and give the Gospel to Every Creature; as really as they would have given their lives to their King and Country if war had broken out and they had been called up to the Western Front.

Those outside the College will never realise what those three weeks cost to about one hundred and twenty students and staff in order to prevail with God. These young people dedicated themselves in a most active and practical sense to the College Vision. They "presented their bodies a living sacrifice, holy, acceptable unto God" (Romans 12:1). What individuals had done in other generations (William Carey for India, David Livingstone for Africa, and J. Hudson Taylor for China), a whole company of young men and women now did for all the nations of the world.

RUMOURS – NOT WARS

As soon as the College prevailed with God and came through to victory, God spoke through His Word: "Ye shall hear of wars and rumours of wars, see that ye be not troubled, for all these things must come to pass, but the end is not yet.... This Gospel of the Kingdom shall be preached in all the world for *a witness unto all nations*, and then shall the end come" (Matthew 24:6, 14).

From that day on there has been nothing but wars and rumours of wars; but not one of those who offered themselves as intercessors at that time has ever been troubled. The College Vision is based on the Word of God: "This Gospel...shall be preached...for a witness unto all nations, and then shall the end come," and the Saviour will return to reign for the Thousand Years. So the prophecy of "No European War" was the result of the three weeks of intercession in the College, and a message from the Word of God. It was clearly seen then and predicted that *all the dictators in Europe could never make a European War –* until the Vision was fulfilled. At that fervent time the second Psalm became a great reality in the College: "The kings (dictators) of the earth set themselves, and the rulers take counsel together against the Lord.... He that sitteth in the heavens shall laugh; the Lord shall have them in derision" (Psalm 2:2, 4).

God said to His Son: "Ask of me and I shall give Thee the heathen for thine inheritance, and the uttermosts parts of the earth for Thy possession" (Psalm 2:8).

From 29th March 1936 – the end of the three weeks of prayer – the Bible College of Wales became a new spiritual force. From henceforth we knew we could prevail upon God to keep His hand upon Hitler and his Storm Troopers, and prevent them from causing a general European War. So every time that Hitler made a new swoop, such as that on Austria, the College set aside days for prayer, to prevail upon God to prevent a war which, while bringing hell on earth, would hinder the College Vision from being put through in thirty years. Every time the enemy challenged the democracies and the Vision, all those who had dedicated themselves by a covenant of sacrifice, were as soldiers marching to the field of battle.

THE DARKEST HOUR

When the Munich clash came in September 1938, we knew that Hitler would not make a European War. In the darkest hour, when bloody conflict seemed inescapable, world leaders of religion – the Archbishop of Canterbury, the Pope and the Chief Rabbi – called for a Day of Prayer for Sunday, 18th September. But God had previously told the College to call for a *Day of Praise,* because they had prayed through to victory. And so the public Opening Day of the Session was one of Praise and Thanksgiving. The following excerpt from the "South Wales Evening Post" of 17th September 1938, is illuminating:

THE BIBLE COLLEGE OF WALES
OPENING of the First Term of the FIFTEENTH SESSION
THURSDAY, 22nd SEPTEMBER 1938.
Meetings at 3pm and 6pm.
THANKSGIVING AND PRAISE

The Meetings will take the form of Praise and Thanksgiving because God has again averted, a European War. The College belief and prophecy is that there will be no European War for the next Twenty-Eight years, until the College Vision of reaching Every Creature with the Gospel will be accomplished.

And what a day of praise it was – hundreds gathered in the Conference Hall [on the Derwen Fawr Estate] in the darkest hour thanking God beforehand, that there was not going to be a European War! The Lord then told the Director to do, as Jeremiah had done, send the prediction out to the country in writing, and let the millions hear it! So an article was sent to the "Evening Post" and the "Western Mail," and, on 29th September, the day before the Munich Pact was signed, a general holiday was given to the College and Schools. The same afternoon, a gift of £500 [£33,720 in 2020] was received at the College from an unexpected donor. It came direct from our Heavenly Father, because of our obedience in making the prediction known.

At the time when war seemed certain, a week before the Munich Pact, on 23rd September 1938, the "Western Mail" published the following noteworthy statement.

HE PREDICTS NO EUROPEAN WAR FOR THIRTY YEARS
DIRECTOR OF BIBLE COLLEGE TELLS OF VISION

Saying that he had had a Vision whereby the Gospel would be given to Every Creature within 30 years, the Rev. Rees Howells, Director of the Bible College of Wales, predicted at a meeting on Thursday that there would be no European War until the Vision was accomplished. The meeting was one of "thanksgiving to God for *averting a war over the Czechoslovakia dispute.*"

The following is from a further article which appeared in the "Western Mail" on 30th September 1938.

BIBLE COLLEGE CHIEF'S "NO WAR"
PREDICTION FOLLOWED BY GIFT OF £500

There was also a very great joy in the Bible College of Wales when the news came over the wireless (Hitler had invited Mr Chamberlain to meet him again), and at the same time the Director opened a letter with a gift of £500.

SLEEPLESS NIGHTS

The world at large will never realise what it cost the Director to obey God by committing himself and the College Vision, and making it known through the Press that there would be no European War while there was not one chance in a thousand to escape war. The Director had more than one sleepless night before he committed himself to the public through the *Western Mail* that there was going to be no European War, and the reason why God pressed upon him to do it was because of the hundreds of thousands of mothers who would break their hearts to see their sons going to be slaughtered on the battlefield....

Picture those fearful days, and picture the man in the street, who had probably read of the £10,000 prophecy and its fulfilment, now reading on the placards of the leading newspapers the further prediction of "No European War." For this latter prediction was not only displayed on the news-bills of the "Evening Post" and the "Western Mail," but also on those of the "Daily Mail" and other London newspapers, which, following the great publicity given to it by the local press, had also been impressed by the prophecy. People read it in Germany, Italy, and even in the Holy Land.

Sent out in the darkest hour of the crisis, the prediction became the subject of discussion among all classes of people, Members of Parliament, dockyard workers, and busy housewives, too. After the fulfilment of the prophecy and the signing of the Munich Pact, the Director was congratulated by all classes.

COLLEGE JUBILATION

The Director, be it remembered, had established the College, Schools, Hospital and other branches of the work, without any committee, council or denomination, looking only to God to guide and provide for everything. And people began to say that the man who could bring into being an institution representing in capital value over £100,000 [£6,744,000 in 2020] and who could rely on his God for a sum of £10,000 in one gift, was a receptive channel for the revelation of God's will. His other predictions must be worthy of attention.

When the general holiday was given to all branches of the College the day before the Munich Pact was signed, over two hundred day children from the Schools alone, went home to tell their parents that there was to be no War; one of the most striking of lessons in faith that could be given either to children or parents. Photographers from town came down to the College, and photographed an assembly of over five hundred people. The daily papers who had previously announced the prediction now published the photograph of the fulfilment jubilation. It was a triumph of faith in the God who is a Revealer of secrets. Thus a prediction in which the great nations of the modern world were directly concerned, a prophecy reminiscent of those mighty prophecies of the Bible, was fulfilled. It was, we repeat, given as a sign that God is going to give The Gospel to Every Creature in this Generation.

In the next chapter it will be shown how another Prediction, that concerning "Danzig and the Corridor" also triumphantly survived the great test.

The Munich Prediction College Jubilation with Glynderwen Manor in the background. 29 September 1938. The Munich Pact was signed the following day and war was averted, giving Britain time to re-arm.

Chapter IV

THE DANZIG PREDICTION

The greatest menace of 1939 was the conflict over Danzig and the Corridor, which Hitler had pledged himself to annex. Moreover, if he failed to acquire them as he acquired Austria and Czechoslovakia, he intended to take them by force of arms. As Poland had two million trained soldiers, and their bravery, shown in repulsing the Russian Army from Warsaw in 1920, was known all over the world, it was thought they would be able to withstand an attack by Germany, and carry on a war, at any rate for many months.

Britain and France had pledged themselves to the Poles, to defend Poland if Germany attacked her. It was understood, on the other hand, that Italy, Spain, and Japan would stand with Germany against Britain and France, if these countries should declare war on Germany. It seemed certain, therefore, that when Germany attacked Poland, nothing in the world could prevent a General European War. But the College had predicted that there would be "No European War" until the Vision of taking "the Gospel to Every Creature in thirty years" was accomplished; and then the real Armageddon would be fought. So sure were we of the prediction of "No General European War" that, after the September victory, when we gave a holiday before the Munich Pact was signed, the College was then led to buy one of the finest properties in South Wales, the [Penllergaer] Estate of the late Sir John Llewelyn, and prepare for fruitful years of peace.

Meanwhile, Hitler, finding that the crisis created over Czechoslovakia did not lead to a European War (because Britain and France allowed him to have his own way), turned his wrath on the Jewish people, and caused thousands of their little children to become homeless (the number has been given as seventy thousand). The sufferings were so great, that the parents were even willing to give their children away, rather than see them starve.

THE REASON BECOMES CLEAR

Thus it came about that God revealed to the College that they were to take over Sir John Llewelyn's Penllergaer Estate, and make there a home and schools for Jewish children. (This will be explained in a later chapter). During 1939 the College spent thousands of pounds in making all preparations to receive the refugees while at the same time, waiting for the Danzig question to lead up to another crisis.

Germany under Hitler, like the Assyrian army under Sennacherib had never been checked nor defeated, and so was now like a roaring lion after its prey. German generals were visiting Italy, Spain, and other countries discussing war; and British generals were over in France, Poland, and Russia, making plans to combat the raging aggressor. Europe was preparing for the greatest war in history!

The responsibility and the tension of the prediction of "No European War," in face of the preparations for it, were so intense at times, that there was neither rest nor peace, except in the "cleft of the rock" (Exodus 33:22) and "under the shadow of the Almighty" (Psalm 91:1). Scores of times the Director [Rees Howells] made it known in the meetings, that when God confounded the dictators, it would be the greatest miracle of the ages, because only thus would a European War be avoided. More than once, when the dictators were rampaging over the wireless as to what they were going to do when the final test came, God had to comfort us, as He did Jeremiah, saying: "Behold, I am the Lord, the God of all flesh, is there anything too hard for Me?" (Jeremiah 32:27).

Was it possible for God to break the Axis, that diabolical union that the Devil had made between these dictators? Yes, the God who came down and confounded the tongues of those who were building the Tower of Babel, would easily be able to confound the plans of the puny dictators of 1939.

WAS IT OF GOD?

During the past seventeen years, God has led the College to make many predictions, some of which are given in this book. It has gained many thousands of followers and supporters, who for years have offered sacrificial gifts, as they were moved by God to do so. Last year alone, nearly £20,000 [£1,348,800 in 2020] was thus received. The fact that he had spent years in building up a work of this kind, and held properties in his hands to the value of about £150,000 [£10,116,000 in 2020], was in itself enough to make the Director very careful in all his predictions, because one real mistake would cause hundreds of supporters to lose their confidence in him. He knew well that the crisis over Danzig and the Corridor, would be the final test of the prediction of "No European War." So – was it of God or of man? Was God able to confuse the plans of the dictators, who appeared to be as firmly united and forged together as were Britain and France?

The College had staked its all on the God of Daniel, in whose hands even the great King Nebuchadnezzar found that "All the inhabitants of the earth are reputed as nothing: and He doeth according to His will in the army of Heaven, and among the inhabitants of the earth, and none can stay His hand, or say unto Him, what doest thou?" (Daniel 4:35).

When the clash came and Germany invaded Poland, some may have doubted. But the first ray of God's light was soon apparent, showing that God was surely working out the prediction.

ITALY AVERTS HER GAZE

After all her protestations of undying friendship, Italy and her dictator backed out. Incredible but true. Spain and Japan also declared their neutrality. In other words God broke asunder the Devil's league, and no power of evil in this world could bring the dictators together again. Mutual trust between the Axis powers was finally shattered. So God had confused the plans of the dictators! What a day of victory for the Bible College! The prediction had been vindicated. No general European War! Not until God permits the Armageddon. Victory beyond value. Although Britain and France, to carry out their pledge to Poland, declared war on Germany, the College knew that so long as Italy and Spain remained neutral, this would never lead to a general European War. When Germany made a league with Russia it was confirmed that both Italy and Spain would remain neutral. The Catholic countries have the greatest respect for their religion and their Sabbath, and they would never join Russia, who had done away with the Sabbath, even bringing her own pagan calendar into Poland.

To those who have eyes to see and ears to hear this joining up of Russia and Germany is a miracle, for they were the two most unlikely countries in the world to make a league with one another. Evil was designed, but here again God overruled it. The greatest enemies of the Nazis were the Reds, as Hitler has repeatedly said. But, just as Daniel made known, after he had seen the great image, whose feet and toes were part of iron and part of clay that "They shall not cleave one to another, even as iron is not mixed with clay" (Daniel 2:43), even so has it been with the four dictators in the day of battle, and so will it be with the Nazis and the Reds.

DISCOMFITED DICTATORS

The three great powers (Germany, Italy, and Japan), who had joined together under the cloak of an anti-Comintern pact, [Comintern was an international association of Communist parties, established in 1919] to work for a world war against Soviet Russia, posed as champions against Bolshevism. Hitler in one of his speeches, said: "The rulers of Russia today are blood-stained common malefactors, and the scum of humanity, who, favoured by the circumstances of a tragic hour, over-ran a great state, butchered and wiped out in wild blood-lust millions of their intellectual classes, and have now for years been exercising the most cruel tyranny in history. Nor let us forget that these rulers belong to a people in whom is combined to a degree seldom attained, bestial cruelty with unique fluency of lying, and which today more than ever believes itself called to the destined extension of its bloody tyranny over the whole world.... One cannot conclude any treaty with a partner whose sole interest is one's own destruction."

Germany, under the cloak of a crusader against Communist menace, was forging the Berlin-Rome-Tokio Axis, and claiming East Europe, as far as the Ukraine and the old Prussian colonisation areas leaving Italy to demand Tunis, Algiers, [in North Africa] etc., and Japan to do as she would in China. By making a pact with Soviet Russia, "the scum of humanity," as he called them, Hitler, to quote another writer, "broke the Humpty-Dumpty Axis beyond mending, and he can never put Humpty-Dumpty together again!"

AN AMAZING BREAK-UP

When it was predicted, through the College, that the Devil, through all the dictators of Europe cannot make a European War, God had already foreseen this. Russia only came in to take all the spoil from Germany, and then settled down to remain neutral. Molotoff affirmed Russian neutrality by saying: "No one can draw Russia into war." No one but the Almighty God could have planned this amazing break-up, and have made it known before-hand.

Britain and France have become one in motive and aim, like parts of a living organism; but the league between Russia and Germany is merely an organisation, a union they try to make outwardly, when inwardly there is nothing but fear and enmity. So, from the day war was declared, and God proved the weakness of the dictators, the College saw that the prediction of "No European War" was safe; and it will shine more and more as the days and years go by, and the Vision is made known in every country of the world.

Yes, this confusion of the dictators is one of the greatest proofs that the College Vision is of God, and that He will give the Gospel to Every Creature in the next twenty-five years.[1]

"Sing ye to the Lord, for He hath triumphed gloriously" (Exodus 15:1).
> Blessed and glorious King,
> To Thee our praise we bring,
> This glorious hour....
> *War now has vanquished been,
> Dictators all are seen –
> Ne'er to unite again.
> Due to Thy power.[2]

*European War.

Editor's note: The above hymn and many others can be found in: *Rees Howells, Vision Hymns of Spiritual Warfare & Intercessory Declarations: World War II Songs of Victory, Intercession, Praise and Worship, Israel and the Every Creature Commission* by Mathew Backholer. *Vision Hymns* gives a rare insight into the prophetic declarations, hymns and choruses used in spiritual warfare by Rees Howells and his team of intercessors at the Bible College of Wales. Spanning the pivotal years of 1936-1948 and brought to life for the first time in more than seventy years.

Chapter V

THE GREAT PREDICTION

GOD WILL INTERVENE TO END HITLER'S WAR

When Hitler in 1933, became Chancellor, he became like Haman of old, the Jews' enemy. As Haman did, he appointed a day (1st April) to make a national boycott against the Jews. It was probably the greatest act of folly ever committed on April Fool's Day, for the Nazi Brown Shirts began to show the dragon's teeth which are destined to grind them to pieces. The world's press termed this blended violence and mendacity "Nazi savagery against Judah." The excesses committed then and since have shocked civilisation profoundly. Jewish doctors born in Germany were dismissed from public service, teachers from their schools, and lawyers from the Law Courts. Business houses were induced to dismiss Jews from their staff, and Germans were forbidden to buy in Jewish shops. Mobs ran amok, robbing Jewish stores, and committing acts of brutal ferocity; and the police did not intervene to restrain the terrorists.

Hitler, aware that the nations of the world were disgusted with his régime, defied humanity, declaring there was no cruelty in thus purging the German nation of an alien and a *Criminal Race,* which had brought ruin on Aryan Germany. The behaviour of the fanatical despot, not only shocked the civilised world, but assuredly shocked God as well. Hitler's treatment of the Jews, and his reference to them as a *Criminal Race,* could not escape the notice of Him who inhabiteth eternity and weighs all acts of men in His balances.

When Balak sent for Balaam he said: "Come, curse me Jacob, and come, defy Israel" (Numbers 23:7), and Balaam said: "How shall I curse whom God has not cursed? Or how shall I defy, whom the Lord has not defied? Surely there is no enchantment against Jacob, neither is there any divination against Israel" (Numbers 23:8, 21). "I shall see Him, but not now; I shall behold Him, but not nigh: there shall come a *Star out of Jacob,* and a Sceptre shall rise out of Israel" (Numbers 24:17).

It would have been well for Hitler had he been guided by that saying from the history of the people he blasphemously branded as a *Criminal Race.* Compare the prophets of the Gentiles, who have lived during the last two thousand years, since the Day of Pentecost (the Dispensation of Grace) with those of the Jews who lived for two thousand years before Pentecost (back to the time of Abraham). Is there one among the Gentiles who can be put alongside of Joseph, Moses, Elijah, or Daniel?

Even Martin Luther saw only the truth of "Justification by Faith," which the Apostles experienced and preached; but Luther did none of the miracles that Peter and Paul did; nor has any other Gentile ever repeated any of the Acts of the Apostles, such mighty works as the calling of Dorcas back from the dead, opening of the prison doors, etc., etc.

HISTORY WARNS HITLER

We dare not treat lightly God's promises to the Jews – His Chosen Race. God's Covenant with Abraham was: "...I will multiply thy seed as the stars of Heaven...and in thy seed shall possess the gate of his enemies; and in thy seed shall all the nations of the earth be blessed" (Genesis 12:2-3 and 22:17-18).

Israel was to be a blessing to the world, but let him who offends the Chosen Race – beware! Though God allowed two nations, Egypt and Babylon, to chastise Israel, He did not thereby endorse all the ways of those nations. Rather did He bring those nations into His judgment and they were overthrown. How then can Hitler, who persecuted the Jews without cause, hope to escape the fate which befalls those who lift up their hands against the Lord's anointed? God said to Abraham: "Thy seed shall be a stranger in a land that is not theirs, and shall serve them; and they shall afflict them four hundred years; and also that nation, whom they shall serve, will I judge" (Genesis 15:13-14). And in Egypt God fulfilled that prediction to the letter – not only killing the firstborn, but drowning Pharaoh and his army in the Red Sea. To this day Egypt is but a third-rate nation.

Again God said to Jeremiah: "These nations shall serve the king of Babylon seventy years. And it shall come to pass, when seventy years are accomplished, that I will punish the King of Babylon, and that nation. I will bring upon that land all My words which I have pronounced against it. I will recompense them according to their deeds..." (Jeremiah 25:11-14). So shall it be with the Nazis. The Lord has made known to the College that He is going to destroy Hitler and the Nazi régime, and the College has predicted it beforehand through the Daily Press, that the world may know that it was God, and God alone who scattered the dictators, and bound the Devil that he could never unite them to fight side by side against God and the right.

God isolated Germany, and caused to go against her, England and France, who have repeatedly said that they are not fighting against Germany as a nation, but against Hitler and the Nazi régime, and they will not make peace with Hitlerism. After our prediction had gone out to the country, there came the Prime Minister's reply to the Hitler peace proposal. Speaking on behalf of the Empire, Mr Chamberlain said: "We unitedly reject it." He added that it would be impossible to make peace with the present German government, for Hitler and his Nazis could never be trusted again.

It was on Saturday, 9th September, and Monday, 11th September, 1939, in the columns of the "South Wales Evening Post," and the "Western Mail," that our new prediction was first published. The article from the "Western Mail" is given here in full:

GOD WILL INTERVENE TO END THE WAR[1]
WELSH BIBLE COLLEGE DIRECTOR'S PREDICTION

Very soon God will intervene in a miraculous way and come to the aid of England and France, who have sacrificed all to defend liberty, especially religious liberty, and put down the Antichrist which has thrown its spell over Germany and caused all the outstanding evangelical ministers to be put in prison and concentration camps.

This is the view expressed by the Rev. Rees Howells, hon. director of the Bible College of Wales, Swansea; in a circular he has issued dealing with the international situation.

Mr Howells continues: "Although England and France have declared war on Germany to carry out their pledges to Poland, God has kept out the German allies – Italy, Spain, and Japan – who before the crisis were as much in league with Germany as France and England were in league with Poland, and through another mysterious way Russia, at the last moment, became neutral.

"So after a week of hostilities, and after a week of prayer and waiting upon God in the College, it is now clearer than ever to us in the College that the prediction of "No European War" is from God, and that He has isolated Germany so that He may get at this system of the Nazi régime, which is the AntiChrist, and release Germany, 'the land of the Reformation.'

"WILL DEAL WITH NAZI RÉGIME"

"The College for weeks and months prayed this prayer three-and-a-half years ago, and we firmly believe now that God will answer that prayer; that God will intervene in a miraculous way just now, and will deal with Germany as he dealt with the Egyptian Army in the time of Moses and with the Philistines in the time of the Prophet Samuel when he raised his Ebenezer.

"We are stronger than ever in the belief that God is in this crisis, and that God has singled out Germany to deal with the Nazi régime (Hitlerism), which is the Antichrist, which would be the greatest opposition to the College Vision of giving the Gospel to Every Creature, because this system of the Nazi régime has caused the best of the evangelical ministers to be put in prison.

"DEADLY BLOW TO HITLERISM"

"Moreover, no missionaries would ever be able to go from Germany as the Moravians[2] of old did, and before this war will go much further God will intervene in a direct way and put this system down, and end the war, and release Germany, the land of the Reformation. He will deal a deadly blow to Hitlerism, and the prediction of "No European War" will stand out clearer than ever. Our Prime Minister will soon see the day when his hopes of peace, instead of being shattered, will become true in Europe again."

The College believe, adds Mr Howells, that God allowed England and France to go to the aid of Poland so as to hold Hitlerism in check, and that God will cause Hitler to fall on the battlefield, or by a mutiny, or a great rising in Germany against the Nazis. The words of David regarding King Saul will soon become true: "The Lord shall surely smite him; or his day shall come to die; or he shall descend into battle, and perish" (1 Samuel 26:10).

It was on 12th September, the day following the publication in the "Western Mail" of the foregoing article that our Prime Minister made it known to the world that "this country can never again accept terms of peace coming from Hitler or the Nazi régime."

- 103 -

So, after a month of hostilities, when the offer of peace came, the world waited and watched to see whether the Prime Minister would go back on his word or not. Thousands of leaflets were published by the "Peace Pledge Union," calling for peace and a conference. But, because of the prediction of "the downfall of Hitler and the Nazi régime," the College was bound to stand with the Prime Minister in stating that the war must be continued "until Hitlerism is overthrown."

BRITAIN ON GOD'S SIDE

History will show that the College stood firmly with the Prime Minister in 1938, when he was inspired to go direct to Hitler, and avert a European War; for *Mr Chamberlain was acting in accordance with the prophecy.* When some people blamed the Prime Minister for flying to Germany, saying that by taking things into his own hands, he had broken every law of diplomacy, the Premier's answer was: "*I am man of peace,* and war to me is a nightmare." There was no other way to avert war, and save millions of lives, and he would follow the same course again. But a year later, in October 1939, the College was confident that God guided Britain and France to refuse Hitler's peace proposal; even though, like so many more, the College had much to lose by the continuance of war. For, we repeat, the Founders are now holding in trust for God, freehold properties to the value of £150,000 [£10,116,000 in 2020], as well as that which is infinitely more valuable than property – the Vision of giving the "*Gospel to Every Creature in thirty years,"* with which is linked the prediction of "No European War" during that period.

If Italy, Spain, and Turkey had joined Germany and made it a *general* European War that would have belied [contradicted] the College Vision. But God isolated Germany, so as to get at this Nazi system, which is the Antichrist, and give it a death-blow. For it is His will to release Germany, the land of the Reformation, and to release the land of the Moravians, that hundreds of missionaries may again be called out of both countries to share in the Vision of giving the Gospel to *Every Creature* in this generation.

How often of late has the College been encouraged to believe in its own Vision by reading the story of Isaiah's prophecy about the Assyrians, who came down like a wolf, like Hitler today. The College prediction is like that of Isaiah, who predicted of that great boaster, King Sennacherib, that God would put a hook in his nose, and a bridle in his lips, and turn him back-and that night, God smote in the camp of the Assyrians 185,000 people (Isaiah 36-37).

Was there not ample reason for God also to intervene against the Nazis? Into what a state our country has been brought! For over a year people have had to keep gas-masks to hand. And now, through fear of air-raids, the King and Queen, down to the lonely peasant and his wife in the remotest parts of the country, have to take their gas-masks with them in case of poison gas from the air. Everywhere death is threatened.

Hitler boasts that he will destroy the one thing he fears most – the British Empire. He can never do it. If Britain and France were to make peace with Hitler and the Nazi régime, people would have to keep their gas-masks indefinitely, so long as the Nazi Government existed. For, as we have said, they could never be trusted not to break out again. Because our new prediction will be fulfilled, and "God will intervene in a miraculous way," our nation must now hasten to turn back to God, must keep her Sabbaths yet again, according to the Fourth Commandment, and must restore the old Puritan England of the past. In short, we must now build Jerusalem in England's green and pleasant land,[3] which was the Vision of the late King George the Fifth.

ARMAGEDDON

All who have read the book "Hitler Re-arms" – which is an exposure of Germany's War plans – will praise God as long as they live, that He has isolated Germany, and divided the dictators, who would otherwise have plunged Europe and the world into the bloodiest war in history. All their preparations for war, their guns and bombs, their poison-words and poison-gas have given millions of people a taste of what the coming Armageddon will be like. But then, alas, God will not intervene, as He is going to do now, by bringing about the speedy downfall of the Nazi régime.

The Bible has predicted the world conditions that will precede the Master's "*Second Coming.*" The two great *signs* are:

1. "And ye shall hear of wars and rumours of wars, see that ye be not troubled, for all these things must come to pass, but the end is not yet. This Gospel of the Kingdom shall be preached in all the world for a witness unto all nations; and then shall the end come" (Matthew 24:6, 14).

2. The Jews will return to the Holy Land. "The Land of Promise." "Then the Lord thy God will turn thy captivity, and

have compassion upon thee, and will return and gather thee from all the nations, whither the Lord thy God hath scattered thee" (Deuteronomy 30:3).

The College Vision is that the Gospel will be given to all nations in the next twenty-five years (for five years have already gone since it was received), and then – the Prince of Peace will come to reign on the Earth. Even so come Lord Jesus!

The next chapter records the prediction that God would make a Home for the children of the Jewish refugees, to educate and train them and send them back to the Holy Land to wait for the Lord's Coming.

Chapter VI

THE £100,000 PREDICTION

HOMES FOR JEWISH CHILDREN IN WALES AND THE HOLY LAND

Yet another remarkable prediction, given to the College, has been confidently noised abroad, though as yet it has only been partially fulfilled. It is that God will send £100,000 to the College to be used for the benefit of Jewish refugee children. The College, believing that this £100,000 will arrive in due course, has evolved a scheme which will operate on the Barnardo [a children's charity] principle. The main features of this scheme are as follow:
1. No destitute refugee child to be refused, but promptly admitted.
2. The children are to have a home and education until they qualify as teachers, nurses or missionaries.
3. There will be no distinction made between Christian and orthodox Jewish children, if the parents or guardians will trust their upbringing to the College.

The following is an article which appeared in the "Western Mail" on 29th May 1939, when the persecution was at its height, in which the prediction and scheme are explained more fully:

£100,000 EXPECTED BY BIBLE COLLEGE

NEW SCHOOLS FOR 1,000 JEWISH REFUGEE CHILDREN

Two prophecies are made in the report of the Bible College of Wales, Swansea, to be presented at the fifteenth annual meeting today. They are: 1. "That the Lord will give the College during the coming year £100,000," and 2. That schools will be built to take in between 1,000 and 2,000 Jewish refugee children so that they may have four years' training in the Secondary Schools and three in the Bible College.

The report states that just as "the £100,000 gift from God's treasury" and the prediction of no European War were made known in the last annual report and by now had been fulfilled, so in the present report the Holy Ghost was making the two further prophecies known.

It is also prophesied that God will again keep back a European War until the College Vision of reaching Every Creature with the Gospel will be accomplished and homes established in the Holy Land for hundreds of Jewish refugees.

PENLLERGAER BOUGHT

Since the crisis last September, says the report, the College has been buying estates on which to build schools for the Jewish children: 1. Twenty-one acres of freehold land adjoining the Bible College estates were taken over last September. 2. Penllergaer, the estate of the late Sir John Llewelyn, has been bought. This estate is of 270 acres. "All this land has been bought so that God may fulfil His promise to give the College £100,000 to be used for the refugee Children." Each refugee child will cost at a minimum £1 a week because those who adopt them must sign that they will be responsible for their education, clothing, food, and a home until they are 18 years of age. Therefore, in addition to the thousands of pounds which the new schools, colleges, and hospital will cost, 1,000 Jewish children will cost £1,000 a week (£50,000 a year).

£50,000 GUARANTEE NECESSARY

"The College," says the report, "will have no claim upon any source for a penny towards maintenance of these children but on God, who has promised to be a father to the fatherless. Since the College bought these 21 acres near Derwen Fawr and the estate of the late Sir John Llewelyn a law has been passed that with each adopted refugee child there must be a bank guarantee given of £50 [£3,250 in 2020] for those up to 16 and £100 [£6,500 in 2020] for those over 16. Therefore, by taking 1,000 Jewish children the College will have to guarantee £50,000, this money to be used for their migration to another country. So the Holy Ghost has foreseen that the College would need £100,000 for buildings and bank guarantee besides the £50,000 per year which will be needed for the maintenance of the children in this country.

The Bible College after 15 years in Glyn Derwen [the first site bought in 1924 and originally spelt as two words but later contracted to one word: Glynderwen] and Derwen Fawr will move to its new home, Penllergaer, shortly. In the College today are students of many nationalities, including Russian and Spanish refugees, Jewish refugees, and a Prince of Abyssinia [Ethiopia].

£360 A WEEK IN GIFTS

The money that came in gifts last year was more than three times greater than the money received in College and School fees. The financial report shows that there was received in gifts alone £18,771, [£1,266,000 in 2020] an average of £360 [£24,346 in 2020] a week. One gift alone was for £10,000 [£674,400 in 2020]. All the money was received "through prayer alone." From fees £5,327 [£359,260 in 2020 from the College, Schools, Hospital, Home of Rest for Missionaries] was received, so that the total receipts amounted to £24,101 [£1,625,400 in 2020].

"Here is a College," states the report, "which was founded on 2s [£6.74 in 2020], without a committee, council, or denomination or any appeal being made in any shape or form, with a turnover of £24,000 for last year, and most of that money has come from outside Wales and nearly all of it spent in the borough of Swansea."

The founders of the College (the Rev. and Mrs Rees Howells) have decided to give their home in Derwen Fawr for use as a Girls' Secondary School and Glyn Derwen as a Boys' Secondary School in order that Derwen Fawr, Sketty Isaf, and Glyn Derwen may be devoted entirely to the refugees. The director is inviting Lord and Lady Baldwin to open Penllergaer because of their great interest in Jewish refugee children.

CITY OF REFUGE

Our new Home for the Jews is an estate of nearly three hundred acres of freehold land; it has a large mansion with many outbuildings; and the latter are being reconstructed to provide lecture-halls and class-rooms, and fifty additional bedrooms.

There are seven other dwelling-houses on the estate, a home farm, and the market gardens where Sir John Llewelyn once employed fifteen gardeners. The estate is famous for its collection of trees and shrubs, which is one of the best in the country; it was here that the Swansea University used to send their students for classes in botany, before the town built their Educational Gardens.

The river and the lake of eighteen acres have long been popular for their trout fishing, and round them are the lovely woods where Sir John entertained shooting parties. The beautiful drive up to the mansion, through masses of rhododendrons and azaleas is over a mile-and-a-quarter in length. When the persecuted little ones are driven up through these banks of rhododendrons, ablaze with bloom, they will feel they are more than half way already to their Home of Destiny, the Land of Promise, which is yet again to flow with milk and honey. This then is the estate on which it is purposed to establish a "City of Refuge" in Wales for Jewish refugee children, where they may "flee from the slayer."

The evidence already apparent that God Himself has planned and led us to take in hand a schemes such as this, has increased our conviction that He will send in the hundreds of thousands of pounds that will be needed to establish a "City of Refuge," not only in Wales, but also in the Holy Land and elsewhere. It also buttresses our belief that He will intervene to prevent a general European War and to smash the diabolical Nazi régime.

Remembrance of recent horrors may help people to realise something of the feelings of God, who is a "Father of the fatherless," when He called the Founders of the College to launch out on this colossal scheme. In Britain, thousands of little children have been evacuated from London and other great cities [from 1st September 1939], for protection against air-raids, and from such a disaster as overtook the mothers and children of Warsaw [in Poland], where over twenty thousand civilians were killed in a few weeks. Over seventy thousand helpless refugee children need homes, education and protection. Will the fathers and mothers of our country pray that all these will have homes, even as our own children had when they were evacuated from our cities?

We give here the photograph of our first Jewish baby, who came to us from Vienna, with several other children, when he was just a year old. Like Moses, found in his ark of bulrushes on the banks of the Nile, and subsequently brought up in a palace, so little Herbert Grunhut[1] travelled here in a tiny basket to be cared for like an infant prince in one of his Father's earthly mansions.

Herbert "Bert" Grunhut (1938-2019) from Vienna, Austria with Lizzie and Rees Howells in front of Derwen Fawr Manor 1939

FAITH'S GOLDEN RULE

There is a golden rule in the life of faith, that the Christian can never prevail upon God to move others to give larger sums of money towards God's work, than he himself has either given, or proved that he is willing to give if it were in his power to do so. The rule applies to a Bible College as well as to an ordinary Christian. It came within the power of the Founders of the College to offer to God the first £100,000 towards establishing the "Cities of Refuge" in Wales and the Holy Land, and so that offering was made, although it would have meant selling up all that they had.

When the Conscription Bill [3rd September 1939] was passed and the young manhood [aged 18-41] of our country was mobilised, the Government bought the freehold land adjoining the College [on Derwen Fawr Road, Sketty, Swansea]. On this they began to erect large buildings for the use of the Territorials and the new Militia Army, [later known as the Home Guard] and there was the possibility of their needing all the College properties. These were very suitable for Government purposes, because they included a Hospital, Laboratory, Gymnasium and Bakery; and by adapting some of the class-rooms and lecture-halls room could have been made to billet a thousand men.

It was even suggested that when the Government decided to take over the three estates [Glynderwen, Derwen Fawr and Sketty Isaf] that the College should have the honorary chaplainship. The College had already bought Penllergaer [six miles north of the three other estates], where there is room to build a town of about two thousand houses. So it was settled that if the Government should decide to take over our College with the fifty acres of freehold land surrounding it, we would move all our work out to Penllergaer, and there begin to build on faith again Colleges, Schools, Missionary Home, Hospital, Bakery, etc., which would cost over £100,000.

There would then be no money or realisable [gain or profit] property for rebuilding, because the £100,000 or so raised from the sale of the properties would be dedicated to the "Cities of Refuge" for the Jewish children. In other words we were prepared to make an offering to God of £100,000 – the value of our College property – for helping the children of His Chosen People. Because we were prepared to do this, we were observing a rule of faith whereby we might confidently look to God for an equal sum for our genuine needs. Prayer was made to God to allow us to use this £100,000 realisable on College property in this way. However, at the last moment, the Government decided not to take any more land in our neighbourhood, as the War Office wrote to us: "The military authorities in the Western Command have, however, been asked whether they wish to acquire any of these properties for any other purpose. As soon as a report is received Mr Hore-Belisha [British Secretary of State for War 1937-1940] will write to you further."

So the Lord allowed us to retain the estates on which the College stands, Glyn Derwen and Derwen Fawr; the former to be continued as a Boys' Secondary School, and the latter to established as a Girls' Secondary School, but College itself will be moved to Penllergaer.

Thus the path is now clear for the Lord to make the College the needed gift of £100,000. We have not a shadow of doubt that the money will come, or that the vision of its coming will be fulfilled. God has said in Psalm 68: "A father of the fatherless, and a judge of the widows, is God in His holy habitation. God setteth the *solitary in families*, He bringeth out those which are bound in chains."

When God made this Promise to be a Father to the fatherless, He bound Himself to be more of a Father to the orphans than the father and mother they had lost, and by becoming their father, He pledges Himself to provide for them. The Word of God says: "If ye then, being evil, know how to give good gifts unto children, *how much more* shall your Heavenly Father" (Matthew 7:11). If He told us to consider the ravens and the lilies, and He feeds and clothes, *how much more* will He feed and clothe these children?

THE SOLITARY IN FAMILIES

Dr. Barnardo (1845-1905) had a revelation of God to set the Solitary in Families, and so he built the Girl's Village Home, and rescued, clothed, fed, mothered and educated over nine thousand girls in one village alone.

Although he died at the age of sixty, he rescued, during his lifetime, over *sixty thousand orphans.* Since Dr. Barnardo, by becoming a channel through whom God could fulfil His Promise to the Orphans, rescued sixty thousand in thirty years, the Lord can, and the College believes will, through then, rescue fifty thousand little Jewish children in twenty-five years. What a company to meet the Saviour in the Holy Land at His Second coming as their Messiah, The Prince of Peace.[2]

Through the Prophet Isaiah God gave a special promise to the orphaned Jewish Children: "Thus saith the Lord God, behold, I will lift up Mine hand to the Gentiles, and set up My standard to the people, and they shall bring thy sons in their arms, and thy daughters shall be carried upon their shoulders. And kings shall be thy nursing fathers, and their queens thy nursing mothers.... Shall the prey be taken from the mighty, or the lawful captive delivered. Thus saith the Lord, even the captives of the mighty shall be taken away, and the prey of the terrible shall be delivered: for I will contend with him (Hitler) that contendeth with thee, *and will save thy Children*" (Isaiah 49:22-25).[3]

GOD'S GREAT DELIVERANCE

Let us look again at Hitler, this time in Rome. Only in May 1938, when Hitler visited Rome, and Mussolini Berlin, Hitler stressed "Colossal unity of Germany" with Mussolini saying "So long as the united community with its front to the world, *nobody will war on us.*" And Mussolini said: "No one can weaken the Berlin-Rome Axis. The friendship between the two countries is everlasting."

"Everlasting" was hardly appropriate. "Ephemeral" was surely the word for an Axis that lasted hardly a year. Yet Mussolini – at the time of the Hitler visit – spoke on racial purity, and opened a campaign against the Jews; he also imposed military training upon all boys from the age of eight until they entered the army, and at the same time he took steps to strengthen the Italian Fleet. Just then it really looked as though nothing could save the world from the dictators. They seemed invincible. Yet the break-up has come and gone, and little has so far been said about it. The world will never fully realise how great is God's deliverance from these ruthless dictators, men whom the Devil would have used to plunge the world into the bloodiest war in history, and for the slaughter of many millions of people.

Already we breathe more freely again. And although the struggle may be great, the sun will again shine in the heavens upon the democracies who will come to understand that they were all the time fighting on the Lord's side, while but feebly hoping that the Lord was with them, and so would enable them to overthrow their powerful enemy. This strange war then is not our war, but God's, and the victory is the Lord's.

The best thank-offering that we can give to God for deliverance from black-outs and gas-masks, from shot, shell and explosion, is to succour these little helpless Jewish children, innocent victims of the Devil's violence, whose despairing parents are willing to give them to the Gentiles, rather than see them perish exposure, bestial cruelty and starvation, and help them we can and will. Thus we shall help God to fulfil His Promise "I will save the Children" (Isaiah 49:25). Thus we shall earn the welcome benediction: "Inasmuch as have done it unto the least of these…ye done it unto Me" (Matthew 25:40).

PART II

Chapter VII

PREDICTION OF THE LARGEST BIBLE COLLEGE

Nowadays there is a great scarcity of mighty men of faith. For this reason it was difficult seventeen years ago to convince the country of the prediction to build the largest Bible College by prayer and faith alone, especially as it was our first great prediction.[1]

Of the millions of Christians in our country in the last generation there was only one, a German named George Müller, who, trusted God, and God alone, to supply hundreds of thousands of pounds to carry on a work that God had committed to him. George Müller was the outstanding man of God who never looked to man, who made no deputation work of any kind, although his needs ran up to £90 a day. Consequently only George Müller and the Old Testament Prophets were able to supply the Founders of the College with the necessary examples to trust God alone day by day to supply the financial needs for this monumental work.

In August 1922, without any seeking on the part of the Founders, God revealed to them that it was His will and purpose to build a large Bible College in Wales, to be founded, and sustained by prayer and faith alone. The idea therefore originated with God, without premeditation or even desire on the part of the Founders. It would seem that in our time God wanted to give another visible proof that He is the living God, and that we can still rely on His Word and His promises. So the College was to be without a committee, council, or denomination; it would spring up with no visible support of any kind, no human patron, no endowment.

God wanted to prove that faith and prayer, are efficient agents, along with implicit trust in His Word for meeting all needs. He wanted to raise up a College to be a testimony to the world that God's work carried on by the Holy Ghost, needs not the patronage of the world; and that God's work, carried on in God's way, will never lack finance, because God is the Owner of all "the silver and the gold" (Haggai 2:8).

The call to build a College on Faith came quite unexpectedly. The Founders were on furlough from Africa, where, for nearly ten years (1914-1923)[2] they had laboured as missionaries with the South African General Mission. During two fruitful years of this period they had travelled over 11,000 miles conducting special meetings round all their Mission stations in South Africa. It was directly after this most successful period of their missionary work that God's call came to remain at home and build the largest Bible and Missionary Training College in the country. Why the largest? Time will show. Anyway, the call was clear and definite. Judge the work by its fruits. Already there has been harvest. But there are plenteous harvests yet to come.

MONEY MIRACLES

Surely one of the most fascinating of tasks is to trace back a story of God in His faithfulness, searching out His Almighty power and wisdom in fulfilling a promise made to one of His servants to whom He has given a commission to undertake beyond his range and power.

When God inspired the building of this College, by faith alone, He gave two promises.

1. "Fear not... He will not fail thee, nor forsake thee, until thou hast finished all the work for the service of the house of the Lord (the College). "There shall be with thee 'of workmanship' every willing skilful man, for any manner of service" (1 Chronicles 28:20-21).

2. The promise of "A Talent of Gold" (Exodus 25:39, the figure given then was £6,150) [£374,600 in 2020].

As already stated, when the call came from God to buy estates on which to build the largest Bible College in the country, the Founders had only two shillings. [The cost of a 1939 *God Challenges the Dictators'* hardback]. So from a human standpoint, without a council or any visible support during the greatest period of commercial scarcity of money in history of the country (1920s), it appeared to be a hazardous and even a crazy venture. It was a time when, through financial and strain in the business world, banks and men's heart's everywhere failed them. It would therefore seem that the call came to build the College of Faith at that time so as, among other things, to encourage businessmen to trust in God, because a living trusting faith in God is above all circumstances.

- 116 -

No delays can discourage faith, no loss of friends or depression in trade can touch it; faith goes on its steady course, and triumphs over all difficulties. That is one reason why it is so necessary to stress that the only thing on earth to fear is – *estrangement from God.*

THE FIRST PURCHASE

The first estate bought by faith for the College was Glyn Derwen, the home of Mr Charles Eden, an uncle of the Right Hon. Anthony Eden, where in past years Mr Eden must have spent many a happy holiday. This estate, with its large mansion, comprised many acres of land, and incidentally a public-house.

The property had been laid out in lawns, tennis-courts and gardens, allowing a commanding view of Swansea Bay and the Mumbles. Since, during the summer months, visitors pass it daily to the Gower Coast, it would also seem that God had planned this College of Faith to be a silent witness to multitudes of passers-by of what He will do in answer to believing prayer.

Like some of the others, this property, which cost over £6,000 was bought when there was hardly a penny in hand. Yet on the morning of the day when the deposit had to be paid, three cheques came in from some distance away and from unknown people. One of the cheques was for £126 [£7,630 in 2020], and the three together brought the amount in hand up to the last shilling required for the deposit!

This was our first convincing victory in finance; in an unmistakable way God showed what He was able to do, and what He would do in the future, if we looked to Him alone. "Let your requests be known unto God.... My God shall supply all Your need" (Philippians 4:6, 19).

OUR PUBLIC-HOUSE

The next few months [of 1923] were spent alone with God, learning further how to prevail on Him to move His stewards to send the thousands of pounds needed to complete the prophecy. During those stern days of waiting and learning in the School of Faith, an offer came to buy from us the public-house and the four acres of land attached to it. *No new licence had been given in Swansea for many years, so the licence itself was worth over a thousand pounds, and acceptance of the offer to buy the public-house would supply the extra money needed to complete the first purchase of the property.* It was the first serious temptation, in finance, to take an easy way of deliverance.

Days were spent waiting upon God in prayer to find His will regarding the selling of the public-house, but there was no possibility of compromise on principle. The unequivocal answer came: "Trust ye in the Lord for ever, for in the Lord Jehovah are everlasting resources" (Isaiah 26:4).

So the offer to trade the public-house and thus to have an easy deliverance for the purchase of the property was politely turned down. Instead, the public-house was closed down and the value of the licence completely lost. But the licensee was compensated for clearing out. Fair is fair to all – saints and publican alike. Then, by the addition of eight rooms, the public-house itself was converted-into a men's hostel!

Thus the second victory was gained; and God, as a reward for our faith and trust, sent in many hundreds of pounds in large and small gifts. When completion of purchase was made, it was found that the price, with costs, amounted to £6,150 7s. 4d. The very amount that God had promised! What a wonderful God to serve!

GOD'S COLLEGE

The College was dedicated on Whit-Monday, [Pentecost-Monday, 9th June] 1924, and hundreds gathered in the grounds for the special service. Long articles, describing the unique event were published in the daily Press, especially in the "Daily Leader," and the Welsh National newspaper, "The Western Mail." The Press head-lines read:

BIBLE COLLEGE OF WALES
A TRIUMPH OF FAITH
FERVENT INAUGURATION

The Press called it "God's College" – a happy title.

God had indeed given the College, for the funds had come from Him. God had stirred the hearts of His stewards to give freely, and so what was done in the Dedication Service was but reverently to hand the College back to God's care. He had given it, and it was given back to Him; the Founders would continue to look to Him to take care of His own, and were confident that He was going to do it.

Thus was founded the largest College of its kind in the country, with, at one time, more than one hundred and forty students in residence. In the first seven years, the Lord sent in thousands of pounds and supplied our needs day by day. Deliverances repeatedly came in at the very hour of need, and urgent needs for the next meal were frequently met only after the last meal had been cleaned away.

But space will not allow of full details to be given; it is only desired to show here how the prediction of building the largest Bible College in the country by prayer and faith alone was fulfilled; that it is now an accomplished fact, and that the evidence is there for all to see. This College has already been a blessing to thousands of people, especially as an incentive to faith in God in all times of distress and financial difficulties.

HALF FEES FOR STUDENTS

Hundreds of students have passed through the College to different parts of the Mission Field – young men and women who because of lack of funds, could never have taken a three years' course – had not the College opened its doors to them, and provided training, board and residence at less than half the actual cost. Students were only required to find the first £10 [£610 in 2020, for one term's fees of which there were three terms per year] and then to enter the School of Faith, there to learn, during three years' residence, to change God's promises into current coin [a phrase popular with Rees Howells]. Many are now missionaries in the foreign field. So again a fulfilled prediction made us raise our Ebenezer: "Hitherto hath the Lord helped us" (1 Samuel 7:12).

After some years of learning in the School of Faith and Prayer at the new College, God called us to further advance by making known that we were to buy Derwen Fawr, the estate of Sir Charles Ruthen. How this new marvel was accomplished will appear in the next chapter.

Chapter VIII

PREDICTION OF BUYING DERWEN FAWR

God had told the Founders to buy Derwen Fawr, the estate of the late Sir Charles Ruthen, who had been Director of Housing for the Ministry of Health. This estate was famous, for among its guests had been Mr Lloyd George (and family) when he was Prime Minister, Lord Melchett (Sir Alfred Mond), and other Cabinet Ministers. It had also been the home of members of the well-known Richardson family. Sir Charles had spent thousands of pounds on the estate, buying all the land between Derwen Fawr Road and Mumbles Road to prevent any buildings being put up in front of Derwen Fawr. Thousands of pounds had also been spent on laying out acres of land in lawns and gardens; and Sir Charles had displayed great architectural skill in altering the mansion, and in making the beautiful Italian gardens, for which he had costly stone-work brought from Italy.

When this estate came to the market, it included seventeen acres of freehold land in the best part of Swansea. Every acre could be turned into building land, for the town was moving down towards Singleton Park and the University; and soon afterwards the Swansea Corporation [local Council], having bought Sketty Park Estate, built their fine Civic Buildings near Singleton.

A TILT WITH ROME

When the Lord revealed [in 1929] that we were to buy Derwen Fawr Estate, the Director found that the Church of Rome were already negotiating for it. It was against the same Church that the College had previously to fight when they bought Glyn Derwen. To make known beforehand, while still without money, that God, through the College, would again oppose the Church of Rome, and a Syndicate also in the field, and would buy Derwen Fawr, at a time when the country was in a state of financial embarrassment, was surely a most daring exploit of faith.

The purchase of Derwen Fawr with no money and against double odds was as much in the impossible as that other unlikely prediction that there would be no general European War. The natural man can never understand these predictions with his unenlightened reason; for they are not in the realm of reason, but in the realm of Faith, which is the realm of God. The Master said: "When He, the Spirit of Truth, is come, He will guide you into all truth...and He will show you things to come" (John 16:13). As we have said, it was the Holy Ghost Himself who made known beforehand that Glyn Derwen should be bought, and a Bible College built there by faith. Again it was the Holy Ghost who said beforehand, and had the prediction made known, that the College should buy Derwen Fawr Estate, even against such great opposition.

At the time the negotiations were going on, a few thousand leaflets were published [the exact number was 4,000] making the prediction known to the public. The conflict lasted for months. There were days of tension when it was touch and go between the College and the Syndicate, for Derwen Fawr was one of the most desired and desirable building estates in Swansea. The only claim we had on Derwen Fawr was that some months before, Lady Ruthen had promised the refusal of it to the College. When the sale of the property was put in the hands of Lady Ruthen's solicitor, who did not know of this promise to the College, he was naturally on the side of the highest bidder, the Syndicate, which had made a slightly higher offer than the College.

None of us will ever forget the day when the depressing news came that Derwen Fawr had been sold to the Syndicate. We brought it before God, asking why He had given the prediction and caused us to make it known all over the country that He was going to buy Derwen Fawr for Himself, seeing that He had permitted it to be sold to another? As a result, and against known facts, the College refused to believe that Derwen Fawr had been sold to the Syndicate.

OUR RED-LETTER DAY

The day of the climax is one which we shall long remember. It was a Monday morning, and the Director's cousin, a doctor in Swansea had gone with him to the solicitor's office, where the two heard from one of the clerks what seemed to be final, that "Derwen Fawr is sold." That was definite enough. The solicitor himself was ill in bed, but had phoned the message through. Now indeed was the prediction sorely tested. Was it really from God, or from man? If it was from God, Derwen Fawr could never be sold to another person. So sure was the Director that it was from God, that he then announced, "Derwen Fawr is not sold. God's Word can never fail!"

At once his cousin visited the solicitor at his home and stressed that the College was entitled to the estate, because it had been definitely promised the first refusal of it. It was then learned belatedly that the Syndicate had merely been given a promise of the estate, provided they closed with the offer on the morning that the solicitor was too ill to attend to the deal. As they had not been able to close, this opened the way for the College to come in on the promise previously made by Lady Ruthen, as it was rightly entitled to do. In other words, this prediction too, was fulfilled, because God had intervened at the last moment to honour His promise.

Even so, Derwen Fawr was also secured when there was not a single penny in hand to pay for it. Fortunately, the solicitor had only stipulated that the Director should go to his office next day, and put down £25 [£1,590 in 2020], which would suffice until he had time to make out a regular contract. Fortunately, too, that very day two gifts were received, one of £5 and the other of £20. So Derwen Fawr was bought by faith in just that simple, unflinching faith which achieved those stirring exploits recorded in the eleventh of Hebrews:

By Faith they passed through the Red Sea as by dry land.
By Faith the walls of Jericho fell down.
By Faith they subdued kingdoms...stopped the mouths of lions.
By Faith they quenched the violence of fire...turned to flight the armies of the aliens.

THE TRUE PROPHET

By simple faith God took these beautiful estates, erected handsome new buildings on them worth thousands of pounds, and so proves to the world that He is the same today as yesterday, and that He will repeat what He did yesterday through the Prophets, when He will find a man with faith equal to that of the Prophets. Today the word prophet has come to mean a preacher only. But the prophets of old predicted the future as well, God making known to them beforehand what He was going to do. So to the prophets the future was like the past to the historians.

But who can understand these things today? For "the natural man receiveth not the things of the Spirit of God, for they are foolishness unto him, neither can he know them, because they are spiritually discerned" (1 Corinthians 2:14).

The Saviour said: "I thank Thee O Father, Lord of Heaven and earth, because Thou hast hid these things from the wise and prudent and hast revealed them unto babes" (Luke 10:21).

In the next chapter we show how, by faith, which is foolishness to the world, we received from God those thousands of pounds required to pay for this new acquisition, the Derwen Fawr Estate.

Derwen Fawr Mansion, c.1934 with a small section of the Italian Gardens on view with the FAITH IS SUBSTANCE / JEHOVAH JIREH plinth on the right in white. The two-storey building on the left was an extension that Rees Howells added and upstairs was used as staff rooms. Downstairs was a small meeting hall with a piano and a pulpit and could accommodate around eighty people, more if they sat on the stairs.

Chapter IX

MONEY LIKE MANNA

The title of this chapter was a sub-title to an article published by the "Evening Post" and the "Western Mail" to describe the buying of Derwen Fawr by faith. The article ran:

FAITH WORKS WONDERS FOR
SWANSEA BIBLE COLLEGE
MONEY LIKE MANNA

Blackpill Bible College[1] continues to present a spectacle of money pouring into a religious institution like manna from Heaven. Money coming in to the extent of thousands of pounds in spite of bad times. The College is one of the strongest and most impressive examples of faith manifested by works in modern religious history.

The supreme aim of the College was the glory of God. One step taken in faith and prayer always prepared for another; and each new experience of trusting God emboldened us to step out on a larger venture, proving that there was no risk in confidently leaning on the Word and faithfulness of God. So long as we were single-eyed to the glory of God, and the extension of His Kingdom, we could claim the promise: "All these things shall be added unto you" (Matthew 6:33), because "Your Father knoweth that ye have need of these things" (Matthew 6:32).

In leaning upon the living God for some years to supply every need, we proved that prevailing prayer was largely conditioned by constant obedience; so every new step had to be promptly taken in faith as soon as fresh leading was given. The largest amounts of money that God would have to provide, would still further prove to the watching world the power of prayer offered in faith.

When God commanded Moses to build the Tabernacle in the Wilderness, He also stirred the hearts of the people to bring in "free offerings every morning," so much so that the people had to be "restrained from bringing, for the stuff they had was sufficient...and too much" (Exodus 36:3-6).

Again, later, when David desired to build a House for the Lord, the people were so stirred that they brought in *princely* gifts until silver in Jerusalem became like stones for abundance. So, likewise, for years God had stirred the hearts of His stewards to give large gifts to the College. But from that time on we looked to Him to send *princely* gifts.

Advance steps in the Bible College were often taken when there was a lack rather than an abundance of money. At times, when needs were most pressing, God would suddenly call us to launch out on an undertaking that would involve thousands of pounds of additional expenditure; as in the buying of Derwen Fawr.

LARGE GIFTS – ON THE NAIL

As by faith we took the challenge to buy Derwen Fawr when we were without a penny, and the deposit had to be paid next day, our prayers were consequently much increased and our faith did not fail under the test; rather was it strengthened. And so, in three days we received five gifts: £250 [£15,900 in 2020], £300 [£19,080 in 2020], £50 [£3,180 in 2020], £25 [£1,590 in 2020] and £50. This abundantly enabled us to pay the sum required for the deposit, and so to secure legally the property for the Lord.

During the following month, among other gifts, there came in one of £400 [£25,460 in 2020] and another of £1,000 [£63,650 in 2020]; and each of these arrived on the very day the money was called for. When God is the deliverer, He frequently plans the supplies to arrive on the nail, the very day when they are needed.

What a shout of victory there was in the College when, after four days of waiting upon God in believing prayer the first gift of £1,000 came in! After that the College received no less than nine further gifts of £1,000 each; and though rejoicings followed the arrival of each £1,000 not one gave us the thrill of the first. We had imagined the joy of receiving the first thousand pounds, but imagination at best is as shadow to substance, in comparison with the real joy of receiving the actual cheque with the certain knowledge that it had come direct from our Heavenly Father.

The joy of such a large deliverance, meeting an urgent and essential need, must be experienced before it can be appreciated. In reading the Song of Moses, one can readily understand the feelings of the Patriarch, for it was the outcome of his own personal joy for the deliverance of his oppressed people from Egypt, and his exploit of faith in opening the Red Sea, and rolling it back upon the discomfited Egyptians.

Those who have not experienced great deliverances of faith, cannot know the joy of them, or how blessedly near they bring one to God; especially large deliverances such as gifts of £1,000 and £10,000. Receiving such bounty direct from the hand of our Heavenly Father, in the very nick of time, brings back the Word of the Master: "If ye then, being evil, know how to give good gifts unto your children, how much more...your Heavenly Father" (Matthew 7:11).

Think that while He meets the needs of millions who appeal to Him in their distress, He can also give, just to one of His children, who is extending His Kingdom, a *princely* gift of £10,000. Suppose His children all had faith, how rich God would have to be even to give £1,000 to each of them! But the Prophet said: "The silver is Mine and the gold is Mine, saith the Lord of Hosts" (Haggai 2:8), and while He is the Owner, our source of supply will never be exhausted. Such large gifts impress us with the Majesty of God. The sensation they give is like that experienced on visiting the Niagara Falls[2] for the first time; an overwhelming feeling of awe and reverence, for one is conscious of standing in the presence of the Great Father – Creator Himself.

FAITH WIELDS A TROWEL

While we were praying for the Derwen Fawr Estate, and still looking constantly to the Lord for the daily needs of the College, the fresh command came from God to: "Go forward and erect new buildings." The first two to be built were a College Chapel to seat two hundred [opened in January 1931], and a Conference Hall [completed in April 1931] to hold five hundred. Then came two men's hostels and afterwards a women's hostel to house over one hundred students in residence.

At the time when the workmen were engaged to start their labours, again there was not a penny in hand; but, although they were regularly employed for over eighteen months, entailing a weekly wage of between £30 [£1,910 in 2020] and £40 [£2,546 in 2020], not once did they go away without receiving their full pay. Even so, on Friday, it was a rare thing to have any money in hand for the Saturday's wages; and very often the Lord would allow the first post on a Saturday morning to go without the deliverances, so that we should have a time of prevailing prayer before the second post. Yet our loving Heavenly Father never once failed us, and every Saturday we were able to pay our workmen and to raise our Ebenezer, and gratefully proclaim: "Hitherto hath the Lord helped us" (1 Samuel 7:12).

"CHRISTIAN" SCEPTICS

Buildings worth thousands of pounds were erected on the new estate, proving daily that he who leans upon the living God alone, is beyond disappointment, for "No good thing will He withhold from them that walk uprightly" (Psalm 84:11). But even with such a monument of faith and these wonderful visible proofs, blind unbelief and jealousy even in ordinary Christians is sure to err; it will always attribute God's workings, however wonderful, to some natural means of influence; and, instead of giving the glory to God, will persist in explaining away the miracles of prayer and grace. In the sight of God it is surely almost blasphemy to attribute His work to some natural means, instead of rejoicing and praising God that the Holy Ghost has come again to do the "greater works" (John 14:12). Did they not say to the blind man: "Give God the praise: we know that this Man (the Lord) is a sinner" (John 9:24).

FAITH THROUGH DISCIPLINE

When Derwen Fawr Estate had been added to Glyn Derwen, and the College enlarged and re-opened [in 1930] on the two estates, there were over one hundred and thirty students in residence, but it was just as easy for God to carry the double burden, as it had been for Him to shoulder a single one. All that He asked of us was implicit faith in Him, then nothing would be impossible. As faith was constantly exercised it grew stronger still, so that it now became as easy to ask God for a thousand pounds, as it had been to ask for a hundred pounds ten years before.

Faith once strengthened through discipline, can never be made to doubt, however great the delays and testings.

The Word of God says that the trial of your faith is "much more precious than of gold that perisheth" (1 Peter 1:7). "Count it all joy when ye fall into divers testings...that ye may be perfect and entire, wanting nothing" (James 1:2-4).

The Saviour said: "Have faith in God. For...what things soever ye desire, when ye pray, believe that ye receive them, and ye shall have them" (Mark 11:22, 24). This has been the experience of the Bible College of Wales from its foundation, "and the half has never been told" (1 Kings 10:7).

- 127 -

Derwen Fawr Mansion c.1932. Behind this Mansion was Derwen Fawr
Road and the Sketty Isaf Estate

Chapter X

PREDICTION OF A THIRD ESTATE

SCHOOL FOR MISSIONARY CHILDREN

The time soon came for yet another advance by faith. This new "push" would mean an outlay of some further thousands of pounds to buy a third estate, and to erect on it the requisite new buildings; also thousands of pounds more each year for upkeep. A large staff of "degree" men and women would be needed before the school could be recognised by the Board of Education. Without money or an influential supporting committee, no sane man would have undertaken such a gigantic scheme as buying an estate and erecting thereon buildings worth thousands of pounds to establish Preparatory and Secondary Schools, much less have undertaken to work the scheme out, unless his faith was unshakably fixed on an Almighty God, whose financial resources were unlimited. *Furthermore, no man could ever have been driven by such a self-seeking purpose to venture on such an impossible scheme.*

Only a conviction that he was doing the will of God could have prompted such an extraordinary action. So that, in the greatest test and the darkest hour, the Founder was always able to say: "I am following One who is leading me."

Again let us stress that the human impossibility of such an undertaking only served to reveal more clearly the wonderful hand of our Guide. A man, without money, in sole dependence upon God, able to add thousands of pounds a year to his, present great liabilities, was an unusual figure. He was bound to convince many ordinary men, as well as some eminent business men and financiers, that it is surely not a vain thing to trust in the living God; and these have not been backward in saying so.

And still, through the College and its branches, the Holy Ghost again says, as the Master once said: "I have greater witness than that of man, for the works which the Father hath done, the same works bear witness of Me" (John 5:36).

Verily God at work in Swansea for all to see!

GOD'S OVERFLOWING TREASURY

By now, through the witness of the daily Press, the attention of millions of people has been drawn to this Faith Monument, which is drawing thousands of pounds each year from God's Treasury. This last year (1939) gifts totalling nearly £20,000 [£1,348,000 in 2020] came in, proving once again without a doubt, that there is a living God in Heaven that rules in the affairs of men, who can easily move donors to send gifts both small and great.

Very often God moves the most unlikely people, just as He moved Cyrus, a heathen king, to provide means for the rebuilding of His temple. We are assured that this same God will yet provide millions of pounds for the College Vision, and so extend the offer of the Gospel to Every Creature.

At the time when God revealed His will to provide both Home and Education for the Missionaries' Children, the College began to negotiate with the Swansea Corporation for Sketty Park, but at the last moment the Corporation decided not to sell. However, just at that time the Dowager Lady Swansea died, and Sketty Hall became vacant. As Sketty Hall is a part of Singleton Park, and is so near the Swansea University, it would be a most convenient estate on which to build a large Secondary School; for after matriculating, the missionaries' children could go on to the University to study for their degrees, using Sketty Hall as their home, and so finishing their education under our care.

So the late Sir Percy Molyneux, who had often befriended us, appealed to his friend, Lord Swansea, to sell Sketty Hall to the Bible College of Wales, but the reply was that Sketty Hall was not in the market just then. Yet what a challenge of faith to bid for another estate worth thousands of pounds. Again, with an empty bank!

THE COST OF PROPHECY

Those who have never been called to believe and to prove God in the seemingly impossible, have no idea what the prophets of old went through, or what it cost a man like Moses, who had to look to God alone to provide for over two-and-a-half-millions of ungrateful people (the population of Wales) in a sun-baked wilderness. The man in the street, like certain scholars, does not believe in miracles; for no one in the present generation has been able to repeat them, or give any visible proof that God can do them today. Common-sense and reason say that if God is the same today as yesterday, then why does He not repeat Himself as the Great Miracle Worker?

The correspondence between Sir Percy Molyneux and Lord Swansea made it plain that Sketty Hall could not then be sold. But later, when the Swansea Corporation made an appeal for Sketty Hall, Lord Swansea wrote to Sir Percy saying that, as he felt indebted to the Town, and had been a member of its Council, the Swansea Corporation had the first claim on it; and so the Council are building a large Secondary School on the estate today.

Although unforeseen obstacles prevented the College from becoming the owners of Sketty Park or Sketty Hall, yet we always knew that all hindrances were under God's control; and that if He did not give this estate for the missionaries' children, it was because He was about to give a better or a more convenient one. Truly "He gives the very best to those who leave the choice to Him." At this time of launching out, another estate, Sketty Isaf, came onto the market. This was an estate of seventeen acres of freehold land adjoining the Bible College at Derwen Fawr, and the owners were willing to sell the house standing on it, with five acres only, and give the option of purchase on the other twelve acres at a later date. So the College bought Sketty Isaf with the five acres, and have since bought the other twelve, and also a still further seven acres of adjoining freehold land.

Since then the College has acquired Penllergaer, the 270 acre estate of the late Sir John Llewelyn. The details of the purchase are given in another chapter.

So instead of Sketty Park and Sketty Hall the Lord has given us Sketty Isaf and Penllergaer. When the prediction of *great extensions* was fulfilled by these important purchases there was again great joy in that College – the Bible College of Wales.

TENSION

The reader, even if he is not a business man, may realise what tension there is when negotiating for properties worth thousands of pounds. Imagine then the increased tension when habitually negotiating without money. Frequently it was touch and go for months. At any time we might be tempted to abandon an inspired vision of the future, because of the lack of so many thousands of pounds in the bank. Although God has said that He is the Owner of "the silver and the gold" (Haggai 2:8), and "the cattle on a thousand hills" (Psalm 50:10), and "all the fowls of the air are His," (Psalm 50:11), yet everyone knows that the money God needs may be invested in other things.

Often it takes time for His stewards to change their stocks and shares into hard cash, for few people have sums like £1,000 or £10,000 lying loose at their bank. That is why the College has always had to pray beforehand for the very sum that the donor will have to give. (Prayer went up daily for months for the gift of £10,000). The Lord has to move the donor first, and then the donor has to release his stocks and shares, or some other property. So there are many processes going on in the spiritual realm before Faith becomes Substance, and the prayer-warrior obtains visible evidence that his prayer is answered. Yet faith is still "the substance of things hoped for, the evidence of things not seen" (Hebrews 11:1). We know for God has proved it so.

LAWS OF GOD'S SUPPLY

Like everything else the life of faith has to be learned. It took George Müller nearly twelve years of living daily from hand to mouth before he learned it. Conditions had to be fulfilled; laws that neither the natural man nor the average intellectual man knows anything about, had to be inflexibly obeyed. It takes many years before a man can become as confident in a life of faith, as an ordinary business man is confident when he has a large surplus in the bank. To those who have never entered this School of Faith, the thought of trusting God and not a bank balance for money is indeed frightening. But as time passes and God proves again and again that He never faileth, fear changes to calm reliance. The Waves and the Winds beat upon the Rock of Faith but the Rock stands firm, serenely confident. For is it not the Rock of Ages?[1]

After seventeen years of laying foundations, and learning more and deeper lessons daily in the School of Faith our confidence in God has become unshakeable. We have branched out, without one anxious thought. We have opened a new Bible College in Paris [bought in January 1939] and expect to open more in many other countries, including the Holy Land and India.[2]

In the next chapter will be shown how the money came to establish the Secondary School, and how we received a still greater blessing. For, in answer to believing prayer there came to us the consecrated staff to run it. True indeed was the prediction that God would meet our urgent need by sending us the assistance of the servants of His choice.

The Glynderwen Estate with Glynderwen House at centre back c.1935, with classrooms and accommodation buildings. The two buildings in the distance (top right) were not part of the Bible College of Wales.

Chapter XI

GOD'S HUNDREDFOLD

When God called Abraham to leave his country, his kindred, and his father's house, the Covenant He made was to bless him *and his seed:* and the Saviour gave the same promise to every missionary – "there is no man that hath left house…or father or mother, or wife *or children* for my sake and the Gospel's, but he shall receive a hundredfold, *now in this time*" (Mark 10:29-30). So if the missionary can leave his children because he believes that God will through him offer the Free Gift of Eternal Life to the heathen, surely he can believe that God will give the hundredfold more to his children, than to the children of the ordinary believer who has never left anything or anyone for the Gospel's sake.

When the Lord called the Founders to leave their only son, Samuel, who was not a year old, in order to become ambassadors of the Cross in Africa, they did as Hannah of old did with her Samuel – "lent him to the Lord as long as he liveth" (1 Samuel 1:28). So God became responsible to provide him a home, education and everything he needed;[1] and as the old coloured man in America said: "When God does a thing, He does it handsome." God gave their son the very best home, and provided for his schooling, and for three years in Oxford, where he graduated; he is today on the College staff, and is Deputy Director. The ordinary believer can never provide for his child as God can, and few of them have been able to send their sons to Oxford or Cambridge, as many missionaries have done, because it is God who provides the hundredfold.

God commanded the Founders to make a Home and Secondary School for Missionaries' children, as He commanded the widow woman of Sarepta / Zarephath to feed Elijah (1 Kings 17:9 and Luke 4:26). She only provided the first meal, for that was all she had: it was God that caused the barrel of meal and the cruse of oil not to fail until the rain came. The God who commanded to build the Schools was the One who gave the money for erecting new buildings and to maintain the staff. All the new buildings of the College have been built by direct labour, because God only provided by the day and by the week. So God had to give the plans to us in detail, as He did to Moses for the erection of the Tabernacle and to David for the building of the

- 134 -

Temple; and He also had to provide men like Bezaleel and Aholiab, "skilled in all manner of workmanship" (Exodus 31:2-6 and Exodus 35:30-35). In this way, new buildings worth over £30,000 [£2,022,000 in 2020] have been erected on the four estates.

THE WAGES OF FAITH

It was decided to turn Glyn Derwen [later contracted to a single word Glynderwen], the first estate, into a Secondary School, and the day came when the Lord said: "Arise and build." As usual there was not a penny in hand when the builders arrived; God did not deliver the money for their first week's wages until the second post on Saturday, when a cheque for £20 [£1,400 in 2020] came. The following Saturday, He did not deliver by post, but sent a donor to the College with £25 [£1,750 in 2020]. In a similar way He provided each Saturday for the first month. Then, one day, when money was required to pay for materials, and there was not a penny in hand, a cheque for £350 [£24,500 in 2020] was received. Again, one Monday, a day when gifts are not really expected, the three posts brought in three anonymous gifts, £100, [£7,000 in 2020] £50 [£3,500 in 2020], and £10 [£700 in 2020], from different parts of the country.

What object lessons these were to over a hundred young missionary students! Along with studying Greek, Hebrew, Theology and Church History, they were able to take part in prayers for money and to see God answering them in a direct way; and they agree that "an ounce of experience is better than a ton of theory" [a phrase popular with Rees Howells.] In a College of Faith like this, where the needs have to be provided for by the day or by the week, the students, after completing their three years' course, are able to say with the Apostles of old: "That which we have heard, which we have seen with our eyes...and our hands have handled, of the Word of life...declare we unto you" (1 John 1:1, 3).

Because this is a work of faith, the Lord has not allowed us to be slack in coming up to the requirements of the Educational Boards. Two residential buildings had to be erected for the staff and the missionaries' children; also nine class-rooms, a large gymnasium and the science laboratory. The work of building went on steadily for about two years, so that faith was kept in constant exercise to bring in the weekly wages, and provide thousands of pounds for materials. When the first £1,000

[£70,000 in 2020] came in towards the School, there was a great shout of victory, and another when the second £1,000 followed. God's hundredfold. Then, the beginning of August a third £1,000 was received, and before the end of the month still another £1,000 came in. August is usually regarded as a lean month, because many of those who have means are on their holidays, but – God never goes on holiday: "He that keepeth Israel shall neither slumber nor sleep" (Psalm 121:4). Thus God sent four gifts of £1,000 during that summer. All we could say was: "Blessed are those who put their trust in the living God." So, in answer to believing prayer, the Lord sent in all the money required to provide the necessary buildings for the School to be *recognised by the Cambridge Board [*July 1937].

GOD SENDS THE STAFF

As God had promised the hundredfold to the missionaries' children even in their education, He had to provide the very best staff for the School, and give each one a personal call to the work. As of old His promise was: "There shall be with thee for all manner of workmanship every willing skilful man, for any manner of service" (1 Chronicles 28:21). The first one called to the School staff [Miss Doris M. Ruscoe] had been a Senior Mistress in Matlock Secondary School for nine years. She came on a visit to the College, and received the College blessing, which has enabled every member of the staff to forsake all and follow the Nazarene – to be a disciple not only in word but in deed. Then the Head Master, [Mr Kenneth McDouall] who is a Cambridge man, and the son of a Missionary, after receiving the blessing, had the call and forsook all to follow the Master.

The Head Mistress [Miss Elaine Bodley] of the Preparatory School is an Oxford graduate who had honours in Modern Languages. [She joined the staff of the Bible College of Wales in 1931 and transferred to the Preparatory School in September 1934]. Others followed, so that by today there are over twenty on the Educational staff of the schools – without counting the Home side, men and women with some of the best degrees in the country, who are out-and-out for God, and have dedicated themselves in a most practical way to be fathers and mothers to the missionaries' children.

The School and the tutors have made such a name in the district that over two hundred children from the best homes in Swansea are attending as day scholars; and a large number of them have been converted in the School. So the Lord is raising up a new generation as He did with the Israelites in the wilderness, where all those who were under twenty when they left Egypt were taught by Moses. They became those faithful followers of Joshua, who walked like one man into the Jordan, and never flinched at the walls of Jericho. So the children who have been brought up in our Schools will be among the ten thousand picked men and women whom God will use to take the Gospel to Every Creature. God's ways are "past finding out" (Job 9:10 and Romans 11:33).

Sketty Isaf Mansion c.1932. The Bible College School began in this building with eleven children and two full-time teachers and one part-time teacher in September 1933. In 1935, the School had outgrown Sketty and moved to Glynderwen, less than five minute walk down the road towards Blackpill. The School was later renamed Emmanuel School, then Emmanuel Grammar School and included a Preparatory School which worked out of Sketty Isaf and Derwen Fawr.

The Schools belong to the Lord, and although they were recognised by the Cambridge Examinations Board a couple of years ago, we have not applied for any grant. This is open for us, as for the Catholic Schools, but we want the Lord to have the honour and glory of providing for His own School. Not only in the last Cambridge School Certificate Examination did the Bible College School have the average passes of the country, seventy percent, but also in the three exams, in the past two years.

No child whose parents have left their country for the Mission Field is to be refused admission; and the parents are only required to find half the actual cost of maintaining each child £30 [£2,100 in 2020] per annum for education, board and residence, holidays included.

Last year the College only received through fees from all sources (College, Schools, Conferences, etc.) a little over £5,000 [£337,200 in 2020], but the gifts from God were almost four times as much as that, nearly £20,000 [£1,348,800 in 2020].

Sketty Isaf Mansion 2011. The three-storey extension is on the left plus a *garage underneath (*out of view) and was built under Rees Howells. Sketty Isaf Mansion and out-buildings were demolished in 2015 and the Sketty Isaf Estate is now known as Howells Reach with fourteen houses with an average value of around £550,000 each.

BABIES' HOME

As God has promised to be a "Father to the fatherless" (Psalm 68:5), and especially to those whose parents have died in His service on the Mission Field, their children are to have a home and education in the College, and God, in answer to prayer, will provide the means of sustaining them. That is why the College has also established a "Babies' Home." The first orphans received were two little girls [Joan and Christina Partridge] whose parents had died in Central Africa, [Belgian Congo] and – whose last wish was that their children should have a home in the College. They came a few years ago [in 1936], when the younger one was under twelve months old; both are in the School today, having a home and all their needs provided for by their Heavenly Father.

Because Dr. Barnardo put out that notice "No destitute child to be refused," God, through the Barnardo Homes, is providing today for a family of over eight thousand. So the Lord, through the College, is ready to provide a home and education for all those children whose parents have died on the Mission Field. The Lord has also purposed to build a Normal Training College, and a large Hospital on the new estate of Penllergaer; so that, after taking the Matriculation and School Higher, the missionaries' children will be able to complete their training, and qualify as teachers or nurses, and then go straight to the Mission Field.

The Schools, therefore, are great monuments of faith, and have already been a blessing to hundreds of homes including those of many of the day scholars. By the completion of the Schools we saw the fulfilment of another great prediction. And again we raised our Ebenezer, and sang another song, like the Song of Moses – a Song of Victory, for Him who commanded His thoughtless disciples to let the little ones come unto Him.[2]

Chapter XII

PREDICTION OF HOME AND HOSPITAL
FOR MISSIONARIES

As we have emphasised already the promise that they will receive a hundredfold more in this present time applies to all missionaries who have left their homes for the Saviour's sake, and have taken the Gospel to foreign lands. Abraham, by stepping out in obedience to God, had thereby a claim on God to give him "the land of Canaan," and to make his seed as innumerable as "the stars of the heavens" (Genesis 22:17); for this was God's promise, and when Abraham believed it, "it was counted unto him for righteousness" (Romans 4:3).

Similarly, the missionary, *called* and *sent forth by God,* who has "forsaken all" (Luke 14:33) to answer the call; when he comes back to this country, has a claim on God to provide a home for him, for the Master promised him "the hundredfold" (Matthew 19:29). Because God promised Eternal Life as a gift to anyone who believes in His Son, the worst sinners, like the thief on the Cross or Jerry McAuley, who becameth a Spirit-filled evangelist, can receive it.[1]

The moment they believe, God is honour bound to give them the gift of Eternal Life, and that only because He promised it. By merely believing God, millions have received this gift, and they:

"Shall never perish" (John 10:28).

"This is the record that God hath given to us eternal life, and this life is in His Son" (1 John 5:11).

"He that believeth on the Son *hath* everlasting life" (John 3:36).

Why is it that the same missionaries who have forsaken all to go out and offer that gift to the heathen, have often failed to believe the promise the Saviour gave to them, that of the hundredfold now in this life for everything they gave up?

The man who has believed and claimed it, enjoys the benefit of it *now,* just as the sinner who has claimed the gift of Eternal Life, reaps the benefit, and has the joy of it, from the moment he receives it.

FAITH AMONG LIONS

The Founders of the College forsook all to become missionaries in Africa. They broke up their home, left their only son, and their country and went to live among the heathen. For one period of eighteen months they never saw a white man; and during that time they lived in a two-roomed house of unburnt brick, with a mud floor. At another time, they were without a home for nearly two years, while they covered eleven thousand miles, travelling from one mission station to another. For about two months of every winter, they lived in a tent, travelling through the wilds of Portuguese East Africa, where they could not even take their dog, because of the tsetse-fly, which gives the sleeping sickness. They would travel about six hundred miles on foot, sleeping by night in the same forest as the lions, and other wild beasts. The only sound to break the silence of the night was the roar of a wild beast; and very often, when awakened by the king of the forest [the lions], they used to repeat to one another heartening verses from that wonderful ninety-first Psalm: "Thou shalt not be afraid of the terror by night.... There shall no evil befall thee...for He shall give His angels charge over thee.... Thou shalt tread upon the lion and the adder because he hath set his love upon me, therefore will I deliver him" (Psalm 91:5-14).

The joy of believing and proving these promises often made them break forth into singing; as Paul and Silas did in the prison at Philippi, when the angels came down to join them, and shook the prison and burst the doors open. (Was it to make room for so many celestial visitors?)

Many a time they sang:

In God I have found a retreat
Where I can securely abide;
No refuge nor rest so complete,
And here I intend to reside.

The pestilence walking about
When darkness has settled abroad,
Can never compel me to doubt
The presence and power of God.[2]

In the greatest danger, they never once doubted His Word or His Promise, but were always able to say: "Where He leads me I will follow."[3]

ONE LARGE FAMILY

Called back from Africa to found a new work in this country, can they not now say that God has given them, too, "the hundredfold?" The recent National Registration affords striking answer. To go out to the Mission Field, the Founders had left their one and only son behind.[4] But when recently the College family was registered the number then in residence was two hundred and fifteen; and there were other students who had not returned from their holidays. What an increase – from one absent child to a family circle which may soon be one thousand!

The youngest child on the register, Baby Herbert, only fifteen months old, had come from Vienna in his little basket about two months before.[5] He is only one of the hundreds of thousands of the Seed of Abraham who have had to flee from Hitler and Germany. From his birth he had to be fed from a soup kitchen, his father having been thrust into one of those concentration camps, ill-famed for so many abominable excesses, his only crime being that he was of Abraham's seed. But the promise still holds: "I will curse him that curseth thee" (Genesis 12:3). So Hitler and his Nazi régime cannot escape this time, for God has predicted their downfall. Surely for them it will be better that they had never been born.

To the missionaries who founded the College God has added "the hundredfold" in property as well as in children. He has given three estates, with mansions, other large buildings and nearly fifty acres of freehold land, to provide a home for their large mixed family. And this does not include the estate of the late Sir John Llewelyn, which the College has recently *bought, and which is nearly eight times as large as the other three estates put together. [*Penllergaer Estate].

Evidently God means that our family is soon to increase to eight times its present size! Already we have in residence a huge staff of ninety-five, which includes over twenty "degree" people on the educational side, and five qualified doctors. Among the sixty children already in residence are many Jewish refugees and children of missionaries.

The money spent last year on our family was £24,101 13s. 4d. [£1,625,400 in 2020] as shown in the Cash Statement; and this family, although so large, has only one Father, their Heavenly Father, to provide and care for them. And yet they have neither fear nor trepidation for the future. What a laughable thing it would be, if every family – following the lead of modern organisations – had to get a committee or a council, to handle their affairs, and then appeal to the outside world for money to provide food for them! Such a family would resemble Russia or Germany, where every bleak and half-starved home is organised by the State. But the Bible College community is like the large families of old Puritan England, where all looked to their father to provide for their daily needs, and their father looked direct to God. And God then, as now, "never faileth" (1 Kings 17:13-16).

THE CRUSE THAT NEVER FAILS

Although there was already a large family in the College to provide for, God revealed that we would not be any poorer, if we added a Home of Rest for Missionaries and also a Hospital in which to nurse them. At Sketty Isaf, God has already provided the Home of Rest, and missionaries staying there are only expected to contribute half the actual cost of their maintenance – *one guinea weekly [*£1 1s or £78 in 2020]. A few thousands of pounds have been spent already for the addition of ten bedrooms, a dining-room, a kitchen and a large garage. [This was an extension on Sketty Isaf House]. Here again the Lord has provided an excellent staff. The matron, [Miss Gwen Roderick] who is a trained nurse, joined the College years ago to use her skill for this purpose; and the other members of the staff, who have received the College blessing, have also dedicated their lives to minister to the missionaries.[6]

Here then, there are no quarrels; only loving service. Here we know in practice the wisdom of the exhortation to esteem others better than ourselves, and that it is indeed a privilege to serve those who have spent their lives in serving the Lord. The Master said: "Whosoever will be great among you, let him be your minister; and whosoever will be chief among you, let him be your servant" (Matthew 20:26-27).

When the prediction of a Home of Rest for Missionaries at Sketty Isaf was fulfilled, we were again able to raise our Ebenezer and say once more that "Hitherto hath the Lord helped us" (1 Samuel 7:12). May He help us to continue to be worthy ministers to those who minister Salvation.

HOSPITAL FOR MISSIONARIES

On the same principle, and because of His promise of the "Hundredfold," God had also to provide for those who had lost their health by working in unhealthy districts in tropical countries. Missionaries often need medical attention and careful nursing for months, after returning to the homeland; but many of them have no home of rest, nor the means to pay for proper medical treatment. This Hospital is for them, and for expectant mothers who, instead of going to maternity Hospitals, and paying about four guineas a week [£4 4s or £312 in 2020] for some weeks, can have free medical attention in God's Hospital, by only paying a guinea a week [£1 1s or £78 in 2020] for their board.[7]

To staff the Hospital God has had to call out the best doctors and nurses. The senior resident doctor gained honours in his final M.B. (Lond.), and he had held several hospital appointments before he was called to the College. But, realising the needs of those missionaries who were coming back from the Foreign Field, he went up to London for a further six months course in Tropical Medicine, and gained a diploma in that subject.

A young surgeon who was on the staff of the Cardiff Royal Infirmary, when called to the College, decided to take his F.R.C.S. so as to be better qualified for surgical practice in the College Hospital. Two other young doctors – a man and his wife – who had been practising for some time, were about to take up a large and lucrative practice in an industrial district. While on a visit to the College, they received the College blessing of forsaking all to follow the Lord Jesus, and were called to the staff of the Hospital. They broke up their lovely home, to become medical servants to the missionaries.[8]

One other, our first lady doctor, who came; five years ago, is Medical Officer for the women students. The present Hospital was intended to accommodate thirty-five patients, but owing to lack of room in the College and School, part of it has been used for class-rooms and sleeping accommodation.

The large Hospital, for two hundred patients, is to be built on the new estate, Penllergaer. There, the doctors, who are already lecturing in elementary medicine and surgery to the missionary students, will train the nurses for the State examinations, and the present nursing staff will also move to the new Hospital.[9]

Already we see the signs of greater days and greater service and greater blessings to come. But as yet we are only in the Preface of our Book of Faith and Service. The Book itself is yet to come. What a marvellous Book that Book of God's Full Dealings

with the Bible College, is destined to be. Surely it will be the Book
of the Future!

The Hospital built on the Derwen Fawr Estate 1939. The bungalow on
the left was originally used as the Kindergarten (a pre-school)

Chapter XIII

THE SUM OF IT ALL

The Founders of the Bible College dedicated their lives to be an object lesson to all, of what may be accomplished by prayer and faith alone; their aim was to teach men and women that it is safe to trust God's Word and His promises. When the Lord called the Twelve and the Seventy, and sent them out in a small country like Israel, He charged them, saying: "Carry neither purse, nor scrip [knapsack]...for the labourer is worthy of his hire" (Luke 10:1-7), and on their return He asked: "When I sent you without purse, and scrip...lacked ye anything?" and they said: "Nothing" (Luke 22:35).

This ideal of faith and complete trust in the living God, has not been generally followed since the days of the Early Church, though in every generation a few outstanding men, like George Müller, have lived up to it. Thirty years ago, the Founders were called to "forsake all" (Luke 14:33), "to sell all that ye have" (Luke 18:22), and to trust God for temporal as well as for spiritual needs. So, after proving God day by day for the first few years of their married life [from December 1910 onwards], it became as easy to live upon God's Promises, as previously it was to live on a salary or on money in the bank.

Many a time the Founders had to walk to the Railway Station without money for their tickets, and once or twice they had to enter the queue at the booking-office, without money or tickets. Yet both were forthcoming before the train departed. Who can forget hearing the story of how the Director had to stand in the queue at the booking-office for tickets to London when he and his wife were on their way to Africa, and how he only received his fee [his deliverance] when he was next but one to the top of the queue, where he would ask for his tickets. With what a shout of victory he came away, saying: "The God of Moses who opened the Red Sea can never, never fail!"

Hundreds of similar instances could be related of how God has answered believing prayer; the very amount needed arriving at the right moment; so there was no loophole for the Devil to say that it came by chance. Now, after thirty years, we are as much at home in asking God for a thousand pounds, as in those days we were in asking Him to meet an essential need of ten pounds.

RECENT ANSWERS

Here are some instances of answers to prayer in the last two or three weeks, while these chapters were being written. For weeks past every Monday has been a Day of Prayer; and two weeks ago there was a need of £100 [£6,550 in 2020] on the Monday. That day a letter came from Chicago, [in America], with no name given, but enclosing a draft for £100 to be paid to us through the Westminster Bank. The next Day of Prayer came with a need of about £50 and that very day a cheque for £50 [£3,275 in 2020] was received, and last Saturday (November 8th, 1939) £1,000 came to hand! [£65,500 in 2020] And this week another £1,000 has been released for the new estate, Penllergaer.

WHY DON'T WE TRUST?

This life of trusting God for temporal needs has been lost in the Church. Christians pray daily: "Give us this day our daily bread" (Matthew 6:11), and yet are unable to trust God to give it day by day. If young people, who have been called to forsake all, and become the Lord's disciples, have a claim on Him to supply their daily needs, what sense is there in their throwing up their salary, and going round the country on deputation work for the sake of getting their need, or their Mission's needs, supplied? The Promise is: "Seek ye first the Kingdom of God; *and all these things shall be added unto you*" (Matthew 6:33).

The Lord built the Bible College of Wales, so that young men and women, who have had the "Call" to be ambassadors for Him in foreign lands, should look to Him alone to supply their personal needs. What a disgrace it would be if our Ambassador in Washington, going round America, should appeal to people to supply his needs, because he was not able to trust the King of England. How much more then should we trust the King of kings, who is the Owner of "the silver and the gold?" (Haggai 2:8).

Young men and women, who have had three years training in the College, have been able to trust God for their board and residence (which is given to them at less than half the actual cost), and then to trust Him still when they reach the land of their adoption. The Word of God says: "Be careful for nothing, but in everything by prayer and supplication, with thanksgiving, let your requests be made known unto God.... My God shall supply all your needs" (Philippians 4:6, 19).

FAITH COLLEGES EVERYWHERE

There are many who have been trained in the College – the School of Faith – working in nearly all foreign lands where there are Missions. There will be room on the new estate, Penllergaer, to train hundreds, who will, after training, go out, "taking nothing from the Gentiles" (3 John 1:7).

The Lord is going to prepare hundreds of young people, who, after spending three or four years in the Bible College of Wales, will go out and found Colleges in every country to reach Every Creature; men and women, who will not only be able to teach Greek, Hebrew, Church History, Nursing, etc., but teach the students to trust God to supply their personal needs. Then, instead of only a few missionaries and native workers, working on lonely stations, there will be thousands (including natives), trained in the Colleges, available for missionary work. These too, will by learning in the School of Faith, will find that living faith becomes substance. They will be like Pastor Hsi in China, who was able to trust God to supply his personal needs and to inspire many Christian Chinese to do the same, just as men like Müller, Chapman and others inspired their friends and followers.

The College has already bought a freehold property in Paris[1] where there is a large Mission Hall and room for students in residence. There we have opened a College, which is staffed by those who have spent three or four years in the Swansea College. We are convinced that the Holy Spirit will bring the College Vision (the Gospel to Every Creature) to fruition, God will train His own missionaries in the Colleges and will send them out by the hundreds. There will be no conflict with those Christians who are not able to live the full *life of faith,* and therefore have not seen the Vision as 'we have seen it.'

Our Secondary Schools, for all missionaries' children, will enable these little ones to join the College, and learn the life of faith and become teachers and nurses in the Colleges in foreign lands. And so follow worthily in the footsteps of their parents. Our Home of Rest for Missionaries; and the Hospital, will be enlarged as the years go on. No one will be asked to pay more than half the actual cost of maintenance (God supplying the other half through us by gifts which last year, were nearly four times as much as all the fees received put together).

Every summer there is held on the College estates, the "Every Creature" Conference, and scores of persons have been blessed in these Conferences and many thousands are destined to be blessed in future.

So then these predictions are an outcome of a walk with God for over thirty years, of treading a path of complete reliance on Him for temporal as well as spiritual needs, during which time: "We have lacked nothing" (Luke 22:35), having taken out of God's Treasury thousands and thousands of pounds in gifts without a single appeal to man. We can say: "We love our Master, and we will not go out free" (Exodus 21:5-6).

PEACE AT EVENTIDE[2]

One last word to everybody. Be of good cheer. After the prediction of God's settlement with Hitler and the Nazi régime is fulfilled, the countries for some years will not be troubled with further menaces, similar to that of Hitlerism. It will then be, as in King David's time, after God gave him peace on every hand, when he established the nation, and prepared to build a House for the Lord, and gathered for it over a thousand million pounds, when silver became in Jerusalem like stones.

The Lord has promised to "open His treasury to the College," and that they are to "lend to nations." And the first nation to receive is to be the Jews. He has promised to give to the College a gift of £100,000 to buy land and houses in the Holy Land[3] (see Jeremiah 32:43-44), and to send back the Jewish children after four years in our Secondary Schools, and three years in one of our Colleges. They will be among the host of evangelists, who will prepare the way for the return of the Lord. Who will be able to withstand their fervent presentation of the Good News of the God of their Fathers? Who will not wish to serve their new-found King, our Lord Jesus Christ? Their Saviour and ours.

The sands of time are sinking,
The dawn of Heaven breaks
The summer morn I've sighed for,
The fair sweet morn awakes:

Dark, dark hath been the midnight,
But dayspring is at hand,
And glory, glory dwelleth
In Immanuel's land.[4]

The Bible College of Wales

CASH STATEMENT for the year ended 31st March, 1939.

Dr.

Year to 31st March 1938 £	Receipts.	£	s	d
-	To Balance at Bank 1/4/38	2	3	4
5,435 435	" Receipts from College, Day School, Boarding School, Missionary Home, Hospital & Conference Fees	5,327	17	9
6,080	" Gifts received	18,771	12	3
£5,035		£5,330	1	1
600	" Capital receipts	-	-	-
£12,115		£24,101	13	4

Cr.

Year to 31st March 1938 £	Payments.	£	s	d
7,849	By Expenses in connection with the College, School, Missionary Home & Hospital, including Rates, Taxes, Fuel & Lighting, Repairs, Salaries & Wages, Provisions & Miscellaneous Expenses	12,270	13	0
3,831	" Purchase of land, New buildings, Additions & Equipment of a Capital nature, & Bank Balances	10,804	10	4
£11,680		£23,075	3	4
435	" Gifts to Missionaries & others	982	13	6
-	" Balance at Bank 31/3/39	43	16	6
£12,115		£24,101	13	4

I certify the above CASH STATEMENT to be in accordance with the books and vouchers of the Bible College and Missionary School.

H. S. W. Seward,
Chartered Accountant.

Derwen Fawr,
Swansea.
11th April 1939.

The Bible College of Wales Cash Statement for the year ended 31 March 1939. Notice the value of the Receipts and Payments were exactly the same income of £24,101 or approximately £1,625,400 in 2020! There was no surplus money held in the bank to draw from, but trust in God who said He would supply all your *need* (Philippians 4:19), not wants or desires. God pays His own invoices, what He has sanctioned. God's work, done God's way in His timing, will not lack His resources. God pays His own bills.

GOD
CHALLENGES
THE
DICTATORS

———

DOOM OF NAZIS PREDICTED

REES HOWELLS

An original hardback of *God Challenges the Dictators* which has been converted into greyscale. The original colour was red with black lettering and framing.

END OF BOOK – *God Challenges The Dictators*

Chapter 7

Hitler's New Year's Gift

'O God, how long will the adversary reproach? Will the enemy blaspheme Your name forever? Why do You withdraw Your hand, even Your right hand? Take it out of Your bosom and destroy them' (Psalm 74:10-11).

'The Lord shall go forth like a mighty man; He shall stir up His zeal like a man of war. He shall cry out, yes, shout aloud; He shall prevail against His enemies' (Isaiah 42:13).

God Challenges the Dictators was translated into a number of languages including French, Spanish and German. The foreign language titles below are from A4 sized typed manuscripts but whether there were any *official* publications like the English editions (in paperback and hardback formats) sanctioned by Rees Howells in foreign languages is unlikely, however copies or portion off were translated, printed and distributed around war-torn Europe.

Through contacts, portions of *Gott Gegen Die Diktatoren: Der Untergang der Nationalisozialisten Vorhergesagt* von Rees Howells (God Against the Dictators: The Fall of the National Socialists by Rees Howells) were sent to leading members of the Nazi party including Adolf Hitler, Joseph Goebbels, Hermann Göring, Joachim von Ribbentrop, Rudulf Hess and Heinrich Himmler! Parts of the book were read out over the Freedom Broadcasting Station – the secret radio which the Gestapo were trying to find!

It appears that it was not until 1st October 1944 that Rees Howells in the 9.30am meeting publicly spoke about foreign language translations and sanctioned them, "Get the book *God Challenges the Dictators* ready in French, German and Spanish."

There is also documentation relating to Portuguese and Italian translations, however at present I have been unable to find any evidence of these translations, partial or complete manuscripts such as the ones in French, Spanish and German languages, though they may have been lost to history.

French Title

Dieu Defie Les Dictateurs: Le Judgement des Nazis Prédit par Rees Howells.

The title translates as: God Defies Dictators: Judgment of the Nazis Predicts.

On the front cover was: (traduit de l'anglais) (tous droits reserves), which translates as: (Translated from English) (All rights reserved).

The translator is not stated however there were many fluent French speakers in the Bible School (later known as Emmanuel Grammar School) and at the Bible College. For many, French was a second language, or third if they spoke Welsh followed by English.

Spanish Title

Dios Reta A Los Dictadores: La Ruina Del Nazismo Predicha por Rees Howells. Translated by P Durnello or P Darnello (Signature is unclear).

The title translates as: God Challenges Dictators: The Ruin of Nazism Predicted.

It is possible that it was translated by Evangelist Parillo whose surname is also spelt Parrilla in the College meeting notes, depending on who typed them. He left Spain in March 1937 with his wife and four children during the Spanish Civil War (1936-1939) and was still at the College in July 1947, but preparing to return to Spain. General Franco did not want any Christian minister who left during the Civil War to return to Spain, so Evangelist Parillo's return with his family was delayed.

German Title

Gott Gegen Die Diktatoren: Der Untergang der Nationalisozialisten Vorhergesagt von Rees Howells. (Please note that "Nationalisozalisten" can now also be spelt using two words: Nationali Sozialisten. It is another term for the ideology and practices of the Nazi party).

The title translates as: God Against the Dictators: The Fall of the National Socialists Predicted by Rees Howells.

On the front cover was (Aus Dem Englischen Ubersetzt) (Alle Rechte Vorbehalton), which translates as: (Translated from English) (All rights reserved).

This was translated by Vrenni, a German and French speaking Swiss citizen who alongside another Swiss student, Paula, arrived at BCW in 1939. During the war they both had the opportunity to return to neutral Switzerland by plane but declined. They chose to stay with the BCW community in Swansea. Rees Howells commended them over several meetings from 28-29th July 1947, including at their Farewell Service. The Holy Spirit had instructed him to lay his hands on them both and Rees was able to declare: "I could see the anointing on these two."

Adolf Hitler's and Senior Nazis' Gift
A cutting from a newspaper, with handwritten blue ink seeping into the page: "The People" (a Sunday newspaper) with the date 7/1/40 (7th January 1940), had the most fascinating story which is typed in full. The type in bold font is how it was printed in the orginal newspaper article.

HITLER HEARS HIS FATE via "The People"

The People's revelations of a Welsh pastor's prophecy that Hitler and his advisers will either meet sudden death or else the fate they meted out to Pastor Niemöller, and hundreds of other German Christians have had amazing results. The story was told by a German-Swiss refugee who formerly held an important position in Germany and he immediately purchased the book "God Challenges the Dictators," written by Rev. Rees Howells, Director of the Bible College of Wales, Swansea.
So struck was he by the prophecy and the author's remarkable record for the accuracy of his predictions, that he translated much of it into German, sending copies to cousins in Lucerne.
Through underground channels they made sure that the copies reached Hitler, Goering, Goebbels, Ribbentrop, Hess, Himmler and Ley in the morning post of New Year's Day!
The refugee also contacted some of his friends connected with the Freedom Broadcasting Station – the secret radio which has been so keenly sought by the Gestapo – with the result that arrangements were made for the German people to be told the probable fate of their leaders.
End of Newspaper Article.

On Tuesday, 9th January 1940 a letter was sent from the Bible College of Wales to a family in London, SW4, England, who were involved in mission work in India. It was not written by Rees Howells but an unnamed senior member of staff.

Dear Mr and Mrs Thrower,
After you left I spoke to the Director [Rees Howells] about Olive's fees etc. and pointed out that your Mission [to the people of India] had hitherto been paying half expenses for her, but that it would be such a testimony for you to be able to tell them that the Director, a man of faith was going to pay all expenses for her. He agreed it would be, and said I was to tell you to do exactly as you wished in the matter.
Did you see or hear of the article in "The People" on Sunday last. I haven't a spare copy of it or I would send you the cutting. It is an amazing story of a German Jewish refugee sending for the book, "God Challenges the Dictators," and being struck with the many predictions that had come true, translated parts of it into German, and Hitler and all his men had a copy each on New Year's Day by the morning post! It was also broadcast by the Freedom Broadcast radio. Another victory for the Holy Ghost....

Frank's Amazing At Nuremberg

"WE TURNED FROM GOD AND WERE DOOMED"

HANS Frank, once the Nazi governor of Poland, asserted before the War Crimes Court at Nuremberg today: "It was not technical hitches and shortages alone which lost us the war, God above all pronounced judgment on Hitler and his system. Hitler's way was the denial of God and Christ. We turned from God and were doomed."

Newspaper Article, 31st August 1946. "God above all pronounced judgment on Hitler and his system. Hitler's way was the denial of God and Christ. We turned from God and were doomed" – Hans Frank, former Governor of Nazi-occupied Poland.

Chapter 8

Swansea During the War

'The Lord is their strength, and He is the saving refuge of His anointed. Save Your people, and bless Your inheritance; shepherd them also, and bear them up forever' (Psalm 28:8-9).

'He who dwells in the secret place of the Most High shall abide under the shadow of the Almighty. I will say of the Lord, "He is my refuge and my fortress; my God, in Him I will trust." Surely He shall deliver you from the snare of the fowler and from the perilous pestilence. He shall cover you with His feathers, and under His wings you shall take refuge; His truth shall be your shield and buckler' (Psalm 91:1-4).

Due to the threat of war with Germany which had been looming since 1936, gasmasks were produced in the millions, beginning in 1938. They were first issued in the summer of 1939 to school children before war was declared, and by September 1939, 38 million gasmasks had been issued to civilians across Britain.

As early as December 1938, trenches were being dug in Hyde Park, London, England, and bomb shelters were being built due to the fear of an inevitable war, which proved all too correct.

By 1939, nearly three quarters of British food came from abroad. During World War II many merchant ships full of cargo for Britain and its colonies were targeted by planes, u-boats / submarines and battleships along Britain's trade routes, even though they sailed in convoys with British battleships and destroyers to help protect them from the enemy. Dig for Victory became a famous poster and phrase, food had to be home-grown; Britain could not rely on imported foods because it was getting more difficult to protect trade routes and ships and their cargo often ended up at the bottom of the sea alongside casualties of war.

Green spaces such as some football and cricket pitches, meadows, and large grass verges, private and public lawns were ploughed or dug over and sown with seeds for growing vegetables and salads. Some public officials were employed to seek out green spaces and encouraged or commanded that food be grown instead of grass or flowerbeds.

War Notes Sermons Extracts by Rees Howells

On 31st August 1939, the evacuation of children in towns and cities at risk from Nazi bombardment began. Rees Howells said, "Outwardly this day, it was as black as midnight. Three million children were going to be evacuated and Germany was asking for more than before. We did not know what was going on in Berlin and had not heard anything officially for seven days."

The following day, 1st September 1939, "was the first night we had with the 'black-out,' " said Rees Howells in the evening meeting. "I brought forward men like Moses, Samuel, Jacob, Esther etc., people who had prevailed on God in a crisis. They did not let Him go until He answered them. We were prepared to go all night and the next day and night for three days if need be, but we meant to prevail.... We came back at 11:30pm that night with the determination to move God to work on our behalf of the Vision. It was the Vision we stood on." The Every Creature Vision.

On New Year's Day 1940, Rees Howells said, "I had been running in the 'Race' for the last thirty years. This was the darkest test in history. The Government called for another million soldiers, all those from the ages of 19-28 to be conscripted. Soon the total will be three million. I advised all for the next six months to live as martyrs, as the Lord had already given this position before there was a need for intercessors for the Kingdom, as this battle was the fiercest in history. If the Lord asked me what I would like as a New Year's gift. I'd like to say, 'Let the war come to an end this year.' As by faith I saw my *uncle walking so I wanted to see by faith this was finishing. I would like to tell God to reveal to me the end of the war and let me see it by faith."

*Uncle Dick was healed on 15th May 1910, having been unable to walk to chapel for 30 years, yet it was only three miles away. Four-and-a-half months earlier the Holy Spirit had unexpectedly spoken to Rees Howells stating that his uncle would be healed. Within fifteen minutes of Rees speaking to his uncle, the Lord revealed to Uncle Dick the precise day and time: 5am, Whit-Sun (Pentecost Sunday), and that he was to walk to chapel.

Beginning on 3rd January 1940, Rees Howells wrote:
I could not take prayers that morning because I was carried away in the spiritual realms reading my book! [*God Challenges the Dictators*]. I could not put it down until I finished it. I stressed on the importance [in the evening

meeting] of praying right prayers, *what* to pray and *when* to pray! I always prayed the right thing at the right time because the Holy Spirit prayed through me. I never once prayed my own prayers, but those He told me to pray and I found those were always answered.

The day the Holy Spirit prayed for the ministers in this country who have received the Specimen copies of the book [Specimen Chapter of *God Challenges the Dictators*], I knew it was *His prayer*. Undoubtedly He wanted to bless them, also the soldiers in our country. I was willing to publish a six penny edition of the book in order that the troops might get a chance of receiving the message. I was willing to be without profit on its sale as long as the men received the message that God had for this country. I prayed for the troops and wanted millions of copies to be sent to them if the Government would permit. "Do good, hoping for nothing in return" (Luke 6:35). I was fulfilling the Sermon on the Mount in a literal way.

When Lord [John] Gort, Commander in Chief [of the British Expeditionary Force in Western Europe in the months that led up to the evacuation at Dunkirk, France], said lately, "To the last man, the last shot, and a bit more," I knew that the "bit more" was the book, *God Challenges the Dictators: The Doom of the Nazis Predicted...*.

Today there is a million and a half troops already called up and another million ready to be called up. The Government was preparing for a war of at least ten years duration. Germany was threatening us with the greatest air-raids in history in the spring [of 1940]. Things were really black.

Rees Howells preached many sermons and gave words of encouragement and testimony before, during and after the war years, and many students and staff members made notes though the College was closed to full lectures until 1946.

The following is from two or more of Rees Howells' sermons, from an unpublished chapter *Fulfilment of the Doom of the Nazis: Scattering of the Dictators*, and relates to the end of December 1939. Rees Howells recalled: 'What perfect guidance He gave me concerning the book [*God Challenges the Dictators*]. I wired to make an appointment with the censor and how quickly it was all done! Then again the Lord worked to get the best publisher in London to take the book without it being reviewed! ...It was wonderful how the Spirit had got over so many difficulties concerning the book, and what seemed a big mistake turned out to be a big victory and blessing. I sent the first 32 pages in a cover as a Specimen copy of the book to the world. What an advertisement it would be! There was a real message in the book, and I thought one day, "Have I ever picked up a book so full of predictions as this one?"

'...The more I read the book the more wonderful it seemed...I used to read my book in the early hours of the morning and was really thrilled with it!'

'Not a single person knew what it cost me to send the new book out to the world. The burden during the last few weeks has been very heavy and I had only about three hours sleep every night.'

Air-Raids Over Swansea and Fear of Invasion

On the night of Sunday, 1st September 1940, at 8:50pm there was a severe air-aid over Swansea which lasted until 3:20am on Monday. The College meeting notes reveal that at the 9am meeting: 'Dr. Kingsley Priddy spoke, the night's air-raid which was really severe and the worst since the war began. Hundreds of bombs were dropped during the six-and-a-half hours they were over and a great deal of damage was done over town. How wonderfully the Lord protected us [the College family which includes the School] again and what peace and victory we found ourselves in. So we can only praise and thank Him for the grace He has given us to trust Him.'

The Western Mail & South Wales News recorded the above raid:

It is feared that in addition to widespread damage, a heavy death-toll was caused by indiscriminate bombing of a South Wales port [Swansea] by enemy raiders over a period of about six-and-a-half hours on Sunday night and Monday morning.

Waves of German aeroplanes carried out the most concentrated attack on a Welsh town since hostilities began. After setting of flares a number of high explosive, screeching and incendiary bombs were dropped, buildings being wrecked and many fires caused.

Anti-aircraft guns put up a heavy barrage and it is believed that one raider [aircraft] was brought down. Some of the main thoroughfares [a road or a path between two places] of the town presented scenes reminiscent of a battlefield as a result of the damage and fire and glass strewn over the roadway. Among the buildings hit were those of a railway company, and a school overlooking the town. A bomb also wrecked a garage near the central police-station; many of the windows were broken by the force of the concussion [a violent shockwave from an exploding bomb].

One of the biggest hotels in the area suffered from four direct hits, three being incendiary bombs and the others high explosives. The first two incendiary bombs were put out with stirrup pumps, but the third caused a fire at the rear of the premises. Another building that was hit was the parish church [St Mary's], the vestry of which was considerably damaged while a big crater was made among the gravestones. Industrial premises and offices were also affected.

It is impossible to give any indications of the likely number of casualties, as it is feared that some persons remain buried beneath houses which have collapsed. One fatal casualty was a police-constable who was only recently married. He was struck by a flying bomb splinter.

All the A.R.P. services [Air Raid Precautions: organisations that enforced the blackout, manned the air-raid sirens, directed people to shelters and reported bomb hits to direct aid] worked efficiently, and the fire brigade and its auxiliaries quickly got the fires in check. They were assisted by a number of other fire brigades. A thick layer of smoke drifted over the town in the morning. Telecommunications were affected by the bombardment as was the electric circuit in certain parts of the town.

A feature about the raids apart from the extensive damage done was the indiscriminate manner in which bombs of all kinds were dropped, far away from military objectives. In fact, it is understood that little damage of a military nature has been caused. It is calculated that 600 bombs were dropped and the fire brigade had to deal with some hundred fires, large and small. Many stories are told of the heroism of the A.R.P. workers, who are stated to have actually been bombed and machine-gunned whilst they were dealing with the havoc caused. It speaks well for efforts of the firemen that by the time most people were going to business in the morning all the outbreaks were under control.

Among the buildings struck by bombs were an institute and annexe to the local hospital used partly for offices and partly for domestic staff. This is further indication of the indiscriminate nature of the bombing attack, as both these places are a considerable distance from any military or industrial objectives. Fortunately there were no residents in the institute, which sustained a direct hit from a high explosive bomb and was badly damaged. A number of person employed there have, however, been rendered idle. Those in the hospital annexe were in shelters and they escaped injury when an incendiary bomb struck the building and set it on fire. Among those who assisted in fighting the flames were the matron and other members of the staff.

A number of stories are told of miraculous escapes. In one case five persons were sheltering under the stairs of a house which sustained a direct hit and they all got out uninjured. In another instance, however, a number of persons sheltering in a cellar were killed when the house above them collapsed.

Other relays of enemy aircraft on the night of Sunday, 1st September 1940 and into the early hours of Monday, subjected other coastal towns to bombardments for several hours. They were: 'Directed against the Bristol Channel and the South Wales area,' announced the Air Ministry and Ministry of Home Security. 'During last nights enemy activity over this country, although widespread was on a comparatively small scale.... And in a town [Swansea] in South Wales a number of fires were caused by high explosives and incendiary bombs and considerable damage was done to houses and business premises.'

A National Day of Prayer was set aside for 8th September 1940 and 'church bells of the South and South West Counties rang this morning in warning of an attempted invasion!' So recorded the College meeting notes.

19th February 1941: 'Three nights of air-raids over Swansea.... The least in the Kingdom of God was greater than John the Baptist. Every time there was a burden for the war, there was a need to get through for something else.'

Swansea Blitz and 44 Air-Raids
It was inevitable that Swansea would be bombed because it was a crucial industrial port and a centre for military-based industries, as the docks handled some tens of million of goods annually. In 1939, the German bombers were more than 500 miles away, but when France surrendered in June 1940; German planes were based less than 100 miles away and Swansea became an easier target.

B. Pugh, a teacher at Emmanuel Grammar School wrote *A Brief Account of the Swansea Blitz* for the school magazine, fifty years on from the Swansea Blitz of February 1941.

The first raid continued on 27th June 1940, a mere twelve days after the French surrender. The pattern of attacks on the town fall into three main phases: the early raids, the main onslaught and the final phases. From 27th June to 10th August there were 10 raids, mostly being classified as 'nuisance.' Lying on the coast, with hills behind Swansea was easy for bombers to find. 'Those who could, would travel to Gower to sleep either with friends or in their summer chalets. School lessons were reorganised and summer holidays were shortened to just two weeks to make up lost time!

By the New Year of 1941 the war had moved into a new phase. German hopes of an invasion had been dashed by the British victory in the Battle of Britain, and thousands of tons of food and war supplies were coming in from the USA and being offloaded at ports in the west of Britain like Swansea.

Forty Acres of Flattened Town

In the worst offensive in February 1941, the Nazi bombers dropped 1,273 high explosive bombs and 56,000 incendiary devices on the town. They missed the docks which were crucial to the war effort, but the town centre was flattened in their place. From 19th to 21st February, bombs fell for a total of thirteen hours and forty-eight minutes. Swansea suffered the most concentrated bombing of Britain in the war and the result was forty acres of flattened town. 7,000 people were made homeless, 857 properties were completely destroyed and 11,000 were damaged. 230 people lost their lives and 400 were injured.

B. Pugh wrote: 'It took over a week for all roads to be cleared and damaged buildings made safe or repaired. Snow had hindered the defenders whiles aiding the enemy by reflecting light from his parachute flares.'

Dylan Thomas and the Swansea Blitz

Swansea poet, Dylan Thomas immortalised his home town in his short stories and poems. After the heaviest bombing of the Swansea Blitz in February 1941, he walked through the flattened town centre with his friend Bert Trick and said, "Our Swansea has died. Our Swansea has died." It took Dylan Thomas six years before he could come to terms with and write down what he had seen. On 28th June 1947, in his broadcast *Return Journey*, Dylan replaced statistics with his meticulous research naming the shops and people who once inhabited the ruins.[1]

The old town centre known by Rees Howells and his contemporaries was gone forever and it was a miracle that the Bible College of Wales remained untouched with its 50 acres of property at Sketty, Swansea over three estates, and its 270 acres of property at Penllergaer, Swansea. Penllergaer as the crow flies is just 7 km north and 5 km west of Swansea Docks, whilst the Bible College of Wales at Sketty was much closer at just 5 km west and less than 1 km south of Swansea Docks! During the air-raids, boarders from the Bible College School, later known as Emmanuel Grammar School, could see the Docks being bombed from the top floor of the El Shaddai building on the Glynderwen Estate. The building was two floors high but had accommodation in the loft / roof area with skylights.

One of the elderly intercessors who lived through the war under Rees Howells and spent more than sixty years at the Bible College of Wales, remembered that one bomb fell on a property *next door* to the Bible College!

B. Pugh in relation to the Swansea Blitz of February 1941 wrote:

In those three nights the town was subjected to bombardment that destroyed virtually all of the old town centre and did great damage to suburban areas as well. During this time hundreds of people walked out to Gower each night, some to sleep in the open if they could find no shelter. Gas, water and electricity services were cut off and with so many shops destroyed; emergency feeding centres were set up. Hundreds of people had to be accommodated in rest centres until they could be found new homes in other areas. Many fires burned right through the day and helped locate Swansea for the bombers on the next night....

After such a severe pounding the enemy must have thought that Swansea was knocked out, for raids resumed the 'nuisance' pattern. Twelve more raids killing seven people followed until June 1941 when Germany attacked Russia and most of the bombers in France were sent there. The final phase of the raids now commenced with virtually no enemy activity during 1942, but the 16th February 1943 saw a vicious fifty minute raid which started at 10pm and

- 163 -

killed thirty-four people. However, many bombs fell on previously bombed ruins and were thus 'wasted.' That was the last raid of the war but the anti-aircraft guns of which there were several hundred by now, including a battery of rocket projectors on the Ashleigh Road golf course [in front of Derwen Fawr House and to the right when looking towards the sea], were in action many times against over-flying planes. The last 'all-clear' sounded in Swansea on 14th May 1944, and the war ended a year later. The centre was rebuilt in the late 1950s, but many people still feel that those three night in 1941 robbed us all of something than can never be replaced.

Raid facts and figures: killed 387. Injured 851. Premises destroyed 802. Premises damaged 27,450. Number of raids 44. Total time town under attack 1,537 hours.[2]

The number of bombs or incendiary devices that fell on the Bible College of Wales' property 0. The Lord protected them as He had promised!

Rees Howells Promoting his Book 1945

Rees Howells never disavowed his book *God Challenges the Dictators*, quite the opposite. At the 7pm meeting on 8th February 1945, Rees Howells said, "I had never had anything to do with war, and here He [Holy Spirit] told me to put this in print [holding up a copy of *God Challenges the Dictators*] and send it out. And if I had only said what I put on the cover of the book *[God Challenges the Dictators: Doom of Nazis Predicted]* it would be enough. Well the dictators have been scattered, they nearly conquered the world. The Lord allowed them to do it, and still He continued to say the doom of the Nazis. Then He came in again and said, 'They will never invade Christian England.' Again He stepped in and said, 'The Nazis will never take the five Bible Lands.'[3] How could He say it beforehand? Then He said, 'The Russians and the Nazis would weaken each other down to nothing.' ...A man had nothing to do with this. On March 29th, [1936] He got the victory over Hitler and at Munich He bent him...."

"....They [the Allies] say they will never sheath the sword [stop the war] until the doom of the Nazis, so if the principle thing is right the other thing must be right. Here every person knows in Germany tonight there will be no terms with Germany until the Nazis are put out...."

Six months after V.E. Day (Victory in Europe) Rees Howells wrote a letter dated, 7th November 1945, to Rev. S. H. Dixon of the Conference of Missionary Societies, Edinburgh House, London, S.W.1.

Dear Mr Dixon,
                    Thank you very much for your letter of the 23rd October. I have no other report printed at the moment, but I am enclosing you a copy of my book, that I sent out the first month of the war. [It was actually the third month of the war when the book was published].

I give you this word of explanation on the book. It was revealed to us that the Devil had entered into Hitler and those followers of his who are awaiting their trial today [Nuremberg Trials of 20th November 1945 to 2nd October 1946], and that this war was not a European War, but that God challenged the Dictators. Keep this in your mind when you are reading it. The book is in two parts, *and the predictions have become true to the letter.* [My emphasis].

The second part of the book tells how the College was built by faith, and we are holding properties in our hands today worth a quarter of a million pounds. I also said in the book that as a thank-offering for victory over the dictators and those systems, that I was to give £100,000 to build Colleges and Schools in the Holy Land. All I need today to get this £100,000 is to sell one of the estates and it will be in my hands to give. Although since the book was written I have been led of the Lord to give Penllergaer Mansion and 54 acres of land to the war orphans. The Mansion itself is valued at £20,000 and I am giving it as a gift to Barnardo's.[4]

We have about half-a-dozen doctors ready to go out with us to the Holy Land. Now there are five of the company who are going out there and who are prepared to go and they are nursing in a sanatorium. They have finished their training as missionaries here and they do not intend to pass as nurses, and we would like very much if they could be released [from their war duties], as each one of them has had three years or four years training with us. You will find their names and ages on the sheet attached. If we can get forms from you for them to fill in, they would return them at once.

The reason I delay to write was because we were expecting Parliament to pass that all over 30 would be free.
   Your Sincerely [Rees Howells]

Chapter 9

Bible College of Wales – May 1945

'You [God] have turned for me my mourning into dancing; You have put off my sackcloth and clothed me with gladness, to the end that my glory may sing praise to You and not be silent. O Lord my God, I will give thanks to You forever' (Psalm 30:11-12).

'Bless the Lord, O my soul; and all that is within me, bless His holy name! Bless the Lord, O my soul, and forget not all His benefits. The Lord executes righteousness and justice for all who are oppressed. He made known His ways to Moses, His acts to the children of Israel' (Psalm 103:1-2, 3-7).

The following is from the *Bible College of Wales, Twenty-First Anniversary Annual Report, Whitsuntide* (Pentecost) *1945*. It was date-stamped '16 May 1945' with a handwritten pencil note of '1,200' which were copies to be printed ready for Whitsun and posted to those unable to attend the meetings. This was just eight days after the end of the war with Germany, V.E. Day (Victory in Europe, 8th May 1945), after they unconditionally surrendered to the Allies. (The war in the Far East continued until 15th August 1945, when Japan surrendered, which became known as V.J. Day, Victory over Japan Day).

For the benefit of the friends and supporters who are too far away to join in Praise and Thanksgiving on Whit-Monday, we are sending out a short account of the marvellous way the Holy Ghost has led and sustained us, and fulfilled the predictions sent forth by the College at the beginning of the war.

In 1935 the Lord revealed:

The College Vision Predictions

1. The Gospel would be given to Every Creature in 30 years.
2. Ten thousand would be called, and filled with the Holy Ghost and sent forth by Him.

3. God would open His treasury and finance the Vision and lend to nations. The first gift to be taken from the Treasury was £10,000.

In 1938 two of these predictions were fulfilled.
1. The gift of *£10,000 had arrived. [*£674,400 in 2020].
2. The Holy Ghost had descended on over one hundred people, as He did on the eleven Apostles on the Day of Pentecost. [These 100+ staff members were the first of 10,000 people that Rees Howells believed that God would raise up].

War Predictions

In December 1939, in the darkest hour of the war, the College sent out a book of predictions with the title:
"God Challenges the Dictators"
and its subtitle
"Doom of the Nazis Predicted"

The Book made Four Predictions which today are fulfilled:
1. The overthrow of the Dictators, and their systems, Nazism, Fascism and Bolshevism.
2. Doom of the Nazis Predicted and the Death of Hitler.
3. That God would deliver Protestant Germany from Hitlerism and deliver the hundreds of Evangelical Ministers from the Concentration Camps, and that their places would be occupied by the fanatical Nazi leaders, if any of these would escape a speedy death.
4. That the College as a thank-offering for the overthrow of the Beast and his systems, would give £100,000 to open Colleges, Schools, and Homes for the thousands of orphans in the Holy Land.

Daniel's Visions
Dictators Coming into Power

Daniel 2:44: "In the days of these kings (dictators) shall the God of Heaven set up a Kingdom, which shall never be destroyed...the STONE was cut out of the mountain without hands, and it brake [break] in pieces these kingdoms of the world."

God said that the war was not the Dictators' European War, but God's War on the Beast [Hitler and the Nazi system], and after the overthrow of the Beast God's Kingdom would be established among all nations. "This Gospel of the Kingdom shall be preached as a witness among all nations" (Matthew 24:14).

The College was warned by the Holy Ghost, that Hitler was the Haman of the day, God's enemy, but like Mordecai and Esther we were prepared, in the power of God, to take part in his overthrow and bring in the Magna Carta [of 1215 under King John of England which resulted in various freedoms and protection for the people] – freedom of conscience and freedom of worship to all people [which Evangelical Christians in Germany had been denied and imprisoned for their faith].

Family of 200 Kept by God

As Elijah and the widow and her son were to be kept by God, until God sent rain upon the earth – "The barrel of meal shall not waste, nor the cruse of oil fail," so the College family were to be kept until the Dictators' Systems were overthrown, and the Nazis brought to their doom.

The Lord has sent, in gifts alone during the years of war, on an average of about £7,000 a year. The barrel of meal has not wasted nor the cruse of oil failed. The Treasury had opened, and the £10,000 came, and no prayer has been made in the College for money during the years of war. All the prayers and intercession were made to overthrow the Beast.

No Gas-Masks or Shelter

When the war broke out, the Word God gave to the College was "Be not troubled" and "Fear not, for they that be with us are more than they that be with them," and the eyes of the 200 (over 70 of them children, and mostly the children of missionaries) were opened to see the "horses and chariots of God" (2 Kings 6). So not one had a gas-mask, and not one went to a shelter. (Some said they were trusting in Psalm 91 in a shelter, but the College people had to trust it outside a shelter).

Not a single bomb was thrown on the College (God's) properties which consist of over 320 acres and the buildings covered acres of land. [270 acres were at Penllergaer, Swansea and the 50+ acres was along the Derwen Fawr Road, Sketty, Swansea, on the three estates of Glynderwen, Sketty Isaf and Derwen Fawr.]

During the worst blitz in Swansea, which was as badly bombed as any town in the country, the meetings went on as usual. The College had two meetings during the war years every evening from 7-9pm and from 10pm-12 midnight, without a single break, like Moses on the Mount, interceding for the war in Europe, and proving: "a thousand shall fall at thy side, and ten thousand at thy right hand, but it shall not come nigh [near] thee" (Psalm 91:7).

New College for London Degree

More than 15 [school students] who have passed their Matriculation and Higher at our Secondary School are preparing for their London B.A. and B.Sc. This Degree College is prepared for hundreds of young people who have had their Matriculation, and joined up, to continue their studies for a Degree, if called to the Mission Field. Through this, God may establish Christian Schools in every country.

Thanksgiving and Praise

Whit-Monday [Pentecost-Monday] will be the greatest day in the history of the College and the Vision. The overthrow of the First Beast, the establishment of the Atlantic Charter with freedom of conscience and freedom of worship, confirm the College Vision given ten years ago, that every country would in the next 30 years be open for the Gospel. The Conference of 46 nations in San Francisco, [America], is establishing this today:- THE GOSPEL TO EVERY CREATURE.
Derwen Fawr, Swansea. 17th May 1945.

End of *Twenty-First Anniversary Annual Report, Whitsuntide 1945.*

Chapter 10

Judgment on the Nazi Régime

Behold, the name of the Lord comes from afar, burning with His anger, and His burden is heavy; His lips are full of indignation, and His tongue like a devouring fire. His breath is like an overflowing stream, which reaches up to the neck, to sift the nations with the sieve of futility; and there shall be a bridle in the jaws of the people, causing them to err' (Isaiah 30:27-28).

'Thus says the Lord of hosts: "The children of Israel were oppressed, along with the children of Judah; all who took them captive have held them fast; they have refused to let them go. Their Redeemer is strong; the Lord of hosts is His name. He will thoroughly plead their case, that He may give rest to the land, and disquiet the inhabitants of Babylon" ' (Jeremiah 50:33-34).

Concentration Camp Film 1945

In 1945, British film makers with the help of Soviet and American film footage began to edit a film in London, England. It was *German Concentration Camp Final Survey,* detailing the atrocities that had been committed under the Nazi régime and the Third Reich. The footage was to be used as evidence to show to the German people and was used as evidence in the Nuremberg Trials of 1945-1946. British and American film crews had been briefed, they needed close shots of victims so that it could be seen how they had been killed, as well as distance shots, with senior officials in some of the footage so that it could never be said that it was staged. The Russians had not been briefed and Soviet film crews arrived a few days after the liberation of Auschwitz-Birkenau. They were shocked beyond belief, as was every soldier that entered the camps. In one of the camps that the Soviets liberated they immediately shot dead every guard they found, such was their anger and disgust over what they saw of man's inhumanity against mankind.

In some areas after a concentration camp had been liberated by the Allies and they saw the devastation, the senior military leader would proclaim martial law and all able-bodied Germans aged

14-80 from the nearest villages or town were ordered to help bury the dead. In some instances the local Germans claimed not to know anything about the camp, or if they did know about them, claimed not to know what went on inside of them. After digging large pits and moving hundreds if not thousands of emancipated corpses into these graves day-after-day, the local citizens without a doubt understood to a small degree the conditions that the prisoners endured in these inhumane Nazi concentration camps.

In some other areas close to a concentration camp German citizens from the surrounding villages and towns were escorted into the camps on foot so that they could see what the German people had been fighting for and supporting, as well as what had been done in the name of Nazism. Camps guards and camps workers were filmed moving, carrying or dragging the 1000s of emancipated dead corpses into deep and large pits.

The British film *German Concentration Camp Final Survey* produced by Sidney Bernstein with the British Ministry of Information was not completed due to the change in British policy toward the Germans, which was against the Russians and Communism. It was abandoned in September 1945. The British felt that it was better to have the Germans as an ally and to utilize them as a buffer against the Soviets, Communism and the looming Cold War. The Americans withdrew from the project in July 1945. They were not pleased with the British response and so used the footage to make *Die Todesmühlen (Death Mills* in English) which was shown in cinemas in Germany and used German narration. The British film was finished by the Imperial War Museum using the original dope sheets (planning sheets) and premiered at the Berlin Film Festival in 2014.

The Fate of Hitler and Six Senior Nazis
Adolf Hitler was one of the most evil people in history whose atrocities knew no limits. He was the leader of the Nazi Party, Chancellor of Germany in 1933 who became Führer in 1934. He was a dictator who tried to annihilate the Jewish race and anybody who opposed him and his ideologies. During the last days of World War II during the Battle of Berlin in his Führerbunker (underground bunker complex) he committed suicide on 30th April 1945 alongside his wife of just one day, Eva Braun, by taking a cyanide pill and then shooting himself in the head.

Hermann Göring was the 16th President of the Reichstag and was sentenced to death at the Nuremberg Trials by hanging.

However, he took his own life by ingesting cyanide the night before (15th October 1946) the sentence was to be carried out.

Joseph Goebbels was the Reich Minister of Propaganda of Nazi Germany from 1933 to 1945. On 1st May 1945, Goebbels and his wife poisoned their six children with cyanide and then killed themselves; just one day after Hitler's suicide.

Joachim von Ribbentrop was Foreign Minister of Nazi Germany from 1938 until 1945. He was sentenced to death at the Nuremberg Trials and was hanged on 16th October 1946.

Rudolf Hess was appointed Deputy Führer to Adolf Hitler in 1933. On 10th May 1941, he flew to Scotland for alleged peace talks with a nobleman and was arrested. After the war he was returned to Germany where he was convicted at the Nuremberg Trials and sentenced to life imprisonment. In Spandau Prison, West Berlin, aged 93, he died by hanging himself on 17th August 1987.

Heinrich Himmler was one of the main architects of the Holocaust and the head of the Reichsführer-SS. He was captured by the Soviets, travelling under a pseudonym with false documents and passed on to the British. During a medical examination he bit into a cyanide pill on 23rd May 1945 and was dead within fifteen minutes.

Robert Ley was Head of the German Labour Front from 1933 to 1945. On 25th October 1945, three days after being convicted at the Nuremberg Trials as a war criminal, he committed suicide.

Belsen Trial 1945

Part of the unfinished 1945 film *German Concentration Camp Final Survey* was used as evidence at the trial of Josef Kramer, who was known as the Beast of Belsen. He was tried along with forty-four other people, men and women associated with Bergen-Belsen and Auschwitz-Birkenau. The trial began in a Lüneburg at a former gymnasium in Lower Saxon, Germany, on 17th September 1945. It was conducted in English and translated into German and Polish with the trial lasting fifty-four days. The verdict was given on 17th November 1945: Fourteen defendants were acquitted, eighteen were found guilty and sentenced to prison of between one to fifteen years, eleven were sentenced to death by hanging and one was too unwell to stand trial. By 1955, as acts of clemency over the years, all of those who had been sentenced to prison had been released.

NAZI CAMP KILLER FOUND HANGED

DACHAU, Thursday.—Lt.-Col. Max Koegel, war criminal facing charges concerning the murder of 46,000 people in Flossenberg concentration camp, was found hanged in his cell at Nuremberg today. He had used a blanket, which he had tied to a door handle.

Koegel, who had been commandant at Flossenberg, was captured yesterday in a Bavarian village, where he was working as a farm labourer.—A.P.

Newspaper Article, 26 June 1946

Nuremberg Trials 1945-1946

The Nuremberg Trials were a series of Military Tribunals that took place between 20th November 1945 to 2nd October 1946 and the world watched with bated breath. It was held under International Law and the Laws of War. The verdicts and results were handed out on 2nd October 1946: Twelve Nazis were sentenced to hang to death, three were given life imprisonment, two were given twenty years, one was given fifteen years, and another was sentenced to ten years in prison.

'The sword of the Lord is filled with blood, it is made overflowing with fatness, with the blood of lambs and goats, with the fat of the kidneys of rams. For the Lord has a sacrifice in Bozrah, and a great slaughter in the land of Edom. The wild oxen shall come down with them, and the young bulls with the mighty bulls; their land shall be soaked with blood, and their dust saturated with fatness. For it is the day of the Lord's vengeance, the year of recompense for the cause of Zion' (Isaiah 34:6-8).

The Charges of the Court

1. Conspiracy – Taking part in a conspiracy to commit crimes against peace, war crimes, and crimes against humanity.

2. Crimes Against Peace – Participating in the planning and waging wars of aggression against: Poland, Britain, France, Denmark, Norway, Belgium, Holland, Luxemburg, Yugoslavia, Greece, the Soviet Union and the United States.

3. War Crimes – Murder and ill-treatment of civilians in occupied territory and on the high seas. Deportations for slave labour, murder and ill-treatment of prisoners of war, killing of hostages, plunder, exacting collective penalties, wanton destruction and devastation. Conscription of civilian labour, forcing civilians to swear allegiance to a hostile power and Germanisation of occupied territories.

4. Crimes Against Humanity – Murder, enslavement, extermination, deportation and other inhumane acts committed against civilian populations, before and during the war. Persecution on political, racial and religious grounds in connection with the common plan mentioned in count 1 (Conspiracy).

The President of the Nuremberg Trials, Lord Justice Laurence pronounced on 1st October 1946, that the following top-ranking Nazis leaders were guilty on all four counts.

Hermann Göring, 53, and former Luffewaffe chief and successor-designate to Hitler.

Joachim von Ribbentrop, 53, ex-foreign minister and former Ambassador in London.

Alfred Rosenberg, 53, intellectual "high priest" and former Minister for Occupied Eastern Territories.

Wilhem Keitel, 64, former chief of the German Armed Forces High Command.

Constantine Von Neurath, 73, Protector of Moravia and Baravia.

Alfred Jodl, 56, Nazi Chief of Staff from 1942 to 1945.

The following were found guilty on some of the counts.

Rudolf Hess, Deputy Führer to Adolf Hitler, 1 and 2.

Albert Speer, Minister of Armaments and War Production, 3 and 4.

Walter Funk, Reichbank President, 2, 3 and 4.

Hans Frank, former Governor-General of Poland, 3 and 4.

Admiral Doenitz (Dönitz), the Supreme Commander of the German Navy since 1943, who succeeded Adolf Hitler as the German head of state for just 20 days in 1945, 2 and 3.

Wilhelm Frick, former Minister of the Interior, 1, 3 and 4.

Julius Streicher, Nazi Jew-Baiter (a vile persecutor of Jews), founder and publisher of the virulently anti-Semitic newspaper *Der Stürmer* and publisher of anti-Semitic children's books, 4.

Fritz Sauckel, Labour Front Chief, 3 and 4.

Baldier Von Schirach, Nazi Youth Leader, 4.

Martin Bormann, tried *in absentina* (while not present) 3 and 4. He is believed to have committed suicide from a bridge on 2nd May 1945. His body was buried on 8th May 1945, but not confirmed until 1973. DNA testing proved it as Bormann's remains in 1988.

Seyss-Inquart, former Governor of Austria, 2, 3 and 4.

Ernst Kaltenbrunner, General in the SS and Chief of the Reich Main Security Office from January 1943 to May 1945, guilty on two counts, 3 and 4.

The following were found not guilty on any of the counts.

Hans Fritsche, 46, Joseph Goebels' propaganda assistant.

Hjalmar Schacht, 69, Hitler's "financial wizard."

Franz Von Papen, 66, Nazi diplomat and former ambassador to Austria and Turkey.

A Prized Possession

Rees Howells and the Bible College of Wales had a prized possession. It was a photo of the Nazi leaders at the Nuremberg Trials, placed in the centre of a large portrait-sized frame, approximately 16 inch high x 12 inch wide. Above and to the left was a cutting "Hitler's Fate." It was taken from *God Challenges the Dictators:*

The Bible College has predicted that the God of Daniel will deliver Pastor Niemöller, and the hundreds of other German Evangelicals who have followed him to the concentration camps (Hitler's dens of lions). It affirms that their places will one day be occupied by the fanatical Nazi leaders, "the power-drunk adventurers," if any of them escape a speedy death. Just as Darius treated those who accused Daniel, so will the Nazis be treated, for they have afflicted Germany and God's servants most sore.

To the right of the frame was a typed list:
Results of the Nuremberg Trials
October 2nd 1946
Twelve   Hanging
Three   Life Imprisonment
Two   Twenty-Five Years
One   Fifteen Years
One   Ten Years

At the bottom of the frame was a triangular cut section of a dust cover (jacket cover) from *God Challenges the Dictators*, with the subtitle and the bottom section of the world. It read:
Doom of Nazis Predicted
Rees Howells

Justice and Closure
The Nuremberg Trials brought some justice to the countless victims and casualties of World War II. However, only when each individual stands before the Throne of God on Judgment Day to give an account of their life will lasting and eternal justice be served. Rees Howells predicted the *Doom of the Nazis* in 1939 when the Nazis believed in a Thousand Year Reign for the Third Reich! This was the Devil's attempt working through Hitler to counterfeit Christ's Millennial Reign (Revelation 20:4-6) and to hinder the Great Commission.[1]

It was Rees Howells trusting in a Living God and in obedience to the Holy Spirit who proved correct and victorious whilst Nazi Germany was proved wrong.

'You are of God, little children, and have overcome them, because He who is in you is greater than he who is in the world' (1 John 4:4).[2]

'For we do not wrestle against flesh and blood but against principalities, against powers, against the rulers of the darkness of this age, against the spiritual hosts of wickedness in the heavenly places' (Ephesians 6:12).

'And the God of peace will crush Satan under your feet shortly. The grace of our Lord Jesus Christ be with you. Amen' (Romans 16:20).

Chapter 11

Saved for a Purpose

Jesus said to the eleven disciples before His ascension, "Go into all the world and preach the Gospel to Every Creature. He who believes and is baptised will be saved; but he who does not believe will be condemned" (Mark 16:15-16).

Jesus said, "As Moses lifted up the serpent in the wilderness, even so must the Son of Man be lifted up, that whoever believes in Him should not perish but have eternal life. For God so loved the world that He gave His only begotten Son, that whoever believes in Him should not perish but have everlasting life. For God did not send His Son into the world to condemn the world, but that the world through Him might be saved. He who believes in Him is not condemned; but he who does not believe is condemned already, because he has not believed in the name of the only begotten Son of God" (John 3:14-18).

Britain and its Allies won the war but we were saved for a purpose. Christian nations, those with a Judeo-Christian heritage that have helped shape laws and society are called to be a light in the darkness; to uphold truth, righteousness and justice.[1] Germany was the land of the Reformation (1517) and Britain with its Empire aided world evangelisation. For Britain, where the flag went missionaries followed e.g. William Carey in India 1793+, or where missionaries went commerce followed e.g. David Livingstone in Darkest Africa 1840s+. Before WWI, Britain and Germany sent out more missionaries than any other countries. But when war broke out in 1914 and again in 1939, men and women were called up into service for the King and Empire. Other Christians were unable to train at Bible Colleges or Theological Institutions and they were expected to do their bit for the war effort. Whilst income dwindled, less money was sent to the mission field and many future Christian leaders were cut down in the prime of youth. The following extract is from R. B. Watchman's autobiography, *The Holy Spirit in a Man: Spiritual*

Warfare, Intercession, Faith, Healings and Miracles in the Modern World.

I entered this world knowing that I was not wanted. World War II (1939-1945) had not long finished and everything was in short supply. Life for millions was an uphill battle, and in Britain, rationing was still the norm for most people, yet there was another war still raging, as it had for thousands of years against spiritual forces of evil in the heavenly realms (Ephesians 6:12). All other wars are a shadow of this one. This is a spiritual war of good versus evil. God has said that in the last days He will pour out His Spirit on all people (Acts 2:17), and everyone who calls on the name of the Lord will be saved (Acts 2:21). The Devil knows he is defeated, but continues to release hordes of demonic forces to blind the eyes of the unbelievers and bring them under demonic bondage (Luke 10:17-20 and 2 Corinthians 4:4).

As World War II drew to a close, more than a few bishops, church leaders, government ministers and military leaders, truly believed that Great Britain had been saved for a purpose. They and others believed it was of a spiritual nature. Victory in World War II was won due to spiritual interventions by God. There was another group led by Rees Howells who fully understood that both these wars were not only linked, but one and the same. Led by the Holy Spirit, they knew that just as the Devil had entered Judas Iscariot (Luke 22:3), the Devil had entered Adolf Hitler to try to stop Jesus' last command, to, "Go and make disciples of all nations" (Matthew 28:19-20 and Mark 16:15). Rees Howells, his son Samuel and over one hundred others, all became channels that the Holy Spirit entered, to fight the Devil's schemes, for our struggle is not against flesh and blood, but against the rulers, against the authorities, against the powers of this dark world, and against spiritual forces of evil in heavenly realms (Ephesians 6:12). God's intent was that now through the Church, the manifold wisdom of God should be made known to the rulers and authorities in the heavenly realms (Ephesians 3:10-11). Rees Howells and his team of intercessors, fully understood this and went to war daily, on their knees. Led by the Holy Spirit they fasted, prayed and interceded, to bind the strong man and pull down his strongholds, releasing angelic forces to do battle with the principalities and powers of darkness (Daniel 10).

Before I reached my second birthday, Rees Howells was called home. His life on earth was over and mine had only just begun. Today, prosperity preachers boast that they will not live in lack, but this was not the world that I was born into. I often went to bed hungry and learnt the value of all that God has given me, and knew that nothing should ever be wasted (John 6:12 and Luke 16:10).

The Holy Spirit had told me to go to the Bible College of Wales (BCW), and it was that plain, that simple. I was told to visit.... I was thrilled to visit the Derwen Fawr Estate in Swansea, where Rees Howells used to live, and where his son, Samuel Rees Howells was continuing the ministry of worldwide intercession. In the early hours of the morning, I walked around these grounds where the Holy Spirit came to visit after Rees Howells presented the Vision that all should surrender their lives to the Holy Spirit, so that Every Creature could hear the Gospel.

Rees Howells had received the Every Creature Vision in the front room of Derwen Fawr House on Boxing Day (26th December) 1934. He explained that if they responded to the Holy Spirit's call, all who accepted would be bondservants for the rest of their lives to this one task – to intercede for every creature to hear the Gospel, to serve those who went as missionaries, and to forever carry this living burden.

Intercession, for Rees Howells and the team he led was not ritualised prayer with little meaning, but it was targeted and specific as they abided in the Vine (John 15:1-11). They were led by the Holy Spirit to intercede on national and international levels concerning any situation which affected world evangelisation. As Every Creature had to hear the Gospel, the doors had to be opened and kept open. In world events, their prayers became strategic and defined. Wherever the enemy used rogue governments or dictators to oppose the freedom to share the Gospel with the unsaved, they had to intercede and become an army fighting on their knees in spiritual battles. They were to wrestle, not against flesh or blood, but against spiritual powers of darkness, principalities, powers, rulers of evil darkness and the host of demonic powers in the heavenlies. Paul used the word 'wrestle' because spiritual warfare can be a long drawn out battle of strengths between the Holy Spirit in His intercessors and the demonic strongholds who resist (Ephesians 6:12-13). Victory belongs to Christ, but the battle continues.[2]

Epilogue

Every Creature Commission

'For the Lord shall build up Zion; He shall appear in His glory. He shall regard the prayer of the destitute, and shall not despise their prayer. This will be written for the generation to come, that a people yet to be created may praise the Lord. For He looked down from the height of His sanctuary; from Heaven the Lord viewed the earth, to hear the groaning of the prisoner, to release those appointed to death, to declare the name of the Lord in Zion, and His praise in Jerusalem' (Psalm 102:16-21).

'Jesus went about all the cities and villages, teaching in their synagogues, preaching the Gospel of the Kingdom, and healing every sickness and every disease among the people. But when He saw the multitudes, He was moved with compassion for them, because they were weary and scattered, like sheep having no shepherd. Then He said to His disciples, "The harvest truly is plentiful, but the labourers are few. Therefore pray the Lord of the harvest to send out labourers into His harvest" ' (Matthew 9:35-38).

This Vision of 26th December 1934 (Boxing Day) given to Rees Howells in the Blue Room of Derwen Fawr House, Sketty, Swansea, became known as the Every Creature Vision / Commission. It was believed that the Gospel should be given to all mankind, to every tribe, nation and tongue within thirty years – a generation. They were to take personal responsibility to intercede for the Gospel to go to Every Creature and to live sacrificial lives in order to train and prepare people for the mission field. By June 1936, there were one hundred and twenty students who had been called out by the Holy Spirit (to lay down their mission callings to intercede for others to go) because the fire of God had fallen on 29th March 1936 – this was revival!
By June 1936, there were one hundred and seventy staff and students praying and interceding three hours a day for the Every Creature Commission to see its fulfilment. First, once every tribe, nation and tongue has heard the Good News then Jesus can

return – the Second Coming. People need an opportunity to hear the Good News to repent, to forsake their sin and to put their trust in the finished work of Jesus Christ. He died and rose again so that we can have eternal life in Him. It is God's grace and mercy, His free gift to mankind that Jesus willingly took the sins of the world upon Himself when He was beaten and crucified, died, buried and rose again after three days; so that we can be forgiven and be reconciled with God through His Son Jesus Christ, who shed His blood for mankind on the cross of Calvary.

The apostle Paul wrote: 'That if you confess with your mouth the Lord Jesus and believe in your heart that God has raised Him from the dead, you will be saved. For with the heart one believes unto righteousness, and with the mouth confession is made unto salvation. For the Scripture says, "Whoever believes on Him will not be put to shame." For there is no distinction between Jew and Greek, for the same Lord over all is rich to all who call upon Him. For "Whoever calls on the name of the Lord shall be saved." How then shall they call on Him in whom they have not believed? And how shall they believe in Him of whom they have not heard? And how shall they hear without a preacher? And how shall they preach unless they are sent? As it is written: "How beautiful are the feet of those who preach the Gospel of peace, who bring glad tidings of good things!" ' (Romans 10:9-15).

Jesus declared, "And this Gospel of the Kingdom will be preached in all the world as a witness to all the nations, and then the end will come" (Matthew 24:14).

Jesus stated, "And the Gospel must first be preached to all the nations" (Mark 13:10).

Peter wrote: '*Looking for and hastening the coming of the day of God,* because of which the heavens will be dissolved, being on fire...' (2 Peter 3:12).

'And they sang a new song, saying, "You [Jesus] are worthy to take the scroll, and to open its seals; for You were slain, and have redeemed us to God by Your blood out of *every tribe and tongue and people and nation*" (Revelation 5:9).

'Then I saw another angel flying in the midst of Heaven, having the everlasting Gospel to preach to those who dwell on the earth to *every nation, tribe, tongue, and people*' (Revelation 14:6).

'So He who sat on the cloud thrust in His sickle on the earth, and the earth was reaped' (Revelation 14:16).

Second, Rees Howells believed that 10,000 people would be raised up like himself, *full* of the Holy Spirit to go into all the world and preach the Gospel in the power of the Spirit.

Third, Rees Howells believed that God would finance these men and women and as a *sign*, a gift of £10,000 would be given to the Bible College of Wales. Up until this time, the largest gift the College had ever been given was £1,000. The £10,000 gift was received in July 1938, worth £674,400 in 2020, and made newspaper headlines in at least three different publications.

Rees Howells was not the first person to believe that the consummation of the age would be in "this generation" (thirty years), as other Christian workers had mentioned it from the 1860s onwards. Men such as J. Hudson Taylor, founder of the China Inland Mission, A. B. Simpson, founder of the Christian and Missionary Alliance and John R. Mott, missionary statesman, all preached the possibility of evangelising the world in their generation. In 1910, the first International Missionary Conference was held in Edinburgh, Scotland, its motto was: 'The Evangelisation of the World in this Generation.'

The Vision Rees Howells received added great emphasis on individuals, for their responsibility in world evangelisation which meant a full surrender and consecration.

The apostle Paul wrote: 'I beseech you therefore, brethren, by the mercies of God, that you present your bodies a living sacrifice, holy, acceptable to God, which is your reasonable service' (Romans 12:1).

This has to be coupled with an enduement of power for service. Jesus said, "But you shall receive power when the Holy Spirit has come upon you; and you shall be witnesses to Me in Jerusalem, and in all Judea and Samaria, and to the end of the earth" (Acts 1:8).

Jesus said, "Go ye into all the world and preach the Gospel to Every Creature" (Mark 16:15) A.V.

The above Scripture became the motto of the Bible College of Wales (BCW) and the Vision was presented to the staff and students of BCW on 1st January 1935.

It was during the war years that Rees Howells and his team of around 120 intercessors played major roles in national and international intercessions for world events. Rees and his team's first international intercession was seen in March 1936 when the Locarno Treaty was broken – Germany went into the demilitarised zone – the Rhineland, but a European War was averted. But their international intercession with a team of around 120 began after Easter 1936 when the Holy Spirit descended on BCW and each individual put his or her life on the line and fully and unequivocally surrendered all. The summer of 1938 (September) saw their intercessions over the Munich Crisis when Hitler invaded Czechoslovakia.

Rees Howells had believed and predicted in January 1940 that war would end by Whit-Sunday (Pentecost) 1940. This was not in *God Challenges the Dictators,* because of its earlier publication date of December 1939. Like all of Rees Howells' major predictions; he announced them to the media as a sign and a testament and they were always printed in the local papers and sometimes the national ones. What we now refer to as World War II did not end until 1945 with an estimated total loss of 55 million lives. In the eyes of many, Rees Howells and the Bible College of Wales (BCW) was deemed a failure and he was labelled a 'false prophet' by some. Some said that the predictions were false, others, that it was another death – the grain which had to die before it could bear fruit; but God had bigger purposes involved. From 1939-1940 BCW lost a lot of its support from those who merely came to the meetings for the wrong reasons. It was a season of sifting, shaking and pruning (John 15), and only the truly committed stood loyal and it was these genuine warriors – the 300 of Gideon's men (Judges 7) who did the real battle through the hard and trying years that lay ahead.

A journalist in an article for the *Evening Post,* 3rd June 1941, wrote about the 17th anniversary of the Bible College, which was the previous day. The journalist recounted much of what Rees Howells had said and done over many years and concluded with: 'Impossibilities have happened in the College, and it would not fail. Unless his [Rees Howells'] critics were men of faith, they are not qualified to criticise him.'

Jewish and Other Refugees

In 1939, £100,000 was a sum the College was praying for as a gift to the Jewish people, as also described in *Rees Howells Intercessor* (chapter 33). In May 1939, Rees Howells was prepared to sell the three sites of Glynderwen, Derwen Fawr and Sketty Isaf which had been valued at nearly £100,000 and then use these huge funds to look after a minimum of 1,000 Jewish refugee children, though they calculated they could take 2,000 children. One thousand children would cost a minimum of

£50,000 per year (£3,274,600 in 2020). Even the local newspapers reported on this 'Welsh George Müller.' Rees would be liable for the children's board, keep and education until their eighteenth birthday. Rees also stated in *God Challenges the Dictators* (chapter VI), that the College would need another £100,000 for all the new buildings to educate and accommodate so many children and staff. The School was going to move to Penllergaer, but this never happened for the Lord never told Rees Howells to sell the three estates, but saw that he was *willing.* Rees Howells said, "There is a golden rule in the life of faith that the Christian can never prevail upon God to move others to give larger sums of money towards God's work that he himself has either given, or proved that he is willing to give, if it were in his power to do so."[1]

The Apostle Paul wrote to the Church at Corinth: 'And in this I give advice: It is to your advantage not only to be doing what you began and were desiring to do a year ago; but now you also must complete the doing of it; that as there was a readiness to desire it, so there also may be a completion out of what you have. *For if there is first a willing mind, it is accepted according to what one has, and not according to what he does not have'* (2 Corinthians 8:10-12).

Due to British Government restrictions on immigration, Rees Howells was unable to take in the large number of Jewish refugees that he wanted to save from the Nazi régime. However, around ten thousand refugee children came to Britain and some were repatriated after the war. Rees received more than one hundred letters from 1937-1940, often accompanied with photos from parents, Jews and non-Jews and older siblings across Europe, begging and pleading with him to accept their children or younger siblings, yet his hands were tied. Many applicants wanted places for their child or children at the Boarding School, others just pleaded for asylum, whilst adults wanted employment, sometimes writing on behalf of another. It took months for the Home Office to grant decisions. The author has read some of these heart-wrenching letters and some of the replies, especially as the fate of most of those concerned was sealed in the concentration camps of Europe under Nazi occupation.

However, some of the child refugees, including German Jews were already in the care of families in Britain and asked Rees Howells if he could admit their refugee children to his school.

A newspaper report of May 1948, stated that Rees Howells soon 'expects a gift of £100,000' – '19 times he has been right' and proceeded to state that up until that point they had received eighteen gifts of £1,000 and one gift of £10,000! The College meeting notes reveal that Rees Howells and the Bible College of Wales were praying for at least three sums of £100,000, all for different projects / gifts and a number of figures for other works.

During the war not a single bomb landed on the properties of the Bible College of Wales which was only five kilometres from Swansea docks, which were heavily bombed, as was Swansea town centre, which was closer. Swansea became a city in 1969.

Final Years and Passing the Baton

Rees Howells' intercession during the war took its toll on his health but along with his dedicated team at the Bible College of Wales, world events were changed by prevailing prayer and the free world was liberated from the tyranny of the World War II dictators. Christian England never gave in and Rees Howells and the staff of BCW never lost faith, but believed and pressed forward in victory!

On Sunday, 15th January 1950 at the 9pm meeting, Rees Howells read the songs of Moses and David and said, "Everything in me is praising God because the Holy Ghost can say, 'I have finished the work Thou gavest Me to do.' Every Creature will hear the Gospel...."

Rees Howells died in February 1950 after suffering several heart attacks in the previous months. For the four preceding days before he passed on, he was in and out of consciousness. His last words were, "Victory... Hallelujah" – uttered on Sunday, 12th February 1950 and he passed into glory the following day on Monday, 13th February at 10am, one day before Valentine's Day. Within one hour, his son, thirty-eight year old Rev. Samuel Rees Howells called the entire staff of the Bible College of Wales and School together and they rededicated their lives to God to carry on with the Vision, to reach Every Creature for Jesus Christ.

In the 1960s, Samuel Rees Howells gave the College a renewed sense of vision and leadership, as he prepared them to continue to be responsible for the Vision of world evangelisation, not in a limited time, but for the rest of their lives. The intercession was now a lifetime commitment to pray, give and go until all are reached. Samuel (known as Mr Samuel to staff and students) also always remained committed to the distribution of the Scriptures and large sums of money were used in printing and distributing Bibles, as well as supporting missionaries in the field across the globe. These were not only former BCW students, but hundreds of other ministries, working and labouring in the harvest fields of the world in a variety of capacities.

A contemporary interpretation of the Vision can be summed up as: Go ye (Mark 16:15), give ye (Luke 9:13), pray ye (Matthew 9:38) and ideally do all three, in the power of the Spirit (Acts 1:8), for the glory of God and the exultation of Jesus Christ. Serve Him, obey Him and abide in Him (John 15:1-11). Go and make disciples of all nations (Matthew 28:19).

When Samuel Rees Howells was promoted to glory on Thursday, 18th March 2004, 'Tucked away in the top right drawer of his writing desk,' wrote Richard Maton, 'were verses of songs composed by Ardis Butterfield, the anointed singer and songwriter, whose ministry in the Spirit would lift the worship during the dark days of World War II. During the darkest hours, the theme had remained unchanged, and Samuel was strengthened through reading them often.'

These intercessions will bear fruit one day
Completed Vision in unlimited way.
Great signs shall follow the Spirit's hosts
To earth's remotest ends and coasts.[2]

Thank you for taking the time to read this book. Please give a shout out on social media and write a short review on your favourite review site. Thank you.

Social Media
Instagram and Twitter: @ByFaithMedia
Facebook, Youtube and Pinterest: /ByFaithMedia

Rees Howells www.facebook.com/ReesHowellsIntercessor
Samuel Rees Howells www.facebook.com/SamuelReesHowells

Also by ByFaith Media: 1. *Rees Howells, Vision Hymns of Spiritual Warfare & Intercessory Declarations: World War II Songs of Victory* by Mathew Backholer. 2. Hardback collector's edition: *God Challenges the Dictators, Doom of the Nazis Predicted: The Destruction of the Third Reich Foretold by the Director of Swansea Bible College, An Intercessor* by Rees Howells and Mathew Backholer. 3. *Samuel Rees Howells: A Life of Intercession: The Legacy of Prayer and Spiritual Warfare of an Intercessor* by Richard Maton and Paul and Mathew Backholer. 4. *Samuel, Son and Successor of Rees Howells: Director of the Bible College of Wales – A Biography* by Richard Maton.

Books by Mathew Backholer

The majority of the following books are available as paperbacks and eBooks on a number of different platforms worldwide. Some are also available as hardbacks.

Historical

- Hardback collector's edition: God Challenges the Dictators, Doom of the Nazis Predicted: The Destruction of the Third Reich Foretold by the Director of Swansea Bible College an Intercessor from Wales (Rees Howells and Mathew Backholer).
- Rees Howells, Vision Hymns of Spiritual Warfare & Intercessory Declarations: World War II Songs of Victory, Intercession, Praise and Worship, Israel and the Every Creature Commission. A rare insight into the prophetic declarations, hymns and choruses used in spiritual warfare by Rees Howells and his team of intercessors at the Bible College of Wales. Spanning the pivotal years of 1936-1948 and brought to life for the first time in more than seventy years. Many of the songs of worship reveal the theology, spiritual battles, and history during the dark days of World War II and the years surrounding it. From Emperor Haile Selassie of Ethiopia, Hitler's predicted downfall, to the Nation of Israel being born in a day and the glories beyond. More than a collection of rare hymns and choruses, including revelations, explanations and historical analysis behind many hymns, coupled with historical events and the authentic voice of Rees Howells.
- Rees Howells' God Challenges the Dictators, Doom of Axis Powers Predicted: Victory for Christian England and Release of Europe Through Intercession. (This is the story behind the story of God Challenges the Dictators, before, during and after publication which is centred around World War II. The book includes letters to Prime Minister Winston Churchill, Press Releases from Rees Howells, plus newspaper articles and adverts, and what Rees Howells said and wrote about his book).

Continued over the page

Christian Revivals and Awakenings
- Revival Fires and Awakenings, Thirty-Six Visitations of the Holy Spirit. (Also available as a hardback).
- Understanding Revival and Addressing the Issues it Provokes.
- Global Revival, Worldwide Outpourings, Forty-Three Visitations of the Holy Spirit.
- Revival Answers, True and False Revivals.
- Revival Fire, 150 Years of Revivals.
- Reformation to Revival, 500 Years of God's Glory.

Christian Discipleship and Spiritual Growth
- Christianity Rediscovered, In Pursuit of God and the Path to Eternal Life. Book 1.
- Christianity Explored. Book 2.
- Extreme Faith, On Fire Christianity.
- Discipleship For Everyday Living, Christian Growth.

Christian Missions (Travel with a Purpose)
- Short-Term Missions, A Christian Guide to STMs.
- How to Plan, Prepare and Successfully Complete Your Short-Term Mission.

World Travel
- Budget Travel, A Guide to Travelling on a Shoestring, Explore the World.
- Travel the World and Explore for Less than $50 a Day, the Essential Guide.

www.ByFaithBooks.org

Appendix A

Two Editions and Errors

The 1939 card cover copy on the first page was originally printed by Western Mail & Echo Ltd., Cardiff and London and published by 'The Bible College of Wales, Swansea.' But the last information in single quote marks is covered over by another piece of paper printed: Simpkins Marshall Ltd. Stationers' Hall Court, E.C.4. which could be read when put up against the light. Also page 164 (last unnumbered page of the card cover) states: Special Note. This remarkable book "God Challenges the Dictators" can be obtained through (and covered over by a piece of rough paper is printed) Simpkins Marshall Ltd. Stationers' Hall Court, E.C.4' but underneath reads: any bookseller or from the from the Western Mail and Echo Ltd., Cardiff and Fleet Street London; or direct from THE BIBLE COLLEGE OF WALES Derwen Fawr, Swansea Wales. Price 1/- [1 shilling] per copy, plus postage 4d., 12 copies sent for 13/- (which includes postage); 50 copies, £2 12s. 6d. (including postage); 100 copies £5 5s. 0d. (including postage).

SPECIAL NOTE.

This remarkable book " God Challenges the Dictators " can be obtained through

Simpkin Marshall Ltd.
STATIONERS' HALL COURT, E.C.4

1939 Card Cover Edition with print errors covered over
(top half of 1939 book page)

- 189 -

By

REES HOWELLS

Printed in Great Britain
by
Western Mail & Echo Ltd., Cardiff and London,
and Published by
Samuel Marshall Ltd.,
STATIONERS HALL COURT, E.C.4,

1939 Card Cover Edition with print errors covered over
(bottom half of 1939 book page)

The text on the spine of the hardback and the dust-jacket is upside down when the book is laid flat on a table with the title on top. I have only ever come across one other book title that does this and it is considered an error in the publishing world where we read from right to left. If you were to rotate the book's spine to face you, whilst the book title is face up on a flat object, you should be able to read the text with ease from left to right. Instead, it was printed upside down and you have to read from right to left, unless you place it title down. If the book is placed on a bookshelf the title of the book should read from top to bottom, but is instead, you have to read it from bottom to top.

www.ReesHowells.co.uk

www.BibleCollegeOfWales.co.uk

Sources and Notes

Foreword
1. The first part of the title of this book: *Rees Howells' God Challenges the Dictators, Doom of Axis Powers Predicted* has been changed from the original 1939 title: *God Challenges the Dictators, Doom of Nazis Predicted* which has been published as a hardback collector's edition and released on 13th February 2020 in commemoration of the seventieth anniversary of Rees Howells' death. This present book was first published as a hardback on 10th October 2020, 141 years to the day when Rees Howells was born in Brynamman.

Chapter 1
1. *Samuel Rees Howells: A Life of Intercession* by Richard Maton, Paul Backholer and Mathew Backholer, ByFaith Media, 2012, 2018, pages 70-71.
2. Compare Proverbs 6:23b and Proverbs 27:5.
3. A prophecy, revelation or prediction can be from God, of the flesh, from the evil one, or a combination of the flesh and the evil one. For warnings and examples of this see: Deuteronomy 13:1-3, 2 Samuel 14:3, 2 Chronicles 18:21-22, Job 32:9, Isaiah 30:1, Jeremiah 14:14, Jeremiah 23:16b, 25-26 and 2 Corinthians 11:4. Jesus warned of false prophets: Matthew 7:15-20, Matthew 24:11, 24 and Luke 6:26, as did the apostles: 2 Peter 2:1, 1 John 4:1 and Revelation 16:3.
4. Prophecy and God's Revelations is based on a chapter in *Prophecy Now, Prophetic Words And Divine Revelations: For You, The Church And The Nations, An End-Time Prophet's Journal* by Michael Backholer, ByFaith Media, 2013, 2017, pages 6-11.

Chapter 2
1. On 15th June 1944, at the 9:45pm service (one of three to four services a day held at the College), Rees Howells acknowledged that 'to save the German nation the Director [Rees Howells] would be willing for God not to make the Divine Intervention. In such an open way, as at first he expected it to be.' The following day at the 7pm service, it was stated, 'the Director is feeling for the people of Germany as he did four years ago for the people of our country [during the blitzes]. An intercession will have to be made for the German nation as Moses made an atonement for the children of Israel. What is the price that will have to be paid?' At the 9:45pm meeting on the same day, the question was asked, 'What intercession does God call for, for Germany to be set free? She is entering into her death now. [The Second Front had begun and 2,000 Allied planes were bombing Nazi-occupied targets every night as well as civilian areas to break the Nazi morale]. Will He tell us what her resurrection is to be?'
2. Rees Howells' liability of over £20,000 relates to a mortgage to buy the 270-acre Penllergaer Estate, guaranteed by the value of less than one of the three other estates in Sketty, Swansea, of: Glynderwen, Sketty Isaf and Derwen Fawr.
3. Each child refugee up to age 16 needed a bank guarantee of £50 per year (£3,250 in 2020), as stated the British government, or a minimum of £100,000 for 2,000 children per annum. For those over 16 it was £100 per year.
4. For more information about Ramallah School see *Samuel, Son and Successor of Rees Howells* by Richard Maton, ByFaith Media, 2012, 2018, pages 78-79, 81 and 83.

Chapter 3

1. *Revival Fires, 150 Years of Revivals, Spiritual Awakenings and Moves of the Holy Spirit* by Mathew Backholer, ByFaith Media, 2010, 2017, pages 39-44.
2. *God Challenges the Dictators – Doom of Nazis Predicted* by Rees Howells, 1939, Simpkin Marshall, Ltd, pages 81, 97 and 101-102.
3. See *Christianity Rediscovered, in Pursuit of God and the Path to Eternal Life: What you Need to Know to Grow, Living the Christian Life with Jesus Christ, Book 1* by Mathew Backholer, ByFaith Media, 2018.
4. *Samuel Rees Howells, A Life of Intercession: The Legacy of Prayer and Spiritual Warfare of an Intercessor* by Richard Maton, Paul Backholer and Mathew Backholer, ByFaith Media, 2012, 2018, pages 10-11.
5. Based on a page in *Samuel, Son and Successor of Rees Howells: Director of the Bible College of Wales, A Biography* by Richard Maton, ByFaith Media, 2012, 2018, page 336.
6. See chapter 32 of *Rees Howells Intercessor* by Norman Grubb, Lutterworth Press, 1952, and *The Intercessions of Rees Howells* by Doris M. Ruscoe, The Lutterworth Press, 1983, 1991, page 17.
7. *The Intercessions of Rees Howells* by Doris M. Ruscoe, The Lutterworth Press, 1983, 1991, pages 18, 20 and 26.
8. To know more about the difference between your surrendered life in God's hands, and the Holy Spirit living His life in your body see: *The Baptism of Fire, Personal Revival, Renewal and the Anointing for Supernatural Living* by Paul Backholer, ByFaith Media, 2017.
9. www.ReesHowells.co.uk and *Rees Howells Intercessor* by Norman Grubb, Lutterworth Press, 1952, chapter 32.
10. *The Intercessions of Rees Howells* by Doris M. Ruscoe, The Lutterworth Press, 1983, 1991, pages 21, 24 and 26. See *Rees Howells Vision Hymns*.
11. The War Office – the military authorities of the Western Command no longer needed more land and buildings in the Swansea area though negotiations had begun. Soldiers were performing training exercises on some fields adjacent to Derwen Fawr and there was a pillbox (reinforced concrete machinegun emplacement) on the Glynderwen Estate next to the stream, close to the Derwen Fawr Road and Blackpill station. There were also rocket launchers at the bottom of Ashleigh Road. At the top end of the road was a side entrance to the Derwen Fawr Estate.
12. See *Samuel Rees Howells: A Life of Intercession* by Richard Maton, Paul Backholer and Mathew Backholer, ByFaith Media, 2012, 2018, chapter 10.
13. *In My Father's Hand, John's Story: An Autobiography by John Kalley Rocha*, privately published, 2013, pages 8-9. See *Rees Howells, Vision Hymns of Spiritual Warfare, Intercessory Declarations* by Mathew Backholer, 2021.

Chapter 4

1. The rest of the quote from Western Mail & Echo Ltd, to Rees Howells from October 1939: 'If bound in stiff cloth, printed title in black, the extra charge for each 10,000 copies will be £175. Enclosed was: Sample of cloth, dummy copy with paper cover enclosed, Annual Report, two specimen books and manuscript returned, and delivered carriage paid to Derwen Fawr.'
2. Rees Howells also sent a book of stamps on a number of occasions to A. J. Russell as portions of the manuscript; different chapters in various stages of revising and correcting were being posted back and forth between Swansea, Wales, and London, England.
3. At the 10pm meeting on 9th October 1942, Rees Howells read excerpts from *God Challenges the Dictators* relating to the Jewish children and the £100,000.

This would have been chapter VI (THE £100,000 PREDICTION: HOMES FOR JEWISH CHILDREN IN WALES AND THE HOLY LAND) and possibly excerpts from chapter IV. He said, "When war broke out I felt like Mordecai." (From the book of Esther). On other occasions Rees Howells read publicly from his book.
4. The solution to German magnetic mines was solved within months by demagnetising them, by girdling them with an electric cable. This was known as 'degaussing' and was applied to all types of ships, military and merchant. It was effective in water over ten fathoms deep. Ships could be degaussed without appreciably delaying their turnaround in most of the major ports, where trained technical staff resided. This work began in the middle of January 1940 and by 9th March 1940, 321 warships and 312 merchant ships were completed with 509 vessels in progress, leaving around 3,150 remaining British ships to be degaussed. The supply of cable initially held up the work and whilst there was talk of using foreign shipping yards this had to be weighed up against the disadvantage of the loss of secrecy. See *The Second World War: Volume I, The Gathering Storm* by Winston Churchill, Cassel & Co. LTD, 1948, chapter XXVIII and Appendix M.
5. This information is from an unpublished document: *Fulfilment of the Doom of the Nazis: Scattering of the Dictators.*

Chapter 5
1. https://trove.nla.gov.au/newspaper/article/42219881. Accessed 24 March 2018.

Chapter 6
1. *Samuel, Son and Successor of Rees Howells: Director of the Bible College of Wales – A Biography* by Richard Maton, ByFaith Media, 2012, 2018, pages 166-167.
2. *Samuel Rees Howells: A Life of Intercession* by Richard Maton, Paul Backholer and Mathew Backholer, ByFaith Media, 2012, 2018, pages 94-95.
3. *The Intercession of Rees Howells*, by Doris M. Ruscoe, Lutterworth Press, 1983, 1991, pages 25-26.
4. *Rees Howells Intercessor* by Norman Grubb, Lutterworth Press, 1952, pages 240-243.

God Challenges the Dictators by Rees Howells

Additional information for Rees Howells' only published book.

Introduction
1. One copy of *God Challenges the Dictators* was owned by a staff member of the Bible College of Wales (BCW) who was present during the war years who passed away more than sixty years later at BCW. Her book revealed that she had pasted in extracts of newspapers columns from during the war and written annotations in the margins aligning what Rees Howells had predicted with what had happened.
2. History records that Adolf Hitler killed himself in a bunker in Berlin, Germany, when he knew that the Nazi régime had been defeated and the allies were closing in.
3. See Epilogue, the Vision was given in December 1934 and the book was published in December 1939, hence five years had elapsed and there were twenty-five years remaining. In 1999, Wycliffe Bible Translators developed and

adopted a project 'Vision 2025' which commenced the following year, where over the next 25 years they planned to translate or to begin to translate the Bible into every language that needed it. It is a *great* vision to have and they have been working hard towards it for the past twenty years, and yet more than 2,100 translations (August 2020) still need to commence.

4. The phrase 'when peace will be upon the earth, and goodwill towards men' is an allusion to the "Christmas" verse in the Bible of Luke 2:14 when the angel of the Lord announced to the shepherds in the fields at night, "For there is born to you this day in the city of David a Saviour, who is Christ the Lord. And this will be the sign to you: You will find a Babe wrapped in swaddling cloths, lying in a manger." And suddenly there was with the angel a multitude of the heavenly host praising God and saying, "Glory to God in the highest, and on earth peace, goodwill toward men!" (Luke 2:11-14).

5. This hymn is the fourth stanza of five of *Who Is On The Lord's Side*, written by Frances Ridley Havergal (1836-1879). She lived in the Caswell district and when Rees and Lizzie Howells were on 'holiday' in the Swansea and Mumbles area in the summer of 1923, they visited the house where she lived and died, on Caswell Avenue, Caswell, Swansea.

Chapter I

1. Czar can also be spelt Tzar and Tsar.

2. See *Revival Fires and Awakenings, Thirty-Six Visitations of the Holy Spirit: A Call to Holiness, Prayer and Intercession for the Nations* by Mathew Backholer, ByFaith Media, 2009, 2017, chapter 3. And *Great Christian Revivals* DVD, ByFaith Media, 2016, which documents the Evangelical Revival (1739-1791), as well as other revivals in the United Kingdom.

3. See *Reformation to Revival, 500 Years of God's Glory: Sixty Revivals, Awakenings and Heaven-Sent Visitations of the Holy Spirit* by Mathew Backholer, ByFaith Media, 2018, chapter 9.

4. Ludwig Müller was a German Theologian who was associated with the Nazis in the 1920s and was appointed Reich Bishop by Adolf Hitler in 1933. As an anti-Christ and anti-Jewish theologian he caused much trouble for Evangelical Christians in Germany and permitted the Gestapo to monitor the churches and youth groups under his care. At the end of the war he took his own life.

5. Martin Niemöller was a u-boat captain in WWI (1914-1918) on a number of vessels and was successful in sinking many British and Allied military and merchant ships. After the war, disillusioned he became a peasant farmer before becoming a Lutheran pastor and quickly rose through the ranks as a popular preacher. He initially embraced Hitler's reforms and had at least two meetings with him to discuss Hitler's views on the Church and reforming Germany. However, as head of the Evangelical Church and because Hitler broke his promises to the Church, Niemöller denounced Nazism in the mid-1930s from his church in Berlin and was arrested in 1937. He was held in two concentration camps from 1938 to 1945. Niemöller was widely known for his poem from 1946 in the German language of which there are several variations in English:

First they came for the socialists, and I did not speak out –
Because I was not a socialist.
Then they came for the trade unionists, and I did not speak out –
Because I was not a trade unionist.
Then they came for the Jews, and I did not speak out –
Because I was not a Jew.
Then they came for me – and there was no one left to speak for me.

Chapter II
1. For more about Martin Luther and the Reformation which began in 1517 in Germany, and spread to other countries across Europe, see *Reformation to Revival, 500 Years of God's Glory: Sixty Revivals, Awakenings and Heaven-Sent Visitations of the Holy Spirit* by Mathew Backholer, ByFaith Media, 2018, chapters 3-5.

Chapter IV
1. See point 3. under Introduction in Sources and Notes.
2. The first two lines of this hymn are the same as *Blessed and Glorious King* by Thomas Hodgson Mundell (1849-1934). However this hymn is probably one composed by Ardis Butterfield, a staff member of the Bible College. She was an anointed singer and songwriter, whose ministry in the Spirit would lift the worship during the dark days of World War II. See *Rees Howells, Vision Hymns*.

Chapter V
1. See point 1. on chapter 2.
2. The Moravians were originally from Bohemia, the native Czechs who had a Reformation in the late fourteenth century under various Bohemian preachers and in the early fifteenth century under John Hus. They were also influenced by the writings of John Wycliff of England and had suffered persecution in Bohemia and Moravia for their Christian beliefs for two centuries until they decided to move. In 1747 and 1749, England passed Acts of Parliament recognising the Moravian fraternity as an ancient Protestant Episcopal Church, and granted it civil and religious privileges at home and in British colonies. There was a revival amongst the Moravian community in 1727 and from that one small village community more than one hundred missionaries went out in twenty-five years. Dr. Warneck, a German historian of Protestant Missions wrote: 'This small church in twenty years called into being more missions than the whole Evangelical Church had done in two centuries.' By 1757, Moravian missionaries were ministering in nearly every country in Europe and they went into Asia, South Africa, Australia and North and South America. For more information about the Moravians, the revival of 1727 and their mission advance see *Global Revival, Worldwide Outpourings, Forty-Three Visitations of the Holy Spirit: The Great Commission* by Mathew Backholer, ByFaith Media, 2010, 2017, chapter 8.
   John Wesley in his *Journal* for 1st January 1739 wrote: 'Mr Hall, Kinchin, Ingham, Whitefield, Hutchins, and my brother Charles, were present at our love-feast in Fetters Lane [in London, England, at a Moravian Society], with about sixty of our brethren. About three in the morning, as we were continuing instant in prayer, the power of God came mightily upon us, insomuch that many cried out for exceeding joy, and many fell to the ground. As soon as we were recovered a little from that awe and amazement, at the presence of His Majesty, we broke out with one voice, "We praise thee, O God, we acknowledge thee to be the Lord." ' Fetters Lane is now known as Fetter Lane in EC4 London. On this site was the above revival and a Moravian Congregation was founded there on 10th November 1742. It became the Moravian Headquarters in 1872 and was destroyed in an air-raid on 11th May 1941.
3. The phrase 'we must build Jerusalem in England's green and pleasant land' is an allusion to William Blake's poem *And Did Those Feet in Ancient Time* (c.1808), as part of his Preface to his epic *Milton: A Poem in Two Books*. It is better known as the hymn, *Jerusalem* with music (1916) by Sir Hubert Parry. The first and last stanzas are:

And did those feet in ancient time,
Walk upon England's mountains green:
And was the holy Lamb of God,
On England's pleasant pastures seen!

I will not cease from mental fight,
Nor shall my sword sleep in my hand:
Till we have built Jerusalem,
In England's green and pleasant Land.

Chapter VI

1. On 18th September 1947, Mr Grunhut of Vienna, Austria, stayed at the Bible College of Wales (BCW) for a holiday, reported a local newspaper. Twice Mr Grunhut escaped the gas chamber in a Polish concentration camp – forty-two of his relatives died in the Holocaust including his own parents. His two children came to Britain as refugees and the Bible College of Wales raised them – Herbert (the baby in the basket) and his older brother, Ervin. Herbert "Bert" Grunhut was a regular visitor to the Bible College and its grounds and died in January 2019 in his eightieth year. The funeral service was held at Siloam Baptist Church, Killay, Swansea, less than three miles away from BCW.

2. Before the Lord Jesus Christ can return to earth, the Second Coming, Jesus said, "This Gospel of the Kingdom shall be preached in all the world for a witness unto all nations; and then shall the end come" (Matthew 24:14). For Rees Howells, if the Every Creature Commission could be completed in thirty years, a generation, or twenty-five years in 1939 as the clock was counting, then there could not be anything hindering the Lord's return, to begin His Millennial Reign on earth. It was Rees Howells' logical conclusion: If this happens (Every Creature) then this can happen (Second Coming). Peter wrote: 'Looking for and *hastening* the coming of the day of God…' (2 Peter 3:12). We can hasten or speed up the Second Coming by reaching the unevangelised of every tribe, tongue, people group and nation, who will stand before the throne of God (Revelation 5:9). Also see point 3 below.

3. When Rees Howells was writing in 1939, the Jews had not yet returned to the Holy Land (another condition for the Second Coming), the Land of Promise, the land of Israel as a nation, when the Nation of Israel was 'born in a day' (Isaiah 66:8) in May 1948. "Then the Lord thy God will turn thy captivity, and have compassion upon thee, and will return and gather thee from all the nations, whither the Lord thy God hath scattered thee" (Deuteronomy 30:3). *The Times* newspaper for 19th September 1938 notes:

> An application is to be made to the Home Secretary to permit the Bible College of Wales at Swansea to accept 40 young Jewish refugees aged between 18 and 20. It is proposed to teach them languages and send them to the Holy Land after three years.

Three years training at the Bible College of Wales was standard. Rees Howells actively and firmly believed in 'hastening the coming day of God' (2 Peter 3:12) and assisting in the re-gathering of Jews back to the Holy Land (Isaiah 49:22, Isaiah 43:6, Jeremiah 23:3 and Jeremiah 30:3). The 'sons of the promise' would be introduced to Jesus Christ the Messiah at the Bible College of Wales (age 18+) or the Bible School (ages 5-18) and it was hoped that they would go to the Holy Land to evangelise and 'prepare the way for the Lord,' as John the Baptist did, calling people to "repent" and look for the coming Messiah.

The newspaper headline from the *Western Mail*, 18th December 1939 stated:

> Bible College Wants Refugees – Jews Instead of Spaniards

Application has been made to the Home Office by the Bible College of Wales, Swansea, for permission to take 20 Jewish refugees who have written from Germany, Austria, and Italy. Among them are four doctors. The College authorities have also asked Swansea Corporation [the Council] for tenancy of the mansion [at Penllergaer] used to house Spanish refugee children, so that it may be used for further Jewish refugees. The College hopes to be able to house 100 refugees. Rev. Rees Howells, College Director, states that a woman in the Holy Land who had read of the prediction from the Bible College that there would be no war, was so stirred that she wrote to him offering terms for taking over a hotel and sanatorium in the Holy Land, for a College and Hospital for Jewish refugees. Mr Howells says he will go to the Holy Land to negotiate for the property and also to try to purchase land for these refugees.

It is important to stress that Rees Howells wanted Jewish refugees as opposed to Spanish ones because the Jews were most at risk from Hitler's wrath and genocide. There were Spanish refugees at the Bible College of Wales' Bible School, later known as Emmanuel Grammar School. In March 1937, Evangelist Parillo from Spain and their four children (Alejandro, Guillermo, Margarita and Elia) found a refuge at BCW. His wife and baby later joined them.

Chapter VII
1. Rees Howells' quote 'to build the largest Bible College by prayer and faith alone,' (my emphasis) can be interpreted in several ways. In 1939, when God Challenges the Dictators was written, Rees Howells owned 270 acres at Penllergaer, Swansea district, and 50 acres at the three sites of Glynderwen, Sketty Isaf and Derwen Fawr at Sketty, Swansea. This is a total of 320 acres, making it the largest Bible College in Britain, (which in addition was run by prayer and faith alone). Also, in 1929 there were 130+ students in residence, 140 students in residence in another year, 90 students in 1935 and in 1936 they had received more than 100 applicants. No other College in Britain had this many students thus making it the 'largest Bible College' in Britain based on the student body. In 1939 there were 95 members of staff, the largest number of staff at any Bible College in Britain, though this included staff for the School etc. whilst some staff members had duties in the College and the School. 20 out of the 95 staff had degrees (very important in academia) and were on the educational side. There were also five qualified doctors because the College had its own Hospital and taught tropical medicine and healthcare for the mission field. The Hospital was commandeered during World War II to help with casualties of the war.

Rees Howells from the Twelfth Session Annual Report of 1936, wrote:
While there is a dearth of students in most Colleges, the Bible College of Wales cannot accommodate all the applicants [my emphasis]. Last year [1935] there were 90 students in residence and over 30 of them joined the same Mission, the Worldwide Evangelization Crusade (WEC), and others went to Japan, China etc. More than a hundred applicants for this new term have been accepted, and others are asked to wait until the New Year. (My emphasis).

In chapter VII of God Challenges the Dictators, Rees Howells wrote:
Thus was founded [my emphasis] the largest College of its kind in the country, with, at one time, more than one hundred and forty students in residence.... it is only desired to show here how the prediction of building the largest Bible College in the country by prayer and faith alone was fulfilled. (My emphasis).

In addition, two local newspapers the *Evening Post* and the *Western Mail* published an article in January 1932 which stated:
The College is one of the strongest and most impressive examples of faith manifested by works in modern religious history.
Chapter IX of *God Challenges the Dictators*.
In addition, Rees Howells commissioned the architect D. Glyn Williams of Swansea in early 1934 to draw up designs for two student blocks, one to accommodate 700 men and the other for 300 women. Rees Howells had his sights set on accommodation for 1,000 students and was inspired by the 900-student, Moody Bible Institute in Chicago, America, when Rees and Lizzie Howells visited in and around spring 1923. This was their third trip to America, having done deputation work for the South African General Mission in 1920.
2. The· *South African Pioneer* (Nov. 1916) notes Rees and Lizzie Howells' employment was from 1914. After nearly two years of preparation and training at separate establishments, they left Britain for the mission field in July 1915.

Chapter IX
1. The Bible College of Wales (BCW) was incorrectly known by a number of names including Blackpill Bible College, Swansea Bible College and Wales Bible College all of which denote the location of the College. Early postcards called the Glynderwen site: Blackpill Bible College or Blackpyl Bible College. The Glynderwen Estate was on the boundary of Blackpill and Sketty (though technically within Blackpill) depending on which entrance you used to access the grounds. Derwen Fawr and Sketty Isaf, were a five minute walk away and were firmly located in (lower) Sketty, however, some early postcards have a photo of the Derwen Fawr Mansion, with 'Bible College – Derwen Fawr Blackpill' in white text written on the front of the postcards. Mail sent from the United Kingdom and abroad (e.g. Thailand) to BCW was sometimes sent to other Bible Colleges in Wales; some were redirected to BCW whilst others were returned to the sender. Samuel Rees Howells sent 100s of letters annually to former students, staff and workers at other Christian organisations. On occasions, those on the mission field (or in the UK) who wrote to thank Samuel Rees Howells had their mail sent to another Bible College in Wales, some mail was forwarded to BCW at Swansea. Some overseas people would have "South Wales" on the bottom of their envelope instead of United Kingdom or Great Britain and one Christian worker had his mail sent to New South Wales (having written South Wales at the bottom) and redirected back to his home in America!
2. Rees and Lizzie Howells saw Niagara Falls when they visited America on a private trip in and around spring 1923. They had a studio photo taken of themselves at the "Falls," this was the driest and clearest option!

Chapter X
1. The phrase and statement: 'The Waves and the Winds beat upon the Rock of Faith but the Rock stands firm, serenely confident. For is it not the Rock of Ages?' is an allusion to the Parable of the Wise and Foolish Builder (Matthew 7:24-27 and Luke 6:46-49). God is known as a Rock (Deuteronomy 32:4, 18, 31, 1 Samuel 2:2, 2 Samuel 22:2, 32, 2 Samuel 23:3, Psalm 18:46 and Psalm 28:1). Jesus Christ is also known as a Rock (Romans 9:33, 1 Corinthians 10:4 and 1 Peter 2:8). In addition, *Rock of Ages* is also the title of a hymn by August Toplady, written in 1763, as he sheltered in the cleft of a rock at Burrington Combe during a storm. The hymn was based on Psalm 94:22 and was first published in 1775. This cleft in a rock in the Mendipp Hills is now known as Rock of Ages and has a plaque in place retelling this famous incident.

The Psalmist declared, "But the Lord is my defence; and my God is the Rock of my refuge" (Psalm 94:22). Jesus said: "And why call ye Me, Lord, Lord, and do not the things which I say? Whosoever cometh to Me, and heareth my sayings, and doeth them, I will shew you to whom he is like. He is like a man which built a house, and digged deep, and laid the foundation on a rock: and when the flood arose, the stream beat vehemently upon that house, and could not shake it: for it was founded upon a rock. But he that heareth, and doeth not, is like a man that without a foundation built a house upon the earth; against which the stream did beat vehemently, and immediately it fell; and the ruin of that house was great" (Luke 6:46-49).

2. The Bible College in Paris was called Maison de l'Evangile (The Gospel House) in Bois-de-Boulogne, Paris, France. Originally it was known by the Bible College of Wales as the Wakefield Bible College after a previous owner Thomas Wakefield Richardson. It cost Rees Howells the equivalent of £10,000 to buy in 1938 (£674,400 in 2020, though the value of the property is considerably more) and officially became BCW property in January 1939. See *Samuel, Son and Successor of Rees Howells: Director of the Bible College of Wales – A Biography* by Richard Maton, ByFaith Media, 2012, 2018, chapter 24. Within the book by Richard Maton are additional references to other Colleges and organisations which were associated to or had ties to the Bible College of Wales (BCW) in Beirut, Lebanon and Ramallah in the Holy Land.

In addition, some former BCW students and staff were sent regular financial gifts (three to six times a year appears standard) by Rees Howells and then under his son, Samuel Rees Howells. Some of these former students founded training organisations or ministries which were often seen as extensions of BCW, being founded and run along the same principles of the 'life of faith' and the 'Every Creature Commission.' Jesus said, "Go and make disciples of all nations" (Matthew 28:19). Finances from BCW were sent to other Bible Colleges and Training Centres in the United Kingdom and abroad. Rees Howells in *God Challenges the Dictators* wrote:

> The Lord is going to prepare hundreds of young people, who, after spending three or four years in the Bible College of Wales, will go out and found Colleges in every country to reach Every Creature; men and women.... Then, instead of only a few missionaries and native workers, working on lonely stations, there will be thousands (including natives), trained in the Colleges, available for missionary work. (Chapter XIII).

Chapter XI
1. See footnote 4. under chapter XII in Sources and Notes.
2. The phrase 'for Him who commanded His thoughtless disciples to let the little ones come unto Him' is an allusion to an incident recorded in the Bible with Jesus, His disciples and multiple parents bringing their young children for Him to bless them. 'Then little children were brought to Him that He might put His hands on them and pray, but the disciples rebuked them. However, Jesus said, "Let the little children come to Me, and do not forbid them; for of such is the Kingdom of Heaven." And He laid His hands on them and departed from there' (Matthew 19:13-15).

Chapter XII
1. Jerry McAuley (1839-1884), along with his wife Maria, founded the Walter Street Mission in New York City in October 1872. It was America's first Rescue Mission, originally known as Helping Hand for Men based at 316 Walter Street,

and is now known as the New York City Rescue Mission. Jerry McAuley was a self-described "rogue and street thief" who in the late 1850s was sentenced to spend fourteen years in Sing Sing Prison in Ossining, New York. He was the son of a counterfeiter from Ireland who fled home, and Jerry aged thirteen was sent to America to live with his older sister. He 'worked' with gangs to survive and was eventually caught and sentenced in 1857. He was converted in prison by reading his Bible and through the visits of a lady missionary who shared the Good News with him. The power of Jesus Christ transformed his life so much that he was released after serving seven years and two months, less than half his time. His Rescue Mission at 316 Walter Street held nightly meetings in the slum area of New York and anybody and everybody was allowed to enter, however drunk, dirty or smelly. The power of Christ to save and transform was preached, testimonies were given and there was singing to rouse the souls of those present.

2. These are two stanzas from the hymn *Under His Wings* by James L. Nicholson and can be found in *Sacred Songs and Solos* by I. D. Sankey, 1878. The hymn is also known as *In God I have Found a Retreat* from its first line.

3. The phrase "Where He leads Me I Will Follow" is a missionary adage and is used in two hymns (Lou W. Wilson's *I'll Follow Where He Leads* and George W. Collins' *I Have Heard My Savior calling*, and is the refrain in a third hymn, E. W. Blandy's *Where He Leads Me*. Many short-term missioners (STM-ers) add as a second line: "What He feeds Me I Will Swallow." For STMs see *Short-Term Missions, A Christian Guide to STMs* by Mathew Backholer, ByFaith Media, 2016.

4. The Founders only child whom they left behind in Wales when they went to Africa was Samuel. If they had taken him to Africa he would have probably died of malaria or some fever. Africa was known as the "White Man's Graveyard" for a very good reason. The author first met Samuel, this man of God, when Samuel was in his 80s and his story is told in: *Samuel, Son and Successor of Rees Howells: Director of the Bible College of Wales – A Biography* by Richard Maton, ByFaith Media, 2012, 2018, and *Samuel Rees Howells A Life of Intercession: The Legacy of Prayer and Spiritual Warfare of an Intercessor* by Richard Maton, Paul Backholer and Mathew Backholer, ByFaith Media, 2012, 2018.

5. See footnote 1. under chapter VI in Sources and Notes.

6. The Home of Rest for Missionaries was in Sketty Isaf whilst the Hospital in which to nurse missionaries was on the Derwen Fawr Estate. These two sites were opposite each other and divided by the Derwen Fawr Road. The Home of Rest for Missionaries was often full and priority for the Hospital was for missionaries. By November 1937 there were around 250 school children at the School and 120 resident students at the Bible College, so very full. Below are excerpts of three letters from April and November 1937, and May 1943.

Evan and Florence Howells (no relation), missionaries to Angola, Africa, wrote to Rees Howells as they were on furlough, desiring to visit, and received a reply by return of post on 14th April 1937:

Dear Mr and Mrs Howells, delighted to hear that you are back in the country…. We shall be very pleased to see you when you come this way. There is always a "Prophet's Chamber" for the Missionaries, so please send me a card when you will be coming. With Christian greetings, yours sincerely, [Rees Howells].

In a letter to Dublin, Ireland, dated 30th November 1937, Rees Howells wrote: Your letter to hand regarding your sister. We regret that the Missionary Home and College are both very full, just now and it will be impossible for anyone to give personal attention to your sister. Nearly every bed is taken up, and although we have to give *a great deal of attention to the missionaries who come back on furlough and are sick*, [my emphasis] but the nurses are giving their attention to them, so that when your sister comes it would be advisable for someone to come with her. So under the circumstances it would perhaps be better for your sister to come later on, as the winter is really the worst time. Yours Sincerely, [Rees Howells].

In a letter, dated 22nd May 1943, Rees Howells wrote to Corporal C. Workman of Shrewsbury, England, and mentions an 86-year-old missionary to Japan, Miss Evans, who 'is enjoying the provision that the Lord has made for her' in the Missionary Home.

7. Many children were born in the College Hospital. This was pre-NHS when healthcare had to be paid for across Britain. After World War II, as a thank you to the nation for the sacrifices that had been made, the National Health Service which became known as the NHS sprang into being and seeing a doctor or receiving medical attention in a NHS Hospital was free.

8. This couple came to BCW in and around the mid-1930s under Rees Howells' leadership. In mid-1964, they were missionaries in South Rhodesia and under the leadership of Samuel Rees Howells he was sending them financial support.

9. Rees Howells intended to build a 'large Hospital, for two hundred patients...on the new estate, Penllergaer,' but this never happened. American officers (and soldiers) were based at Penllergaer from 1943 and officers lived in the Big House, the Mansion was badly damaged during their stay. As examples: Chunks of marble were smashed from the twin marble staircase, presumably by dragging heavy objects like metal filing cabinets down or up them! Whilst the brick astronomical observatory built in 1846, from where some of the earliest photos of the moon (1857) were taken was used as target practice! Evidence of the bullet marks can still be seen in this preserved and recently renovated, historical building.

Chapter XIII

1. See footnote 2. under chapter X in Sources and Notes.

2. The phrase 'Peace at Eventide' means a 'Literary Evening,' an old fashioned phrase for the last section in a book.

3. On 7th November 1945, Rees Howells wrote to Rev. S. H. Dixon in Edinburgh House, London. In part of the letter he wrote: 'I also said in the book [*God Challenges the Dictators*] that as a thank-offering for victory over the dictators and those systems, that I was to give £100,000 to build Colleges and Schools in the Holy Land. All I need today to get this £100,000 is to sell one of the estates and it will be in my hands to give. Although since the book was written I have been led of the Lord to give Penllergaer Mansion and 54 acres of land to the war orphans. The Mansion itself is valued at £20,000 [£864,900 in 2020, and I am giving it as a gift to Barnardo's.' However, even this did not happen due to Barnardo's declining the Mansion and 54 acres of land. See chapter 8, footnote 4. In 1939, the Mansion was valued by insurers at £30,000 [£2,022,000 in 2020] and premiums had to be paid based on this valuation.

4. 'The sands of time are sinking, The dawn of Heaven breaks' was originally a poem of 19 stanzas by Ann Ross Cousin and was first published in *The Christian Treasury* (1857). Rees Howells quoted a single stanza of what became a hymn entitled *The Sands of Time Are Sinking* popular with just six stanzas.

End of Sources and Notes from
God Challenges the Dictators **by Rees Howells**

Continuation of Sources and Notes

Rees Howells' God Challenges the Dictators, Doom of Axis Powers Predicted: Victory for Christian England and Release of Europe Through Intercession and Spiritual Warfare, Bible College of Wales by Mathew Backholer

Chapter 8
1. *Blitz Cities. 4. Cardiff*, with John Humphrys, BBC, 10 September 2015 and *Dylan Remembered, Volume 1: 1934-53* by David N. Thomas, Seren Publishing, 2004, page 92.
2. *Emmanuel Magazine*, Number 46, December 1991, pages 37 and 39.
3. The five Bible Lands that Rees Howells referred to are: Israel, Ethiopia, Syria, Babylon (present-day Iraq) and Persia (present-day Iran). Other Arab nations are presently inside the geographical area encompassed by the Babylonian and Persian Empires.
4. Barnardo's looked at the Penllergaer Mansion and 54 acres and stated that it would be too expensive for them to convert it into a children's home. In addition, large children's homes were becoming a thing of the past, giving way to smaller groups of children in family friendly styled settings. In a sermon from spring 1944 Rees Howells spoke about a building that Barnardo's had bought in Lyndhurst to house 40 children, but the Council would not permit them to use it as a home. However, in the previous year, the Annesley Bank Barnardo's Home in Pinkney Lane, Lyndhurst, Hampshire was opened, Barnardo's having obtained it in 1939. http://www.childrenshomes.org.uk/LyndhurstDB/. Accessed 12 October 2019. There was a Barnardo's Home in Shaftsbury House, Swansea for 'little boys' which was opened in 1902. *Memoirs of the Late Dr Barnardo* by Syrie Louise Elmsie Barnardo, 1907.

Chapter 10
1. See *The Holy Spirit in a Man: Spiritual Warfare, Intercession, Faith, Healings and Miracles in the Modern World* by R. B. Watchman, ByFaith Media, 2015, pages 8 and 196.
2. For more about overcomers see: *Ibid,* chapter 35.

Chapter 11
1. See *How Christianity Made the Modern World, The Legacy of Christian Liberty: How the Bible Inspired Freedom, Shaped Western Civilization, Revolutionized Human Rights and Transformed Democracy* by Paul Backholer, ByFaith Media, 2009, 2016.
2. *The Holy Spirit in a Man: Spiritual Warfare, Intercession, Faith, Healings and Miracles in the Modern World* by R. B. Watchman. ByFaith Media, 2015, pages 7-8 and 106-107.

Epilogue
1. *Rees Howells Intercessor* by Norman Grubb, Lutterworth Press, 1952, page 234.
2. *Samuel, Son and Successor of Rees Howells: Director of the Bible College of Wales – A Biography* by Richard Maton, ByFaith Media, 2012, 2018, page 179.

www.ByFaithBooks.org

ByFaith Media Books

The following ByFaith Media books are available as paperbacks and eBooks, whilst some are available as hardbacks.

Biography and Autobiography
9781907066-14-6. *Samuel, Son and Successor of Rees Howells: Director of the Bible College of Wales – A Biography* by Richard Maton. The life of Samuel and his ministry at the College and the support he received from numerous staff and students as the history of BCW unfolds. With 113 black and white photos. Hardback 9781907066-36-8.

9781907066-41-2. *The Holy Spirit in a Man: Spiritual Warfare, Intercession, Faith, Healings and Miracles* by R. B. Watchman. One man's compelling journey of faith and intercession, a remarkable modern day story of miracles and faith to inspire and encourage. (One chapter relates to the Bible College of Wales and Watchman's visit).

Christian Teaching and Inspirational
9781907066-13-9. *Samuel Rees Howells A Life of Intercession: The Legacy of Prayer and Spiritual Warfare of an Intercessor* by Richard Maton, Paul Backholer and Mathew Backholer is an in-depth look at the intercessions of Samuel Rees Howells alongside the faith principles that he learnt from his father, Rees Howells, and under the leading and guidance of the Holy Spirit. With 39 black and white photographs. Hardback 9781907066-37-5.

9781907066-35-1. *Jesus Today, Daily Devotional: 100 Days with Jesus Christ* by Paul Backholer. One hundred days of two minutes of Christian inspiration to draw you closer to God to encourage and inspire. Have you ever wished you could have sat at Jesus' feet and heard Him speak? *Jesus Today* is a concise daily devotional defined by Jesus' teaching and how His life can change ours. See the world from God's perspective, learn who Jesus was, what He preached and what it means to live abundantly in Christ.

9781907066-33-7. *Holy Spirit Power: Knowing the Voice, Guidance and Person of the Holy Spirit* by Paul Backholer. Power for Christian living; drawing from the powerful influences of many Christian leaders, including: Rees Howells, Evan Roberts, D. L. Moody, Duncan Campbell and other channels of God's Divine fire.

9781907066-43-6. *Tares and Weeds in Your Church: Trouble & Deception in God's House, the End Time Overcomers* by R. B. Watchman. Is there a battle taking place in your house, church or ministry, leading to division? Tares and weeds are counterfeit Christians used to sabotage Kingdom work; learn how to recognise them and neutralise them in the power of the Holy Spirit.

9781907066-56-6. *The Baptism of Fire, Personal Revival, Renewal and the Anointing for Supernatural Living* by Paul Backholer. Jesus will baptise you with the Holy Spirit and fire; that was the promise of John the Baptist. But what is the baptism of fire and how can you experience it? The author unveils the life and ministry of the Holy Spirit, shows how He can transform your life and what supernatural living in Christ means.

Historical and Biblical Adventure plus Archaeology
9781907066-95-5. *Rees Howells, Vision Hymns of Spiritual Warfare & Intercessory Declarations: World War II Songs of Victory, Intercession, Praise and Worship, Israel and the Every Creature Commission* by Mathew Backholer. A rare insight into the prophetic declarations, hymns and choruses used in spiritual warfare by Rees Howells and his team of intercessors at the Bible College of Wales. Spanning the pivotal years of 1936-1948 and brought to life for the first time in more than seventy years. With thirty-one digitally enhanced black and white photos.

9781907066-76-4. Hardback collector's edition. *God Challenges the Dictators, Doom of the Nazis Predicted: The Destruction of the Third Reich Foretold by the Director of Swansea Bible College, An Intercessor from Wales* by Rees Howells and Mathew Backholer. Available for the first time in 80 years – fully annotated and reformatted with twelve digitally enhanced black and white photos. Discover how Rees Howells built a large ministry by faith in times of economic chaos and learn from the predictions he made during times of national crisis, of the destruction of the Third Reich, the end of fascism and the liberation of Christian Europe during World War II.

9781907066-78-8. *Rees Howells' God Challenges the Dictators, Doom of Axis Powers Predicted: Victory for Christian England and Release of Europe Through Intercession and Spiritual Warfare, Bible College of Wales* by Mathew Backholer. This is the story behind the story of *God Challenges the Dictators* (GCD), Rees Howells' only published book, before, during and after publication which is centred around World War II. Read how extracts of GCD were aired over occupied parts of Europe, and how Hitler and leading Nazi officials were sent copies in 1940! The book includes letters to Winston Churchill and Press Releases from Rees Howells and how he sent copies of his book to Prime Ministers plus government officials, and what the newspapers had to say.

9781907066-45-0. *Britain, A Christian Country, A Nation Defined by Christianity and the Bible & the Social Changes that Challenge this Biblical Heritage* by Paul Backholer. For more than 1,000 years Britain was defined by Christianity, with monarch's dedicating the country to God and national days of prayer. Discover this continuing legacy, how faith defined its nationhood and the challenges from the 1960s till today.

9781907066-02-3. *How Christianity Made the Modern World* by Paul Backholer. Christianity is the greatest reforming force that the world has ever known, yet its legacy is seldom comprehended. But now, using personal observations and worldwide research the author brings this legacy alive by revealing how Christianity helped create the path that led to Western liberty and laid the foundations of the modern world.

9781907066-47-4. *Celtic Christianity & the First Christian Kings in Britain: From St. Patrick and St. Columba, to King Ethelbert and King Alfred* by Paul Backholer. Celtic Christians ignited a Celtic Golden Age of faith and light which spread into Europe. Discover this striking history and what we can learn from the heroes of Celtic Christianity.

9781907066-52-8. *Lost Treasures of the Bible: Exploration and Pictorial Travel Adventure of Biblical Archaeology* by Paul Backholer. Unveil ancient mysteries as you discover the evidence for Israel's exodus from Egypt, and travel into lost civilisations in search of the Ark of the Covenant. Explore lost worlds with over 160 colour photos and pictures.

978178822-000-2. *The Exodus Evidence In Pictures – The Bible's Exodus: The Hunt for Ancient Israel in Egypt, the Red Sea, the Exodus Route and Mount Sinai* by Paul Backholer. Two brothers and explorers, Paul and Mathew Backholer search for archaeological data to validate the biblical account of Joseph, Moses and the Hebrew Exodus from ancient Egypt. With more than 100 full colour photos and graphics!

978178822-001-9. *The Ark of the Covenant – Investigating the Ten Leading Claims* by Paul Backholer. Join two explorers as they investigate the ten major theories concerning the location of antiquities greatest relic. Combining an on-site travel journal with 80+ colour photographs through Egypt, Ethiopia and beyond.

Revivals and Spiritual Awakenings
9781907066-01-6. *Revival Fires and Awakenings, Thirty-Six Visitations of the Holy Spirit: A Call to Holiness, Prayer and Intercession for the Nations* by Mathew Backholer. With thirty-six fascinating accounts of revivals in nineteen countries from six continents, plus biblical teaching on revival, prayer and intercession. Hardback 9781907066-38-2.

9781907066-07-8. *Global Revival, Worldwide Outpourings, Forty-Three Visitations of the Holy Spirit: The Great Commission* by Mathew Backholer. How revivals are birthed and the fascinating links between pioneering missionaries and the revivals that they saw as they worked towards the Great Commission, with forty-three accounts of revivals.

9781907066-00-9. *Understanding Revival and Addressing the Issues it Provokes* by Mathew Backholer. Everything you need to know about revival and its phenomena. How to work with the Holy Spirit to see God rend the Heavens and pour out His Spirit on a dry and thirsty land and how not to be taken in by the enemy and his counterfeit tricks, delusions and imitations.

9781907066-06-1. *Revival Fire, 150 Years of Revivals, Spiritual Awakenings and Moves of the Holy Spirit* by Mathew Backholer. This book documents in detail, twelve revivals from ten countries on five continents. Be inspired, encouraged and challenged.

9781907066-15-3. *Revival Answers, True and False Revivals, Genuine or Counterfeit Do not be Deceived* by Mathew Backholer. What is genuine revival and how can we tell the true from the spurious? Drawing from Scripture with examples across Church history, this book will sharpen your senses and take you on a journey of discovery.

9781907066-60-3. *Reformation to Revival, 500 Years of God's Glory: Sixty Revivals Awakenings and Heaven-Sent visitations of the Holy Spirit* by Mathew Backholer. *Reformation to Revival* traces the Divine thread of God's power from Martin Luther of 1517, through to the Charismatic Movement and into the twenty-first century.

Christian Discipleship
9781907066-16-0. *Extreme Faith, On Fire Christianity: Hearing from God and Moving in His Grace, Strength & Power – Living in Victory* by Mathew Backholer. Discover the powerful biblical foundations for on-fire faith in Christ! This book explores biblical truths and routines to shake your world.

9781907066-62-7. *Christianity Rediscovered, in Pursuit of God and the Path to Eternal Life: What you Need to Know to Grow, Living the Christian Life with Jesus Christ, Book 1* by Mathew Backholer. Since the beginning of time mankind has asked, "Why am I alive, does my life matter and is there an afterlife I can prepare for?" *Christianity Rediscovered* has the answers and will help you find meaning, focus, clarity and peace.

9781907066-12-2. *Discipleship For Everyday Living, Christian Growth: Following Jesus Christ and Making Disciples of All Nations* by Mathew Backholer. Engaging biblical teaching to aid Christian believers in maturity, to help make strong disciples with solid biblical foundations who reflect the image of Jesus Christ.

Short-Term Missions (Christian Travel with a Purpose)
9781907066-49-8. *Short-Term Missions, A Christian Guide to STMs: For Leaders, Pastors, Churches, Students, STM Teams and Mission Organizations – Survive and Thrive!* by Mathew Backholer. A concise guide to Short-Term Missions (STMs). What you need to know about planning a STM, or joining a STM team, and considering the options as part of the Great Commission, from the Good News to good works.

9781907066-05-4. *How to Plan, Prepare and Successfully Complete Your Short-Term Mission For Churches, Independent STM Teams and Mission Organizations* by Mathew Backholer. This book will guide you through all you need to know about STMs and includes: mission statistics, cultural issues, where and when to go, what to do and pack, food, accommodation, and more than 140 real-life STM testimonies.

Supernatural and Spiritual
9781907066-58-0. *Glimpses of Glory, Revelations in the Realms of God Beyond the Veil in the Heavenly Abode: The New Jerusalem and the Eternal Kingdom of God* by Paul Backholer. Find a world beyond earth which is real, vivid and eternal. A gripping read!

9781907066-18-4. *Prophecy Now, Prophetic Words and Divine Revelations for You, the Church and the Nations* by Michael Backholer. An enlightening end-time prophetic journal of visions, prophecies and words from the Holy Spirit to God's people, the Church and the nations.

9781907066-80-1. *Heaven, Paradise is Real, Hope Beyond Death: An Angelic Pilgrimage to Your Future Home* by Paul Backholer. Come on a journey to another world of eternal bliss, joy and light, in this enchanting narrative which pulls you in and shows you heaven. Meet those who have gone before into paradise and found eternal peace. Enter into the heavenly Jerusalem, with a man and an angelic guide to discover the truth about immortality, the afterlife and the joy of eternity.

Budget Travel – Vacation/Holiday
9781907066-54-2. *Budget Travel, a Guide to Travelling on a Shoestring, Explore the World, a Discount Overseas Adventure Trip: Gap Year, Backpacking, Volunteer-Vacation and Overlander* by Mathew Backholer. *Budget Travel* is a practical and concise guide to travelling the world and exploring new destinations with fascinating opportunities.

9781907066-74-0. *Travel the World and Explore for Less than $50 a Day, the Essential Guide: Your Budget Backpack Global Adventure, from Two Weeks to a Gap Year, Solo or with Friends* by Mathew Backholer. A practical guide for the solo backpacker or with friends that will save you time and money, with ideas and need-to-know information.

ByFaith Media DVDs

Revivals and Spiritual Awakenings
9781907066-03-0. *Great Christian Revivals* on 1 DVD is an inspirational and uplifting account of some of the greatest revivals in Church history. Filmed on location across Britain and beyond, and drawing upon archive information and rare images, the stories of the Welsh Revival (1904-1905), the Hebridean Revival (1949-1952) and the Evangelical Revival (1739-1791) are brought to life in this moving 72-minute documentary. Using computer animation, historic photos and depictions, the events of the past are weaved into the present, to bring these Heaven-sent revivals to life.

Christian Travel (Backpacking Short-Term Missions)
9781907066-04-7. *ByFaith – World Mission* on 1 DVD is a Christian reality TV show that reveals the real experience of backpacking short-term missions in Asia, Europe and North Africa. Two brothers, Paul and Mathew Backholer shoot through fourteen nations, in an 85-minute real-life documentary. Filmed over three years, *ByFaith – World Mission* is the best of ByFaith TV season one.

Historical and Adventure
9781907066-09-2. *Israel in Egypt – The Exodus Mystery* on 1 DVD. A four year quest searching for Joseph, Moses and the Hebrew slaves in Egypt. Join brothers Paul and Mathew Backholer as they hunt through ancient relics and explore the mystery of the biblical exodus, hunt for the Red Sea and climb Mount Sinai. Discover the first reference to Israel outside of the Bible, uncover depictions of people with multicoloured coats, encounter the Egyptian records of slaves making bricks and find lost cities. 110 minutes. The best of *ByFaith – In Search of the Exodus*.

9781907066-10-0. *ByFaith – Quest for the Ark of the Covenant* on 1 DVD. Join two adventurers on their quest for the Ark, beginning at Mount Sinai where it was made, to Pharaoh Tutankhamun's tomb, where Egyptian treasures evoke the majesty of the Ark. The quest proceeds onto the trail of Pharaoh Shishak, who raided Jerusalem. The mission continues up the River Nile to find a lost temple, with clues to a mysterious civilization. Crossing through the Sahara Desert, the investigators enter the underground rock churches of Ethiopia, find a forgotten civilization and examine the enigma of the final resting place of the Ark itself. 100+ minutes.

www.ByFaithDVDs.org

Byfaith Media Downloads and Streaming

The following ByFaith Media productions are based on the DVDs from the previous page and are available to download: to buy, rent or to stream via Amazon.

Revivals and Spiritual Awakenings
Glorious Christian Revival and Holy Spirit Awakenings: The Welsh, Hebridean and Evangelical Revivals, Evan Roberts, Duncan Campbell and John Wesley. 1 hour 12 minutes. Discover the Welsh Revival (1904-1905), the Hebridean Revival (1949-1952) and the Evangelical Revival (1739-1791), with Evan Roberts, Duncan Campbell, John and Charles Wesley, George Whitefield and others. Filmed on location across the UK and beyond. B07N2N762J (UK). B07P1TVY6W (USA).

Christian Travel (Backpacking Short-Term Missions)
Short-Term Mission Adventures, A Global Christian Missionary STM Expedition with brothers Mathew and Paul Backholer. 1 hour 15 minutes. The mission begins when two adventurers land in Asia, a continent of maximum extremes. After overcoming culture shock and difficult travel, the adventurous missionaries preach in the slums. From India they strike out into Nepal, Bangladesh, Thailand, Myanmar, Cambodia and Vietnam. The mission also touches down in the great cities of Europe: London, Paris, Rome, Dublin, Frankfurt & Amsterdam. B07N2PVZZK (UK). B07PNSWBKN (USA).

Historical and Adventure
The Bible's Lost Ark of the Covenant: Where Is It? Egypt, Ethiopia or Israel? With brothers Mathew and Paul Backholer. 1 hour 10 minutes. The Ark of the Covenant was the greatest treasure in Solomon's Temple, but when Jerusalem fell the Ark vanished from history. Now join two adventurers on their quest for the Ark of the Covenant, beginning at Mount Sinai where it was made, to Pharaoh Tutankhamun's tomb, crossing the Sahara Desert into the underground rock churches of Ethiopia and beyond in an epic adventure. B07MTTHHZ7 (UK). B07R3BMBW6 (USA).

The Exodus Evidence: Quest for Ancient Israel in Egypt, The Red Sea, The Exodus Route & Mount Sinai. Join two adventurers, brothers Mathew and Paul Backholer as they investigate a three-thousand year old mystery, entering the tombs of ancient Egypt seeking the exodus evidence. Discover the first reference to Israel outside of the Bible in hieroglyphics, uncover ancient depictions of people with multi-colored coats, encounter the Egyptian records of slaves making bricks and find lost cities mentioned in the Bible. 1 hour 15 minutes. B07P63BWZ2 (UK). B07Q3ST613 (USA).

Online Exclusive (not to rent or buy)

Christian Revival & Holy Spirit Awakenings. Join revival historian and prolific author Mathew Backholer, as he joins CEO Gordon Pettie in the Revelation TV studios over 7 episodes to examine many powerful Christian revivals which shook the world. Including the: Layman's Prayer Revival of 1857, Ulster Revival 1859-60, Welsh Revival of 1904-05, Azusa Street Revival of 1906-09, Korean Revival of 1907-10, the Hebridean Revival of 1949-52 and more! B07R445S5W (UK). Coming to the USA soon!

Notes

CPSIA information can be obtained
at www.ICGtesting.com
Printed in the USA
LVHW081934230422
717058LV00011B/324